ULTIMATE RISK

Mark Nicol was educated at Belmont Abbey in the SAS's home town of Hereford. His father served with distinction for sixteen years in the 22nd Special Air Service Regiment. Mark graduated from Reading University with a degree in politics and international relations and joined the *Evening Standard* in 1996. He went on to work for the *Sunday Mirror* and the *News of the World*, specializing in military writing and particularly in reports on the SAS. This is his first book.

MARK NICOL

ULTIMATE RISK

SAS CONTACT AL QAEDA

PAN BOOKS

First published 2003 by Macmillan

This edition published 2004 by Pan Books
an imprint of Pan Macmillan Ltd
Pan Macmillan, 20 New Wharf Road, London N1 9RR
Basingstoke and Oxford
Associated companies throughout the world
www.panmacmillan.com

ISBN 0 330 41315 5

3 5 7 9 8 6 4 2

A CIP catalogue record for this book is available from
the British Library.

Typeset by SetSystems Ltd, Saffron Walden, Essex
Printed and bound in Great Britain by
Mackays of Chatham plc, Chatham, Kent

All Pan Macmillan titles are available from
www.panmacmillan.com
or from Bookpost by telephoning 01624 677237

Acknowledgements

I would like to thank the following for their support and friendship: first and foremost, my parents and family. And Jason Beedell, Andrew Buckwell, Mike Cain, Kate Cornish, Sarah Counsell, Gerard Cousens, James Coxhead, Anna and Barbara Gekoski, Rupert Hamer, Jonathan Harris, Poppy Heath, Ryan Herman, Max Innocenzi, Anna Leyns, Ronan McGreevy, John McNally, Jonathan Mantle and family, Mark Osgood, Ian Perryment, Emma Power and Eleanor Simons.

CONTENTS

List of Illustrations

O Lord, who didst call on thy disciples to venture all to win all men to thee, grant that we, the chosen members of the Special Air Service Regiment, may by our works and our ways dare all to win all, and in doing so render special service to thee and our fellow men in all the world, through the same Jesus Christ our Lord.

The Regimental Collect of the
22nd Special Air Service Regiment

Introduction

This is an accurate account of the biggest and most destructive battle in the history of the 22nd Special Air Service (SAS) Regiment, the events leading up to it, and its aftermath. Whatever you may have read or heard, it is also the only battle the Regiment has fought against Al Qaeda. *Ultimate Risk* is based exclusively on first-hand military and civilian sources, many of whose names and backgrounds have necessarily been altered, and my own research in Afghanistan. The conversations between the men are based on their first-hand recollections of what was said and when. In my view this book neither defames SAS soldiers past or present nor poses a threat to the Regiment's future actions; I would have no part in any article or publication that did.

Against a backdrop of US reluctance to engage the enemy, 120 SAS soldiers launched a daring mission against Osama bin Laden's crack forces in Afghanistan in 2001. Although the United States would later deploy 200,000 troops in the Gulf to depose Saddam Hussein, only 1,300 were sent to Afghanistan to hunt down the world's most wanted man and destroy his terrorist regime – a decision which in the light of the failure to capture him seems a grave error. The Americans also favoured a policy of air strikes alone, and only the SAS CO's (Commanding Officer's) and the RSM's (Regimental Sergeant Major's) insistence prevented the destruction of a potential intelligence goldmine and challenged Al Qaeda's view that the infidels were too scared to fight them.

The SAS's argument that Al Qaeda should be fought on the ground was out of kilter with US 'military think' and Operation ENDURING FREEDOM proved hugely frustrating. The war had reached a critical stage; seven weeks of bombing had brought President Bush no closer to his primary war aim – Osama bin Laden 'dead or alive'. Finally, the Americans gave in and in late November Operation TRENT, not only 22 SAS's biggest but also arguably its most politically risky operation, took place.

Prior to deployment the Regiment was gripped with anxiety and uncertainty over its future. With its battle-hardened core at its smallest in the history of the SAS, the Regiment's capability was in question. The 'old and bold', the Falklands, Gulf War and Balkans veterans, were a dying breed, surrounded by 'combat virgins', good enough to pass Selection but untested under enemy fire. Could they cut it against Al Qaeda? Would the CO's willingness to blood them in such a testing environment, when the United States was reluctant to sanction the fight, prove a fatal error of judgement?

The SAS is the world's best-known and most revered fighting force, which was also at the forefront of the invasion of Iraq in March 2003. The live televising of the storming of the Iranian Embassy in 1980 had turned its soldiers into celebrities and triggered the public's insatiable appetite for SAS stories which shows no signs of abating. But Operation NIMROD, as the Embassy siege is also known, was followed by the very public controversy of Operation FAVIUS, when a four-man SAS team shot and killed three IRA terrorists in Gibraltar in 1988, and a string of speculative and inaccurate reports of SAS military and anti-terrorist operations around the world.

Many senior officers within the regimental fraternity still believe the SAS can and should continue trading on the myth factor; that somehow, despite the huge publicity and popular fascination, it can remain a ghost force, lurking in the shadows. This is wishful thinking. In order to 'manage the myth', or what remains of it, preventing disclosure has become a regimental obsession. The DSF (Director Special Forces), an SAS officer with the rank of Brigadier, today employs a staff officer with full-time responsibility for the subject. If only his time could be spent on operational matters.

In the flood of SAS books that followed the 1990–91 Gulf War, the staggering commercial success of *Bravo Two Zero*, published in 1993, and *The One That Got Away* (1995) made their authors, patrol leader Andy McNab and his deputy Chris Ryan, millionaires. Disputes over the authenticity of their accounts brought them and the Regiment into disrepute, and made McNab and Ryan pariahs among members of the SAS community. Ryan's crime was simple: the betrayal of the SAS tradition that all its members are equal and no one member should speak ill of another who has fallen on the battlefield. As SAS founder Colonel Sir David Stirling wrote, 'Man is the regiment and the regiment is the man.'

The failure of the patrol, deployed behind enemy lines in January 1991 to disrupt Iraqi MSRs (Main Supply Routes) through the Western Desert, cost the lives of three soldiers, one of whom, Sergeant Vince Phillips, was harshly treated in the television film of Ryan's book. In his own account of the Gulf War, *Eye of the Storm*, Regimental Sergeant Major Peter Ratcliffe described McNab's and Ryan's books as 'highly fictional'. Former 21 SAS (TA) soldier Michael Asher's book, *The Real Bravo Two Zero*, also questioned McNab's and Ryan's accounts and went some way towards restoring Sergeant Phillips' reputation. The policy of the

Ministry of Defence (MOD) pertaining to UKSF (United Kingdom Special Forces), of disclosure only in exceptional circumstances and with approval at ministerial level, prevented the release of information from the post-operational debrief. In the words of one SAS contact, Ryan would be 'filled in' if he dared drink in a Regiment pub in Hereford.

The SAS and the Government are still pondering whether and how to modernize the Regiment's public relations. The failure of the MOD to challenge publicly the most ludicrous newspaper reports has only encouraged more of the same. On 24 March 2002, the *Mail on Sunday* claimed that a Victoria Cross (VC) was going to be awarded to the RSM (Regimental Sergeant Major) for leading the regiment's soldiers into caves at Tora Bora, Afghanistan, where they supposedly cut Al Qaeda to shreds in a series of knife fights. This action simply did not take place and hence no VC was, nor was ever going to be, awarded. It is my belief that, in order truly to appreciate its finest fighting force, the time has come for the British public to be told of the true events.

My father was badged and served in D Squadron and 264 (SAS) Signal Squadron between 1972 and 1988 and was awarded the MBE by his CO, Lieutenant General Cedric Delves DSO. My father did not, however, contribute to this book. I grew up in the SAS 'family' in Hereford, took an honours degree in International Relations and went on to a career in national newspaper journalism. After clearance by the DA-Notice security committee, on 13 January 2002 the *News of the World* published my first account of the single contact between the SAS and Al Qaeda, the genesis of the story that has become *Ultimate Risk*. Out of respect for the Regiment, its soldiers and their families, I will be making a donation to one of its charities from the proceeds of this book.

Mark Nicol, Hereford, May 2003

1. THE CO'S BRIEF

The SAS's home is a barracks 3 miles from the centre of Hereford, at what used to be RAF Credenhill, now named Stirling Lines after the officer who founded the Regiment in the Second World War, Colonel Sir David Stirling. Further out, near the village of Pontrilas, on the road to Abergavenny, is the Regiment's training area. The world's most lethal small-arms weapons are tested there, from semi-automatics to grenades, pistols, machine-guns and sniper rifles.

Hereford and its surroundings are an ideal home for the SAS, away from prying eyes. The men do their best to avoid deliberately attracting attention or causing trouble. To the amusement of the Regiment's officers and men, a lot of nonsense is written about the ability of this so-called ghost force to mingle effortlessly with the natives of far-flung corners of the earth. SAS troops do not merge into the background in Hereford: and to suggest they do so in Baghdad or Kandahar is ludicrous. In Hereford they are the proverbial sore thumbs, whizzing through the city on their mountain bikes, wearing shorts whatever the weather, with rucksacks strapped to their backs. While some of the Regiment's older members have the weather-beaten faces of sheep farmers from the nearby Black Mountains, they are otherwise, in appearance and character, a breed apart.

The dawn chorus of birdsong and the gentle hum of nature pierced the silence of Herefordshire on 13 September, in marked contrast to the cacophony of cranes, diggers and fire engines at Ground Zero after what was, as President Franklin Roosevelt said of 7 December 1941 when the Japanese attack on Pearl Harbor killed 2,395 US citizens, 'a date which will live in infamy'. Herefordshire is as rural a county as any in England and outside its city centre – city status being bequeathed by Hereford's Cathedral – it is also as beautiful and tranquil as any. In contrast to Manhattan forty-eight hours on, life in Hereford was gripped by still-ness.

From shortly after 8 a.m. a stream of soldiers in cars and on motorcycles passed through the main gates of Stirling Lines. By 9.25 a.m. 350 men had packed into the cavernous MBR (Main Briefing Room) for a 'must-attend' meeting, in Army parlance a 'Scale A'. It had been announced the day before by the CO and its purpose was to discuss the immediate implications of the Al Qaeda attacks. It was a roll call of the SAS's full strength, approximately sixty men each from the four sabre squadrons, A, B, D and G, plus the Regiment's support units, the largest being 264 (SAS) Signal Squadron. Members of the RIC (Royal Intelligence Corps), RAMC (Royal Army Medical Corps), RE (Royal Engineers) and the RAF (Royal Air Force) liaison officer team were also present.

This was an event in itself, for the entire SAS Regiment is brought together at best once a year, the most common occasion being the pre-Christmas cross-brief, an annual analysis of operations and exercises. The meetings are fol-lowed by the 'bun fight', the Regiment's biggest piss-up of the year. Many of the troops had spent most of 2001 away from from 'H' – regimental shorthand for Hereford – some on secondment to the RIC undercover unit, '14 Int', which is part of UKSF, and others with Delta Force, the United

States' closest equivalent to the SAS, but the majority had been away on squadron exercises. Such gatherings were also an opportunity to catch up on life back at the camp. Many otherwise only seemed to return for the fiercely contested inter-squadron rugby matches.

A hum of voices echoed around the vast, brightly lit and sparsely furnished room, bare apart from curtains and carpet, both in regimental shades of light and dark blue, a steep bank of black plastic seating and a large screen for film showings. The majority of the men were standing, some against the building's four concrete pillars, a few gazing upwards above the neon strip lights suspended by wires from the ceiling and through the skylights. All were in uniform except the duty anti-terrorist team, who were dressed scruffily in jeans and T-shirts, ready to jump into a helicopter at a moment's notice. At this time, the main threat was clear: an Al Qaeda strike on Britain.

At exactly 9.30 a.m. two men swept through the swinging double wooden doors, removed their sand-coloured berets and stepped up on to the podium. They were the two most important soldiers in the Regiment, veterans of combat, men hardened and schooled by experiences of war, with the medals and the scars to prove it. They commanded respect, not merely by virtue of rank, as do many commanders, but through their achievements as soldiers which bore testimony to their characters. They were respectively the RSM and the CO, who was a Lieutenant Colonel.

The muttering died down as the RSM, notifying the troops of the CO's presence, gave them the command to 'Sit Up' from their positions in front of the podium.

The CO was a quintessentially dashing commander, tall, dark haired, 'domineering but not arrogant' according to the men. He had joined the SAS from the Light Division, proved himself as a Troop Commander in the Gulf War and became OC (Officer Commanding) D Squadron. In

September 2000, as CO, he accompanied D Squadron when it teamed up with 1 PARA to rescue British hostages in Sierra Leone: a mission which cost the life of Trooper Brad Tinnion, twenty-eight, who later received a posthumous MID (Mention in Dispatches). (At the time of writing Trooper Tinnion is the last SAS soldier to die in combat.) Some twenty-five enemy, the West Side Boys, were killed in the operation and eighteen captured, including their leader, Brigadier Foday Kallay. Ex-SAS officer General Sir Charles Guthrie was the CDS (Chief of the Defence Staff) who approved the jungle mission, codenamed Operation ABLATE.

As the CO flicked through his notes, the winged dagger of the SAS badge on his belt buckle glinted under the MBR's lights. He came straight to the point, speaking into a microphone: 'There is no distorting the seriousness of what has happened, and the intent of America. The word from the briefings at Camp David is that there will be an all-out assault, and there is even the chance that nuclear weapons will be used.' This point was met with many nods of approval.

He continued: 'After the actions of 11 September, the future implications are that when the war starts it will not be short and will probably go on for generations and will probably not only involve us and our children, but their children and probably theirs too.'

The men were keen to know their role in the weeks and months ahead. Some shuffled nervously in their seats as the CO got to the part of his speech they had been waiting for. He said: 'We will be involved, but not directly right now, and our daily routines will not change. The days ahead of us are going to be long, with planning, preparation and a lot of time spent looking at battle procedures. Everything is on a strict need-to-know basis and anyone caught spreading rumours will be severely disciplined and if necessary

RTU'd.* That includes your wives and girlfriends. Be security-conscious and go about your daily routines as per normal in a high standard and fitting with the tradition of this Regiment.'

With that the CO turned and left, the RSM in tow, with as little fuss and ceremony as they had arrived. No one saluted or jumped to attention as this was not the SAS way. The pair left a highly charged atmosphere in which the men's desire for combat was palpable, written on their faces and set in their eyes. The troops took the CO's briefing to suggest that they would soon be setting off for war. With the enormity of the events in New York and Washington, the likelihood that the SAS would be thrown into battle soon seemed high and the SAS man by nature is not a peacetime soldier. He joins the world's elite fighting force to do exactly that and to ensure that at times like these he will be part of the action. The MBR was buzzing although the CO had, in fact, sounded a cautious note, stressing that the fight against Al Qaeda would be a long-term and not necessarily immediate commitment.

The list of possible uses for the SAS inside Afghanistan seemed endless. Putting aside the Regiment's specialist counter-terrorist role, the 'black ops' tasks such as the Iranian Embassy siege, the SAS has deployed with most success deep inside enemy territory, on long-range reconnaissance missions and striking key enemy installations, using stealth and surprise. With these methods it has on countless occasions achieved results belying its size. Surely the Regiment would be used to track down bin Laden?

As soon as possible after 9/11 the CO wanted to establish what the Regiment calls 'operational status', the switch from a peacetime to war role, and a determination of its

---

* RTU'd: Returned to Unit. Punishments range from a year's suspension to the end of a soldier's SAS career.

position in the political climate. The Regiment's primary responsibility was, as ever, the terrorist threat to mainland Britain. D Squadron was in the hot seat on 9/11 and for the remainder of 2001. If the Al Qaeda terrorists struck, its troopers would be tasked with repelling them. There is always one anti-terrorist troop of sixteen men on half an hour's notice to leave Hereford. It is known as First Team.

The pregnant pause before battle was much longer than the troops had hoped and the SAS-obsessed British media expected. All eyes were on President Bush. This was going to be America's war, one in which the SAS would be fortunate to participate. Even so, experience had taught its officers to pre-empt political decisions whenever possible, and being a step ahead after 9/11 intelligence-wise made for more efficient planning and preparation. The Regiment's excellent relations with Delta Force, based at Fort Bragg, North Carolina, ensured it would know what was happening before any MOD mandarins. Once an immediate Allied response was ruled out – the United States could not hit bin Laden as it did not have a clue where he was – the CO and his RHQ (Regimental Headquarters) Cell, including 264 Signal Squadron head shed, RIC and RE representatives began looking ahead.

The assumption was made, based on the Camp David int-brief and in order to prepare for the largest possible SAS deployment, that Afghanistan would be, in Regiment parlance, a 'big party': similar in size and scale to Gulf War I, when two full squadrons were operational and a third waited in the wings. An early question was how much kit the Regiment would have in Oman, its likely infil (infiltration) point for Afghanistan operations. The goal was to get enough weaponry, ammunition, water, rations, fuel and spare parts there for two SAS sabre squadrons as quickly as possible – a huge logistical operation. UKSF – the umbrella group which oversees the SAS and its Royal Navy equivalent, the SBS (Special Boat Service) – wanted the MOD and the Prime Minister to lobby for as large a role for its troops as possible. The Regiment had to be ready to deliver whenever called upon.

SAS activities are divided into four categories and rotated between sabre squadrons on a six-month cycle. These are: the Anti-Terrorist, also known in 'H' as SP (Special Projects), Courses, Standby and Long-Term Training. After 9/11, A Squadron was on Long-Term Training; having spent the first half of the year on SP; B Squadron was on Standby, D Squadron, as mentioned, was the duty SP, ruling it out of contention, and G Squadron was on Courses, its soldiers learning the core troop skills such as languages, combat medicine, mechanics, telecommunications and demolitions.

Each squadron is divided into a headquarters and four specialist troops, each consisting of sixteen soldiers, Air, Boat, Mobility and Mountain. Air is home to the free-fall parachuting specialists, Boat to the combat swimmers, canoeists and divers, Mobility to the highly trained drivers and motorcyclists and Mountain to the climbers, skiers and abseil experts. As soldiers frequently switch troops, and on occasion squadrons, they become experts in many areas in addition to the introduction to Regimental training during SAS Selection.

A maximum of two squadrons are deployed operationally at any one time in any given theatre of operations, though a third may be held in reserve, as was the case in the Falklands War and Gulf War I. The Standby squadron is on permanent readiness to carry out missions such as Operation ABLATE on instant notice, without the luxury of build-up training or acclimatization. It may carry out short exercises, worldwide, on the proviso that they are terminated if an SAS immediate action is required elsewhere. The squadron on Long-Term Training will spend months away from Hereford, in cold climates, the jungle and more often than not, the desert.

A Squadron was in pole position to deploy as its troops were just about to conduct desert exercises in Oman. Much of its kit, vehicles and other hardware were already there, having left the United Kingdom for the Gulf in July from Marchwood military port, Southampton. Oman is the SAS's chosen location for desert exercises and its dusty, mountainous environment was considered excellent preparation. G Squadron hoped to win the CO's sympathy vote after missing out, somewhat controversially, on Gulf War deployment, despite having completed five months of build-up training in the United Arab Emirates. Its troops returned to 'H' dismayed as A Squadron, which had been on exercise in the South American jungle, flew to Saudi Arabia to join B and D Squadrons.

Perhaps the factor which denied G Squadron a role in the Gulf would ensure its ticket to Afghanistan. The CO was under great pressure to put A Squadron in theatre in 1990–91 as it was the only one of the four sabre squadrons not involved in any way in the South Atlantic – Squadrons D and G were on the Falklands while B Squadron remained on Ascension Island. A Squadron was simply unfortunate as the Argentine invasion coincided with its six-month stint as the duty SP. There is, however, unquestionably, a political side to which squadrons are deployed and these decisions can also hinge on the CO's relationship with each squadron's OC and its officers. Another factor in G Squadron's favour over B Squadron was that it had completed desert training – known as an Exercise Barren Land – as part of its Long-Term Training in the first half of 2001.

While much is made of SAS troopers being 'more intelligent and sophisticated' than regular soldiers in the mainstream British Army – they are more often than not the former if not always the latter – ask them what really matters in life and you will be told 'beer, babes and bullets', in no particular order. After 9/11 they were up for a big scrap and in the words of one: 'A piss-up and a shag could wait.' Filing in and out of the MBR, the men were relieved to know that the Americans wanted them on board, at least in theory, if not yet in practice. They would have preferred a clearer idea of when operations might start, though: 'not yet' did not really do the job.

The desert was neither Jock's nor Jason's ideal environment as its flat terrain provided little cover and it was uncomfortably hot by day and cold by night. As the forthcoming training period in Oman would hopefully serve as build-up training for Afghanistan, it mattered not. Heading back across camp to A Squadron HQ, Gulf War veteran Jock, ex-Para like so many in Hereford, was excited by the opportunity of another contact or two. The red-faced Scot, a hulk of a man, had been lucky in his SAS career, having fought in Iraq, the former Yugoslavia and Colombia. Most soldiers in the British Army never see combat at close quarters, and even for SAS troopers it may be a once-in-a-career experience. Afghanistan would be the Sergeant's last hurrah. Now in his early forties, he was one of the seasoned soldiers, the 'old and bold' occasionally referred to in Hereford as 'heavy call signs'.

It was apt that Jason, the best part of twenty years younger, walked behind him, as if in Jock's shadow. The Londoner was a 'combat virgin', incredibly able and keen but as yet untested when it really mattered. The fact that Jock remembered being just as wet behind the ears did not stop him taking the mickey and avoiding Jason's company off camp. Though he had slightly more respect for Jason than he let on – as they were both former Paratroopers, the SAS's dominant breed – even this counted for little against Jason's lack of combat experience.

Jock was confident A Squadron would be selected. 'How's your Arabic?' he asked.

'Er . . . crap,' replied Jason, startled that the dour Scot, a man of few words, had struck up a conversation. 'I know a bit,' he added, then: 'You think we'll be going, then, Jock? Seeing as we've just spent a month in the sand?'

'Aye, I do, laddie, and we're gonnae find out whether you're any good or not when we close in,' he said, smiling. He liked winding Jason up and it did not take much to do so.

What Jason may have lacked in brain cells he compensated for with confidence, thanks to his Parachute Regiment background.

'Hey, Jock, I wouldn't let anyone down when we're in a contact, hope not; anyhow, I'll be switched on when it counts.'

Jock laughed. 'Jason, you wouldnae know "when it counts" if it smacked ye in the face, son. Sure you're not just a wee range-man? You'd better perform. I mean it.'

'Yeah, sure, I will, so I ain't worried. I'm well up for it. You've never been to Afghanistan either so it might be just as different for you too.'

Jock stalled for a second, a little taken aback. 'No . . . I havenae, but one little rag-head looks pretty much like another. And take ma word for it, son, Arabs cannae fight for shite.'

Jason was right. Jock had not been to Afghanistan, but he knew a man who had; a few of them in fact.

The SAS had played a small part in the Soviet Red Army's defeat in Afghanistan in the 1980s after a nine-year occupation. Members of the Regiment and SAS veterans working for private mercenary companies conducted covert operations linked to the supply and training of the US-backed *Mujahideen*, in what was the last proxy Cold War conflict. Afghan warriors backed by tens of thousands of

Muslims from the Middle East were trained by the West to use sophisticated weapons such as shoulder-fired Stinger rocket launchers. Pieces of Soviet equipment were also brought back to Hereford for analysis.

There were a few old sweats from the highly covert Afghanistan missions knocking around Hereford for Jock to tap up. Their role twenty years before had been top secret. If they were shot, injured or wounded it would have been extremely difficult for the British Government to get them out. The SAS's presence in Afghanistan during the 1980s has never been admitted. The troops lived for months with the *Mujahideen* in the harsh, barren environment, some suffering malnutrition and returning psychologically scarred having witnessed the Red Army using fuel-air bombs to wipe out entire villages. The indiscriminate bombing of the countryside was intended to control Afghanistan's lawless rural areas, something the Soviets never achieved. The horrific policy killed tens of thousands of Afghans and caused a flood of refugees.

Like most SAS soldiers Jock kept abreast of world affairs and knew about the Taliban, which had swept across Afghanistan since 1994. It imposed the harshest interpretation of *Shari'a*, or Holy Law, ever seen: women were seldom allowed to leave home and men, among many ridiculous laws, were forbidden to shave, listen to music or play sport. The Taliban's rule was medieval and the more the world came to know it, the more unpopular and isolated it became. The young Talibs, fresh out of the *Madrassa*s, the religious colleges in Pakistan, chose Kandahar as their home and a shy, pious man, Mullah Mohammed Omar, as their leader. Injured four times fighting the Red Army, he ran his own *Madrassa* and had only one eye.

Jock made a mental note to buy one of the Afghan vets a beer the next time he was in town. One in particular could be found propping up the same bar most nights, smoking roll-ups. Political developments apart, Afghanistan had not changed significantly since the early 1980s. Although its population had increased to around 26 million it had always been incredibly ethnically diverse, with at least thirty languages spoken, and its transport and communication links were appalling. It barely had an economy worthy of the name and life expectancy was forty-six years.

Jock pondered how much Al Qaeda would have in common with the Communist *Adoo* – Arabic for enemy – whom the SAS fought from the 1950s to the mid-1970s. These were Marxist, Soviet-funded guerrillas, armed with AK47 assault rifles, RPGs (Rocket Propelled Grenades) and 82-mm mortars. Jock had not fought in Oman, it was before even his time, and his view that the Arabs 'couldnae fight for shite' was harsh. They were well regarded by the SAS as skilful tacticians, resourceful and determined. Al Qaeda were similarly armed but unlike the secular *Adoo* their guerrillas were fuelled by Islamic fundamentalism. They dreamed of slaughtering infidels, martyrdom and living in heaven surrounded by virgins, not of a left-wing nirvana where everyone was as poor as them.

Phil was another combat virgin, but unlike Jason was in G Squadron. He left school at the time of the Gulf War. Since joining the Regiment in 2000 from the RE he had heard the tales of 'G' having to return to the UK to perform the anti-terrorist role when it appeared they would charge into Iraq and, like hundreds of millions of people worldwide, the twenty-eight-year-old from the Midlands had watched with horrified astonishment some forty-eight hours earlier as the Twin Towers fell. Phil was popular, respected by his older colleagues and as eager as any man to cut his combat teeth in Afghanistan.

He had listened to the Prime Minister's speeches on

9/11, in which he described international terrorism as the new global evil and its perpetrators as having 'no regard whatever for the sanctity or value of human life'. Phil agreed with Tony Blair that the world's democracies should come together to eradicate it and that it was 'not a battle between the United States of America and terrorism, but between the free and democratic world and terrorism'. He particularly liked Blair's pledge that Britain would 'stand shoulder to shoulder' with the United States, as that meant British forces and, hopefully the SAS, would be in the thick of the action.

But within a few days Phil was sick of pontificating politicians and as he watched one on television meandering through a series of platitudes he said, 'Come on, man, we've got to get into Afghanistan now, before Bin Laden fucks off.'

Like Phil, Gordon, a G Squadron NCO (Non-Commissioned Officer), wanted the MPs to shut up and the retaliation to start. Walking into the TV room, coffee in hand, the Geordie gave Phil the benefit of his opinion, and not for the first time: 'Britain's under siege, man, there's no planes coming in and out, everyone's fuckin' shitting themselves. On the telly they've talking about global coalitions and all that shite. What the fuck do we need a coalition for? We've just got to go down there, man, and smack 'em, fuckin' simple as that.'

Phil agreed with the former Coldstream Guards soldier but was not sure G Squadron would get the call. G Squadron is so named because when it was formed in 1965, superseding the Guards Independent Parachute Company after the Regiment's Borneo campaign, it consisted entirely of soldiers from the Guards Division. This was no longer the case.

'You reckon we'll get down there?' Phil asked, wondering whether 'Grumpy Gordon', as he was known, had heard a whisper.

'I don't know yet, mate, but we fuckin' better had. You know G got stuffed last time in the Gulf, don't you? The OC has got to give us a big push. We can't get stitched up again, Phil. We only did desert training a few months back and that's what should count.'

Phil did not mind whether G Squadron went to Afghanistan through the front door, on merit, or through the back door as the result of sympathy. The thought of being on the Start Line — a soldiers' term for the imaginary line in the ground from where an advance to contact begins – had kept Phil going through SAS Selection. He wanted to be tested.

'OK, Gordon, let's say we go. What do you reckon we'll do?'

'Ah, don't worry about that, man, the Yanks know we're the business, mate, better than any fuckin' bunch they've got and we work with them all the time. We'll get some good tasks. Definitely.'

Phil was not as sure. 'I don't know about that. The CO didn't say so.'

'Yeah, man, but the head sheds never tell you what's going on, just what they want you to know. He can't have us all getting too excited, can he?'

All the men assumed the Regiment's Gulf War success would stand it in good stead, the SAS having famously destroyed the mobile missile launchers in the Iraqi Western Desert used to fire Scuds towards Israel. B and D Squadrons' attacks forced Saddam Hussein's forces to abandon 'Scud Alley', moving his lethal hardware deeper into home territory towards Baghdad, and, crucially, out of range of Israel. In doing so the Regiment amazed Gulf War US Commander-in-Chief General 'Stormin'' Norman Schwarzkopf who had to be persuaded by the Commander of British forces in the Middle East, ex-SAS CO General Sir Peter de la Billière, aka 'DLB', to approve the operations. The Regiment created a template for Special Forces operations in the

Gulf and its success embarrassed Delta Force out of its slumber.

Much to Jason, Jock, Gordon and Phil's relief, A and G Squadrons were put on standby for Afghanistan deployment. G Squadron included one of the two Falklands War veterans to head there, the other being the RSM – a remarkable nineteen years after their first conflict, and some testament to their fitness and longevity. The squadrons were chosen as a result of their recent desert training. The weeks spent in that arduous climate had paid off.

Prior to the autumn of 2001, the Regiment had seen very little action for a decade; this had not been the case before, as the 1950s, 60s, 70s and 80s were times of almost permanent conflict, with the extent of the fighting reflected in the number of gallantry awards: eighty-four decorations for SAS soldiers in Malaya alone between January 1953 and June 1958.

No other British Army unit needed to worry about a shrinking level of combat experience. But for the SAS, the first unit in line wherever and whenever British interests are at stake, it was a major cause for alarm and pre-deployment nerves. Despite having served as a Sergeant in Hereford since 1992, Gordon had never been shot at. A and G Squadrons were crawling with combat virgins young and old, of irrefutable pedigree but untried nevertheless. Unlike the SAS parties which set forth for the Falklands or the Gulf, A and G's inexperienced troopers could not see many hard-nosed old pros like Jock who had been there and done it.

The SAS had to play a waiting game, what would happen and when being up to the US Generals and the Bush Administration. Tony Blair, who had watched the incredible events of 9/11 in a Brighton hotel room as he prepared to address the Trades Union Conference, was one of the first Western leaders Bush spoke to. The coalition building, which was already frustrating the SAS, began in earnest with the British Prime Minister discussing the threat of global terrorism with German Chancellor Gerhard Schroeder, French President Jacques Chirac and Russian President Vladimir Putin – three men with whom he and President Bush would fall out spectacularly in the build-up to Gulf War II.

2. 'DEAD OR ALIVE'

Like weary soldiers leaving the battlefield, fire fighters trudged through the dusty New York streets. They were mentally, physically and emotionally exhausted after twenty-four-hour shifts spent in snake-like human chains crossing Ground Zero, passing body parts and possessions down the line. Now they were oblivious to the applause of fellow New Yorkers who clapped and shook their tired hands as they passed. The shattered fire fighters had no way of knowing as they worked on 13 September, the day of the CO's brief, that the mountain of debris had already given up its last survivor. Thirty-year-old Port Authority worker Genelle Guzman-McMillan was pulled to safety at 12.30 p.m. the previous day, having lain trapped in an air pocket for over twenty-six hours. Her worst injury – a miracle considering she had fallen thirteen storeys down the North Tower's stairway B when it collapsed – was a crushed right leg. The rubble gave up just eighteen survivors: twelve fire fighters, three police officers and three civilians.

Over the course of the following year some 19,858 pieces of human remains would be found amid the 1.8 million tonnes of concrete and steel. There would be no more tales of miraculous escape from this colossal mausoleum of rubble and fires, the last of which was extinguished on 20 December 2001, two months and nine days after the Towers

collapsed. Once the world's fifth and sixth highest buildings, the Twin Towers had become a tomb for 1,721 men
and women whose bodies were never found. The World
Trade Center had taken six years and eight months to build
but from first impact to the second tower's collapse, just one
hour and forty-two minutes to destroy. No terrorist attack,
at home or abroad, had ever claimed as many British lives.
Some sixty-seven Britons died in New York, their ages
ranging from twenty-two to sixty-two, their jobs from company director to security worker.

Funeral processions became routine. Time and again fire
fighters hunched over stretchers carried their deceased
brethren, the corpses wrapped in the Stars and Stripes.
Against a backdrop of the towering wreckage, resembling a
Gothic cathedral with its stone arched windows and pieces
of metal twisted into the shape of crucifixes, they passed in
silence through avenues of saluting rescue workers. The fire
fighters were America's new heroes, something they never
wanted to be. The desire to avenge their deaths and those
of the other victims of 9/11 would inspire US troops.
Television pictures taken of the US Special Operations
soldiers embarking on raids inside Afghanistan on 19
October captured them slipping images into their rucksacks
of fire fighters raising Old Glory over Ground Zero.

The pre-9/11 deliberations of the US Government, in its
intelligence gathering and law enforcement, were characterized by ignorance, complacency and an underestimation
of Al Qaeda. It assumed the terrorists might hijack a US aircraft but the suicide bomb theory was regarded as unlikely.
Al Qaeda supposedly did not have sufficient agents and
infrastructure to mount a large-scale operation on mainland
America.

The terrorist threat, whether at home or abroad, was not

a key issue for the newly elected President. His foreign policy priorities, which lagged behind tax cuts on his to-do list, were building relationships with China and Russia – one reason why Bush made Moscow expert Condoleeza Rice his NSA (National Security Advisor); she had previously handled Russian affairs for President Bush Senior's NSA, Brent Scowcroft. Having beaten Democrat Al Gore courtesy of 537 votes in Florida, Bush's agenda had a greater domestic emphasis than his immediate predecessor's. Playing global peacemaker did not appear to interest him. The choice of location for his first foreign trip as President spoke volumes: Mexico, home from home for the Texan.

As clouds of thick black smoke billowed from the Twin Towers the blame game started in Washington as White House aides, the CIA (Central Intelligence Agency) and the FBI (Federal Bureau of Investigation) anticipated the wrath of President Bush and the American people for the security failure. They were right to soul-search. The United States expected attacks similar to those on its embassies in Africa in July 1998 and on USS *Cole* in October 2000, which killed seventeen soldiers and injured thirty-nine aboard the billion-dollar warship, not on mainland America. The threat to US installations and its citizens abroad was perceived to be greater.

On 22 June 2001, US forces in the Middle East and Europe were placed on 'Force Protection Condition Delta', the highest alert level. Also in late June, Osama bin Laden warned America it should expect attack in the coming weeks. On 1 July, Senate Intelligence Committee member Diane Feinstein said, 'Intelligence staff tell me that there is a major probability of a terrorist incident within the next three months.' The White House was warned that the G8 summit in Genoa, Italy, on 20–22 July, was one possible target. The meeting passed without incident, however.

On 10 July FBI sleuth Ken Williams, a Bureau agent with

eleven years' anti-terrorism experience, suggested that Middle Eastern students at Arizona flying schools might be linked to Al Qaeda. The FBI deferred action on Williams' memo which did not progress high enough up its chain of command. He was right; one of the hijackers, Hani Hanjour, did train there, but before his investigation. The FBI argued therefore that acting on Williams' advice would not have prevented 9/11. Its response dismayed Senators, with Illinois Democrat Richard Durbin saying, 'The fact that the Phoenix memo died on somebody's desk takes your breath away. They just shuffled it off.'

On 6 August, the CIA briefed Bush on the possibility of Al Qaeda hijacking US airlines or boats and using biological weapons. His administration decided against publicizing details of the briefing and thus knowledge of the unspecified threat to all Americans stayed within the Government community.

On 15 August 2001, a Minneapolis flight school reported Zacarias Moussaoui, later charged with links to 9/11, to the FBI. He wanted to fly Boeing 747s but was not interested in learning how to land them. Moussaoui was arrested on immigration charges but detectives were refused permission to search his computer. The White House was not told. With no intelligence flow, the jigsaw pieces could not be fitted together when on 27 August France tipped off the United States that Moussaoui was a suspected Islamic extremist.

On 4 September, the Principals Committee, consisting of Vice-President Dick Cheney, Condoleeza Rice and other top NSAs, had finally met to pore over White House terrorism Tsar Richard Clarke's Al Qaeda report – submitted nine months previously. He recommended pre-emptive air strikes on terrorist training camps in Afghanistan and sufficient US support for the Northern Alliance to depose the Taliban. The proposals would cost several hundred million dollars, which the Bush administration thought would be better spent on a National System of Missile Defense. Clarke's cause was not helped by an alleged reputation for crying wolf too often and working for the previous tenant of the White House.

On 9 September, Al Qaeda agents assassinated Northern Alliance leader Ahmed Shah Massoud, the talismanic leader of Tajik and Uzbek ethnic groups in Afghanistan who led the opposition to the Taliban. In April, Massoud had warned the European Parliament in Strasbourg: 'If President Bush does not help us very soon, these terrorists will damage the US and Europe very soon.' On 10 September, a CIA plan to hit Al Qaeda was put on President Bush's desk at the White House. He was to look at it on his return from routine business in Florida.

At 9.31 a.m. on 9/11, President Bush gave his first reaction, telling America that all the Federal Government's resources would be directed towards 'a full-scale investigation to hunt down and find these folks who committed this act.' In using 'these folks' to describe Al Qaeda, the Texan sounded as if the hunt was on for youths who had burnt down his barn, not the world's most wanted man.

The catastrophic events pointed to just one organization, as NSA Condoleeza Rice recalled: 'the operation looked like Al Qaeda, quacked like Al Qaeda, seemed like Al Qaeda'. Having left a classroom of bemused seven-year-olds at Emma E. Booker Elementary School, Sarsoata, Florida, minutes after hearing the news, the President was not allowed to return to the White House's Emergency Operations Center until the evening; such was the security threat. His route to the citadel aboard Air Force One took in Barksdale Air Force Base, Shreeveport, Louisiana, and Offutt Air Force Base, Nebraska, the strategic command location from where any nuclear war would be orchestrated.

He was beaten back to Washington, DC by Secretary of State Colin Powell, who took a seven-hour flight from Lima, Peru, where he was attending the Organization of American States (OAS) conference. He told delegates: 'A terrible, terrible tragedy has befallen my nation. I will bring President Bush your expressions of sorrow and words of support.'

The fire which had sparked in the President's eyes when Chief of Staff Andrew Card first whispered news of the attacks in his ear raged that evening when, addressing the US people, he said: 'The search is underway for those who are behind these evil acts. We will make no distinction between the terrorists who committed these acts and those who harbour them.' The forty-third President of the United States, who entered the Oval Office with the narrowest electoral margin since 1876, would have to lead his nation through its darkest hour.

The United Nations would draw no distinction between 'perpetrators, organizers and sponsors' of the terrorist act and 'those responsible for aiding, supporting and harboring' them. United Nations Secretary-General Kofi Annan expressed his 'deep shock and revulsion at the cold-blooded viciousness of the attack' as its members unanimously adopted Resolution 1368 (2001). It was both an unequivocal condemnation of the attacks and a call to arms, the United Nations expressing its 'readiness to take all necessary steps to respond to the terrorist acts of 11 September 2001 and to combat all forms of terrorism, in accordance with its responsibilities under the Charter of the United Nations'.

The Security Council went on to pass Resolution 1373 (2001) which determined that all States should suppress the financing of terrorism, criminalize terrorist fund-raising and freeze the assets, funds and economic resources of any individual or group who participated or facilitated terrorist action. It also said, in a clause particularly relevant to

Afghanistan's Taliban regime, that states had a responsibility to prevent their citizens from making money available to terrorists, and states themselves should offer no support to terrorists by means of safe havens but bring to justice anyone who has participated in the financing, planning, preparation or perpetration of terrorist acts.

The Security Council called on states to afford one another the 'greatest measure of assistance for criminal investigations or criminal proceedings relating to the financing or support of terrorist acts. States should also prevent the movement of terrorists or their groups by effective border controls.' Resolution 1373 (2001) added that the Security Council was 'deeply concerned by the increase, in various regions of the world, of acts of terrorism motivated by intolerance or extremism, calling on states to work together urgently to prevent and suppress terrorist acts, including through increased co-operation and full implementation of the relevant international conventions relating to terrorism'.

This dry diplomatic language was in stark contrast to President Bush's which stoked the fires of revenge, insulted potential allies and, as the 'these folks' line exemplified, failed to capture the enormity of events. Bush gaffed six days later when he described the fight-back in terms of a 'crusade'; not a wise remark as he required the support of Muslim leaders, in Saudi Arabia, Oman, and Pakistan in particular, for military action in Afghanistan. He made the War on Terror seem like a clash between Christianity and Islam, as Arab League spokesman Hanan Ashrawi explained: 'It is an unfortunate choice of word. In English it is used figuratively, but it appears that they do not understand in Washington that the word is very negative in the Middle East and connotes religious zealotry.' Roger Heacock, History Professor at Bir-Zeit Palestinian University, added: 'Crusade in Arabic means a campaign to bring the

cross to the Muslims. By their own account the Crusaders
slaughtered 70,000 Muslims.'

On 17 September, Bush made his most infamous off-the-
cuff remark, one which emphasized his personal agenda,
although contrary to assumptions at the time, it would not
dictate the course of military action. As CENTCOM (United
States Central Command) operations failed to yield Osama
bin Laden, and with his terrorist organization still a global
threat today, it was perhaps a regrettable emotional outburst. Asked about the Al Qaeda leader at a White House
press conference, the President, leaning back confidently in
a black leather chair, and with just a hint of a grin, said, 'I
want him, I want justice and there's an old poster out West,
as I recall, which says Wanted Dead or Alive.' He then
nodded intently and his face filled with an expression of
satisfaction and conviction. It was too much for the First
Lady, Laura Bush, who, it was widely reported, repri-
manded her husband for sounding 'too much like a cow-
boy'. Bush also backed up his blunt, bellicose language with
written authorization for any operation to assassinate the Al
Qaeda leader.

So, in Bush's mind at least, it was a manhunt, in which
the combined forces of the United States, Great Britain and
other allies would come together to find and kill bin Laden.
Vice-President Dick Cheney was just as unequivocal,
remarking that he would accept bin Laden's 'head on a
platter'.

The fact that there was no knee-jerk retaliation post-
9/11 suggests that while Bush knew he must dismantle the
Taliban and confront Al Qaeda, it was bin Laden, talismanic
icon and leader, who dominated his thoughts at this time.
Just as his Presidential predecessor had responded to the
US Embassy strikes in 1998, he could have ordered attacks
on Al Qaeda camps in Afghanistan or on Kandahar, the
regime's home city. The latter option risked heavy civilian

casualties and international outcry; the United States may have conceded the moral high ground before the international coalition required to sustain military operations was secure. The President bided his time.

A division of priorities among his most senior colleagues had to be addressed. Defense Secretary Donald Rumsfeld and his deputy Paul Wolfowitz called for an immediate strike on Iraq, placing Saddam Hussein alongside bin Laden as the leader of a state supporting international terrorism and one which, they claimed, harboured its perpetrators. Secretary of State Colin Powell, who would call so fervently on the United Nations to sanction military action against Iraq in February 2003, won the day, insisting that as Iraq and Saddam Hussein were not going anywhere and Osama bin Laden was, military operations should focus on his capture and Al Qaeda's destruction: for a short while at least.

Predictably, the Taliban rejected the United States' demand to hand over bin Laden, with its Pakistani ambassador Abdul Salam Zaeef boasting that America would make 'more offers' when it had lost the war and adding: 'The world has seen that the Afghans cannot be dictated to.' The last diplomatic gambit was the United States' use of Pakistan as a go-between. Mullah Omar's dismissal of a request by General Musharraf to give up bin Laden for the sake of peace and Afghanistan made war inevitable.

The United States needed intelligence and military support from Pakistan, the opening of ISI (Inter-Services Intelligence) files on bin Laden and use of its airspace and airbases. General Musharraf, who seized power in a bloodless military coup in 1999, held out for, and secured, billions of dollars of debt relief in return. He also insisted that the involvement of bin Laden and Al Qaeda with 9/11 should be proved, not simply assumed. A dossier of evidence was required.

It was simply out of the question for General Musharraf to support the United States if in doing so he paved the way for the Northern Alliance to sweep to power. Pakistan had given birth to, armed and funded the Taliban, in order to counter the threat which it perceived the Tajiks and Uzbeks to pose. It would also be tantamount to Musharraf cutting his own throat: his military dictatorship would most likely have been overthrown if he was seen to be too pro-United States; bin Laden had tens of thousands of vociferous supporters in Pakistan. Siding with the United States was arguably the gamble of Musharraf's political life but confronted with the 'You are either with us or against' stance of the weightlifting, ex-US Navy Seal turned Deputy Secretary of State Richard Armitage, he had little choice.

Such was the danger of a political vacuum in Kabul that some Bush advisors advocated the formation of a government in exile to replace the Taliban, led by Afghanistan's exiled king. But like the SAS soldiers, the President had little time for the diplomatic preamble. There was no guarantee that Pakistan's support would hold and Al Qaeda might strike again in the time required for such an option to be implemented. The SAS was in a hurry to get into theatre and do the job: such a sense of urgency is central to Regimental ethos, although sadly it is easily mistaken for a bloodthirsty attitude.

Whatever Musharraf's concerns, the United States had no option but to team up with Pakistan's enemy, as the Northern Alliance was, in Powell's words 'the only coherent, functioning military organization that we could partner with and use as we undertook our military operations'. Its dubious record on human rights and humanitarian issues seemingly irrelevant at this time, as Dick Cheney admitted:

'You need to have on the payroll some very unsavoury characters. It is a mean, nasty, dangerous and dirty business out there and we have to operate in that arena.' Rumsfeld was characteristically precise: 'Our particular interest is very clear; it is to root out terrorists that exist in that country. It is up to the Afghan people to sort through what happens after that.'

With every day and week that passed bin Laden could plan his escape from Afghanistan. How was Bush going to bring him in? He was sure it was not going to happen by deploying large numbers of ground troops alone, if at all. The President said: 'We learned some very important lessons in Vietnam. Perhaps the most important lesson I learned is that you cannot fight a guerrilla war with conventional forces. That is why I've explained to the American people that we're engaged in a different type of war; one obviously that will use conventional forces but one which we have got to fight on all fronts.'

President Bush was scared of US troops coming home in body bags. But to win he would have to commit ground troops. As former NATO chief General Wesley Clark said, 'The resistance of a fanatical foe may be overcome only by boots on the ground. After Vietnam, the US has become extremely sensitive to casualties. Of all the obstacles the generals are facing this may be the most difficult.'

The Bush administration was hesitant. There was no blueprint for the operations ahead. Through the 1980s, Reagan and Bush Snr had watched with satisfaction as the Soviet Union toiled against the United States and Saudi-backed *Mujahideen* in Afghanistan's deserts and mountains. Poring over maps in the White House, the President and NSA Rice saw a country surrounded by US enemies such as Iran and unstable and potentially hostile states such as Pakistan, Tajikistan and Uzbekistan. As Condoleeza Rice recalled, 'Of all the places to fight a war, Afghanistan would not be our choice. That was what everybody thought.'

The Red Army's first deployment outside the Warsaw Pact since the Second World War had taken Washington by surprise and destabilized Southern Asia and the Middle East. In December 1979, when the tanks rolled into Kabul, President Carter vowed to oppose the Soviet occupation by 'any means necessary'. The conflict cost the United States and Saudi Arabia in excess of $7 billion over the decade and bankrupted the Soviet Union.

The situation demanded a flexible approach and, in keeping with Afghan tradition, the greasing of palms. Advice came from the Russians, who knew the territory best, with retired Major General Alexander Lyakhovski saying, 'The most effective weapon in Afghanistan is money. When I was there we said, "You can't conquer this country, only buy it". But Russia is not the richest country in the world. There are some that are much richer and we know who the richest country in the world is.'

Bush toned down the Wild West rhetoric when he addressed the Congress and Senate on 21 September; a speech which told America that Bush was in command. Prime Minister Blair was there to hear it in person. And Americans were watching, anxiously; 79 per cent of them – almost 30 per cent more than the percentage who vote – saw the televised thirty-six-minute speech. It had senior Republicans gushing in admiration, with former aide to Ronald Reagan Frank Donatelli describing Bush's oration as 'eloquent and almost Churchillian, inspiring the country'.

The President gave way to applause over thirty times during the address, in which he said: 'Tonight, we are a country awakened to danger and called to defend freedom. Our grief has turned to anger and anger to resolution. Whether we bring our enemies to justice or justice to our enemies, justice will be done.

'And on behalf of the American people, I thank the world for its outpouring of support. America will never forget the sounds of our national anthem playing at Buckingham Palace, on the streets of Paris and at Berlin's Brandenburg Gate. America has no truer friend than Great Britain. Once again we are joined together in a great cause. I'm so honoured the British Prime Minister has crossed an ocean to show his unity with America. Thank you for coming, friend.'

But what was Britain's and the SAS's role to be, beyond the symbolic and the diplomatic? This would be determined by the Pentagon and CENTCOM.

At 9.38 a.m. on 11 September, American Airlines Flight 77, which had taken off from Dulles International Airport, 25 miles west of Washington, DC, bound for Los Angeles, crashed into the five-sided and five-storey Pentagon building in northern Virginia. In blowing a hole 65 yards wide in the Pentagon's west side Al Qaeda had struck at what it saw as the heart of the beast, the Pentagon being the US military's headquarters.

CENTCOM, based at MacDill Air Force Base, Tampa, Florida, is the most important of the United States' worldwide combat command centres. Pre-9/11 between 18,000 and 25,000 American troops were deployed in its AOR (area of responsibility), twenty-five states including Afghanistan, Central Asia's former Soviet republics, Egypt and Iraq. These countries were home to 500 million people and at least eighteen major ethnic groups. CENTCOM's Commander-in-Chief (CINCCENT) during Operation ENDURING FREEDOM – the name given to military operations in Afghanistan – was General Tommy R. Franks.

A career artillery officer, fifty-six years old in September 2001, General Franks had completed three and a half decades of military service, including Vietnam, where he was wounded three times, and the Gulf War, where he was an

Assistant Divisional Commander answering to former legen-
dary CINCCENT General 'Stormin'' Norman Schwarzkopf.
Franks' career development had accelerated after Operation
DESERT STORM. In June 2000, the Commander, who like
President Bush hailed from Midland, Texas, was promoted
to the US Army's highest rank, of Four-Star General, and
took command at CENTCOM.

CENTCOM has three specific objectives, enhancing US
security, promoting democracy and human rights, and bol-
stering American economic prosperity. In order to meet
these goals CENTCOM, as Franks, a limited speaker seemingly addicted to military jargon, told the Senate Armed
Services Committee on 22 March 2001, 'promotes regional
stability, ensures uninterrupted access to resources and
markets, maintains freedom of navigation, protects US citizens and property and promotes the security of regional
friends and allies'.

Just three months into Franks' time in office Al Qaeda
shattered that stability when two men in a dinghy blew a
gaping hole in USS *Cole* as it refuelled just off Yemen, a
suicide strike which proved an appetizer for the atrocities
of 9/11.

The USS *Cole* attack prompted Franks to warn Capitol
Hill about the threat of terrorist groups in Afghanistan: 'We
need dedicated, long-term effort with access to all terrorist-
related information, both intelligence and law enforcement,
leveraged by state of the art information technology tools.
Timely warning will generate defensive and offensive
options that we do not currently have. We must concur-
rently ensure that we are postured in the event timely
warning does not come. The volatility of our region requires
CENTCOM remain adaptable and agile. Without a large
footprint in the region, we must be truly deployable.
Responsive command, control and communications during

peace, crisis and conflict will remain key to our ability to accomplish this mission.'

In the wake of the world's greatest terrorist strikes, Franks was under enormous pressure to ensure that Bush got his man 'dead or alive', to destroy Al Qaeda and oust the Taliban; all without sustaining high numbers of US casualties. His country and his President demanded success; with it would come the adulation enjoyed by General Schwarzkopf who in removing Saddam Hussein's forces from Kuwait single-handedly restored the American people's faith in their military after Vietnam and Operation EAGLE CLAW, Delta Force's failed US hostage rescue mission in Tehran in April 1980. Schwarzkopf became America's most popular military figure since Dwight Eisenhower. His boots were a big pair to fill.

The Pentagon promoted Franks as an all-action, tough-talking and cigar-smoking leader straight out of Schwarzkopf's mould, perhaps in a bid to counter the image of the camera-shy, softly spoken man who appeared on news bulletins. Franks was a highly experienced, well-regarded commander with a quieter, academic side. As well as having seen a lot of combat in Vietnam, he had a degree in business administration, a masters' degree in public administration and had passed through the US Armed Forces Staff College and Army War College.

Major General Leo Baxter, a fellow artillery officer who had known Franks for twenty-five years, made him sound as rough and tough as possible: 'Tommy is not a quiet, introverted thoughtful general. Tommy Franks is very outgoing, very opinionated. He is not a guy who flies off the handle, but in the course of a five-minute discussion about how you're wrong and he's right, he'll use words that are and aren't in the dictionary. Having spent lots of time in combat situations he's got this reputation as truly a soldier's general. He's very engaging and delightfully profane. He talks the language of soldiers and the soldiers love him for it.'

The story also emerged of how Franks put his legs up on a desk at the start of a meeting. Asked 'How are you, sir?' by a junior officer about to brief him, the reclining Franks replied in his Southern drawl: 'I'm the best you'll ever meet.'

Although Baxter made Franks seem like Schwarzkopf, this was not the Franks General de la Billière encountered in Kuwait in 1991. At the time Franks was part of the First Cavalry Division and 'DLB' Commander-in-Chief of British forces, some of whom were under Franks' immediate authority. The ex-SAS CO recalled: 'Physically, Franks was the exact opposite of Norman [Schwarzkopf] being small and quiet, and limping slightly on one artificial leg – the legacy of a severe wound received in Vietnam. But he resembled Norman in being intelligent and likeable.'

His background did the SAS's chances of immediate action no favours. Like Schwarzkopf, Franks was not a 'Spec Ops' man. His specialist field was big guns, not the guerrilla warfare-style tactics which the SAS is most adept at employing. At least Schwarzkopf's background was US Airborne. It did not bode well that Schwarzkopf, with more Spec Ops experience than Franks, still needed a pretty hefty dig in the ribs from DLB to be persuaded to use the Regiment inside Iraq. Schwarzkopf thought the anti-Scud role he proposed was too risky. After victory he was quick to recognize DLB was right – as he so often was during his exemplary military career – and wrote to Air Chief Marshal Sir Patrick Hine, Joint Commander of Operation GRANBY, praising the SAS for its 'totally outstanding performance'.

Schwarzkopf's reluctance was based on experiences in Vietnam when Special Forces suffered heavy casualties and failed to achieve over-ambitious targets. His *modus operandi* for victory was conventional and, quite rightly, low risk. His cautious approach, belying his huge physical size and temper, was underpinned by a genuine sense of paternal care towards his troops; in removing the Iraqi Army from Kuwait he was simply not prepared to jeopardize unnecessarily any of his 450,000 soldiers – 45,000 of whom were British.

Strong links between the SAS and the US military existed long before Gulf War I. One should not underestimate the Pentagon's complement to the Regiment in establishing Delta Force in 1977, replicating SAS Selection, continuation training, and squadron and troop structure. The architect was Colonel 'Chargin'' Charlie Beckwith, who was badged and served in Hereford in 1962–3. That this was the case makes the foresight of one twenty-four-year-old Scots Guards subaltern, Lieutenant D. A. Stirling, in 1941 all the more remarkable. Since Delta Force's inception a constant flow of personnel between Fort Bragg and Stirling Lines had fostered generosity and mutual respect which paid off during the Falklands War, the SAS receiving Stinger missiles, which accounted for at least one Argentine aircraft, and of greater importance, TACSAT (Tactical Satellite Communications) equipment which provided the critical Command Net between the SAS CO on the ground, General Sir Michael Rose, and the MOD.

In its early years the SAS was regarded as a peripheral, maverick unit made up of gung-ho misfits. After a half century of unrivalled success in combat it opened the batting for UKLF (United Kingdom Land Forces), and many of its officers, such as DLB, General Rose, the British Army's most decorated officer on his retirement in 1992, who was also CO at the time of Operation NIMROD and later Commander of the UN Protection Force in Bosnia in 1994, and General Sir Charles Guthrie, CDS prior to Admiral Sir Michael Boyce, infiltrated Whitehall's corridors of power and developed excellent reputations across the Atlantic. By contrast, Delta Force and its officers had been unable to make a similar impact on the higher echelons of the US military, two reasons being a lack of comparable operational achievements and the sheer size of the US Army.

Set against the US Defense Department's unilateralist stance, the Bush Administration's fear of body bags affecting public support and General Franks' steady approach, the SAS faced potential exclusion from Operation ENDURING FREEDOM. These factors trumped what the Regiment had to offer, its service record and even the high regard in which it was held inside the Pentagon, CENTCOM and the SOCOM (US Special Operations Command). At least the United States' newly appointed Chairman of the Joint Chiefs of Staff, General Hugh Sheldon, had a Spec Ops pedigree as a former SOCOM CINC and commander of the 82nd Airborne Division; it mattered not from the Regiment's perspective that he got the job only after the first choice, the then Vice-Chairman of the Chiefs of Staff, General Andrew Ralston, withdrew his candidacy after US media reports of his alleged affair with a female CIA agent. Although the CO had been promised an invitation to what his troops would call 'America's Party', he would not be the guest of honour.

3. THE ELVIS OF THE EAST*

If he were to appear on television now, what would he say? All he could say is 'I am alive.' That would seem childish. Remember, this is a man who took years to plan the World Trade Center attack. He is planning another attack and he will be just as meticulous, just as careful. If he succeeds then he will appear on television. For him, it is not enough of a victory just to survive.

Issam Abdullah, expert in the psychology of
Osama bin Laden

Osama bin Laden was born on 10 March 1957 in Riyadh, Saudi Arabia's capital, the seventeenth son of a hugely wealthy and well-connected construction magnate. Mohammed bin Laden was pro-Western, educating his eldest son Salem at Millfield, the exclusive public school in Somerset. Osama's upbringing took place in privileged surroundings but was strict, dominated by religious observance and hard work.

Life centred on his father Mohammed's Bin Laden

* 'I think the most probable outcome is that he [Osama bin Laden] will not be found. We will never know for certain what happened to Osama bin Laden. I don't mean to trivialize it, but he's going to become the Elvis Presley of the east.' Admiral Eugene Carroll, 28 December 2001.

Construction Company, founded in 1931. The BLCC is an incredible success story. Its Yemeni-born founder, Osama's father, started his career as an illiterate labourer who found his way to the court of King Abdul Aziz of Saudi Arabia, where he distinguished himself by building a wheelchair ramp which enabled the partially paralysed King to reach his first-floor bedroom. Mohammed bin Laden's assiduously cultivated royal connections secured the Kingdom's most lucrative contracts, building roads, palaces and Mecca's Holy Mosque. He had twenty-one wives – in accordance with Islamic law, no more than four at a time. His fifty-four offspring included twenty-four sons. After Mohammed bin Laden's death in a plane crash in 1967, King Faisal supported the bin Laden family and paid for the children's education. Osama bin Laden would betray this kindness, dismissing his family's ties with the House of Saud and wishing it forgotten that he grew up in royal circles.

Osama was gentle, quiet and more religiously devout than most of his contemporaries. Friends recall the shy, slight youth's consideration towards others. Whatever his claims to have hated Jews and Americans since childhood, there was no hint of the extremism to come. Anti-Western feelings, if harboured, were well hidden. He was an ordinary boy, his height, not his politics, distinguishing him from his peers. He lavishly praised his father's achievements and was deeply affected by his death. From his late teens and through his twenties and thirties, he sought the company of intellectually superior and older men for spiritual and political guidance.

At the age of seventeen he married Najwa Ghanem, a Syrian relative on his mother's side. In 1977, he enrolled at Jeddah's King Abdul Aziz University to study economics. The gifted student joined the Muslim Brotherhood organization, which advocated a society based on *Shari'a* (Holy)

Law. One of its speakers, the militant Palestinian Abdullah Azzam, lit the touch-paper of bin Laden's Islamic fundamentalism and was his closest ally for the next decade. With a convert's zeal he turned against his affluent homeland. He became increasingly anti-Western and anti-Jewish, convincing himself of the non-Muslim world's corruption and the necessity of Israel's destruction. In 1981, Bin Laden headed for the world's least hospitable country: Afghanistan.

As one of 10,000 Saudis and 35,000 Muslims from forty-three countries to volunteer for the *Mujahideen*, the 'Army of God', Bin Laden insisted that fighting the *jihad* was his religious duty and in accordance with his father's wishes. Some experts claim he was also recruited by Saudi intelligence; this was unlikely, given that he had turned against the ruling Royal Family.

Legend has it that bin Laden was an excellent horseman, but with no military training the lanky twenty-two-year-old was of little use on the front line where between December 1979 and 1989 a staggering one million Afghans and Arabs were killed. Bin Laden saw the *Mujahideen*'s need for greater infrastructure, finance and manpower in order to mount a sustained guerrilla warfare campaign based on surprise and stealth rather than confronting the superpower head-on – these were tactics the SAS also instructed the *Mujahideen* to adopt. He was a peerless fundraiser, providing millions of dollars for BLCC engineers and workmen to build roads, tunnels and caves which would later be used to good effect by Al Qaeda. The CIA dubbed him the *Mujahideen*'s 'financial Godfather'.

With Abdullah Azzam, bin Laden founded the Maktab al-Khidmat (MAK) group, recruiting volunteers and paying for their transportation and training. His first military camp, a forerunner of Al Qaeda's facilities, was established in eastern Afghanistan in 1986, its recruits schooled in infantry and artillery skills by Pakistani and American officers. The

United States supported the flood of would-be warriors as it wanted to highlight global opposition to Moscow's invasion. Many would remain in Afghanistan after the Soviet withdrawal to join Al Qaeda.

In 1986, bin Laden moved to Peshawar, Pakistan. In his flowing white robes he stood out from recruits in their *shalwar kameez*, the familiar baggy trousers and long loose shirts. He had delusions of royal grandeur and enjoyed being referred to as 'the Sheikh'.

By the late 1980s, bin Laden's global ambitions outstripped those around him. He found a new mentor, Ayman Al-Zawahiri, in 1987, who became his Al Qaeda deputy. The podgy, bespectacled Egyptian doctor led the Egyptian militant group Islamic Jihad, which assassinated President Anwar Sadat in 1981. His first mentor, Azzam, was jettisoned and killed by a car bomb in 1989; bin Laden's involvement was suspected.

The imperialists vanquished, Afghanistan's warlords, who had united in a common cause, reverted to their predominant pastime: in-fighting. Bin Laden, meanwhile, basked in personal glory and when interviewed later by CNN dismissed the US role, claiming: 'They were a burden on the *Mujahideen* and us in Afghanistan. We were just performing a duty to support Islam, although this duty crossed with US interests – without our consent.'

The liberation of Afghanistan was won at a huge cost. The tools of war littered the ground: burnt-out aircraft, tanks, personal weapons and 10 million anti-personnel and anti-tank mines which would kill 8,000 civilians a year after the conflict. Every man and boy carried a Kalashnikov AK47 assault rifle. There was little law and order in the major cities and none beyond them. Afghanistan was an aid-based state unable to support itself; its citizens lived in hunger and poverty, with no sense of national identity.

'Success' against the Soviets fed bin Laden's aspirations.

He had a global coalition of radicals at his disposal; they had studied Islam and fought the Russians side by side. He formed Al Qaeda – 'The Base' – in 1988, and returned to Saudi Arabia in 1990, whipping up feverish opposition to the Royal Family's Western-influenced modernization. Thousands of his imported foot soldiers spread their wings, joining Muslim armies in Somalia, the Balkans and Chechnya. In 1991, Al Qaeda merged with Al-Zawahiri's Egyptian Islamic Jihad. There was a surfeit of volunteers for terrorist assignments. Only men of the highest religious devotion, intelligence and skills were chosen for operations. They worked independently, ensuring that Bin Laden could never be directly linked to any one mission. 'Need to know' was another Al Qaeda tenet – as it is in the SAS.

Anticipating his neighbour Saddam Hussein's expansionist ideas, Saudi Arabia's King Fahd spent billions on US fighter aircraft, tanks and Patriot missiles. To bin Laden's fury he favoured 450,000 Allied soldiers to defend the kingdom ahead of his 'Afghan Alumni' when Kuwait was invaded. This snub from the Royal Household led to bin Laden cutting ties with Saudi Arabia. He called Interior Minister Prince Naif 'a traitor to Islam' for allowing tens of thousands of US troops to stay on after Iraqi forces were repelled in 1991.

Bin Laden wrote to King Fahd attacking Saudi Arabia's close relationship with America: 'The core of our disagreement with you is your abandonment of your duties to the religion of the One True God.' He found Saudi Arabia's close ties with America and the presence of its troops on 'Holy Land' – Mecca and Medina – abhorrent. In bin Laden's words: 'The latest and greatest of aggressions incurred by the Muslims since the death of the Prophet is the occupation of the land of the two Holy Places – the foundation of the house of Islam, the place of revelation, the source of the message – by the armies of the American

Crusaders and their allies.' The expulsion of US and Allied forces from the Gulf would become a critical strategic and ideological goal for Al Qaeda.

The Saudi Royal Family's conspicuous wealth and the values of the Kingdom's social elite outraged bin Laden. He regarded the region's oil as Allah's gift to be shared, not to grant the privileged few a life of splendour. Bin Laden had no truck with a secular ideology like Marxism. His belief, albeit socialistic in tone, was in accordance with Islamic teaching that God's subjects lead a humble life.

Saudi Arabia's economic inequality caused social unrest and made the country fertile ground for Al Qaeda. Anti-Western feeling had never been higher. Fifteen of the 9/11 hijackers were Saudis. With oil revenues falling, the country faced uncertainty. Income per head had fallen from $28,600 to $6,800 since 1980 and unemployment stood at 33 per cent in 2001. Of the country's population of 22.7 million people, 77 per cent lived in major cities and 50 per cent were aged eighteen and under. Saudi Arabia had also lost 'best-friend' status in Washington, as America had become less reliant on Saudi oil; in 2001 the United States imported just 8 per cent of its crude from Saudi Arabia, against 25 per cent in 1973. The Saudi Government claimed bin Laden deliberately chose its citizens for the strikes on New York and Washington to undermine further its relationship with America.

Bin Laden spent the years 1992 to 1996 in Sudan, mostly in Khartoum. Under the guise of employing ex-Afghan *Mujahideen* as factory workers and farm labourers, he could continue their military and terrorist training. Sudan, regarded by the United States as a sponsor of international terrorism, rejected calls for bin Laden's deportation, while his fortune paid for an airport at Port Sudan and the Port Sudan to Khartoum highway.

On 26 February 1993, exactly two years after the liberation of Kuwait, six people were killed and 1,000 injured in the first attack on the World Trade Center. Experts considered the date more than a coincidence and pointed the finger at Iraq. The target was considered too big for Islamic fundamentalists working without state sponsorship, a capability which has evolved since that time. The main protagonist, Ramzi Ahmed Yousef, was captured in Pakistan in 1995 and is serving a 240-year prison sentence. He drove the van full of explosives which exploded in an underground garage. Had the detonator been correctly positioned, the bomb might have downed one of the Towers.

Yousef studied at Swansea's West Glamorgan Institute of Higher Education before joining a more traditional Al Qaeda finishing school, the Muslim Brotherhood. His real identity and that of his paymasters remain unclear. Although he trained in Afghanistan for six months in 1988, he was no typical bin Laden foot soldier. Yousef was more of a one-man band: attempting to kill Pakistan's Prime Minister Benazir Bhutto; planning to fly a plane into the CIA headquarters in Langley, Virginia; and to kill Pope John Paul II. Bin Laden was just one of many suspected conspirators further down the list after Saddam Hussein.

By late 1992 Al Qaeda had expanded into Africa and the United States followed suit, committing 28,000 troops to Operation RESTORE HOPE, the United Nations' humanitarian mission in Somalia. Still seething about what he saw as US troops' 'occupancy' of the Gulf, Bin Laden issued a *fatwa* condemning America's move.

In 1996, his three wives and thirteen children in tow, bin Laden returned to Afghanistan. In Kabul, captured by the Taliban in the same year, Pakistani ISI (Inter Services Intelligence) introduced him to the new regime's senior members. The ISI suggested they protect bin Laden and capitalize on his wealth and skills. In return for security, bin

Laden would train Taliban at his terrorist camps and send Al Qaeda to fight the Northern Alliance. From his haven bin Laden issued his first call for *jihad* against Western occupation of Arabia: 'The walls of oppression and humiliation cannot be demolished except in a rain of bullets.'

The Taliban – the 'Students' – emerged as a predominantly Pakistani force in Afghanistan's civil war in 1994, armed and organized by the ISI. They were men aged from fifteen to twenty-five who had congregated at the Saudi-funded *Madrassas*, the colleges in Pakistan's tribal areas offering religious instruction and military training. By 1990 500,000 had graduated. Pakistan exported the Taliban to control its lawless, politically unstable neighbour.

Al Qaeda had become a highly sophisticated multinational organization. Below bin Laden and Al-Zawahiri, the revolutionary council leaders, it separated into four *Shura Majlis*, committees overseeing religious/legal affairs, finance, media and military operations. In the next section down were numerous semi-autonomous cells. Being divided into small working groups made Al Qaeda extremely difficult to infiltrate. A spy could only access information in his own department.

As 9/11 indicated, meticulous planning and preparation characterize its operations, executed by units established in the target country working under limited supervision. Al Qaeda strikes 'high-ball' targets, and unlike Western terrorist organizations such as ETA or the IRA, resists claiming the responsibility and glory.

Bin Laden prefers hinting at his connections to those in custody. He admitted being a friend of one of Ramzi Yousef's accomplices, Wali Khan, but denied knowing Yousef himself, despite of evidence that he stayed in a bin Laden-owned guest house in Pakistan. Bin Laden also denied knowledge of preparations for Yousef's World Trade Center attack, merely warning that there would be 'future Ramzi Yousefs' because of US foreign policy towards Muslims.

The scale and success rate of Al Qaeda's attacks are critical, not their frequency: there is no rush towards execution. Al Qaeda likes its volunteers to strike in their homelands, a request John Walker Lindt, the 'Californian Taliban', refused, insisting he fight in Afghanistan. The story of Ahmed Ressam, on the other hand, is typical. Algerian by birth, he lived in Canada from 1994. He was recruited into Al Qaeda through his Montreal mosque and sent to a bin Laden camp in Afghanistan in 1998. Ressam returned six months later to identify potential US targets, which included plotting to blow up Los Angeles International Airport. He worked independently and did not return to Afghanistan for authorization or further training. Any such movement and communications between Canada and Al Qaeda HQ would have been picked up by intelligence agencies. He was finally arrested on the United States/ Canada border on 14 December 1999 with maps and 130 pounds of explosives in his car.

At 8.46 a.m. on 11 September 2001, Eastern Standard Time, American Airlines Flight 11 from Boston to Los Angeles, a Boeing 767 carrying ninety-two passengers and crew, lodged itself between the ninety-fourth and ninety-eighth floors of the North Tower of the World Trade Center. The Boeing's fuel tanks exploded instantly, creating an inferno and signing a death warrant for everyone on and above the ninety-first floor.

Four of the five hijackers were trained pilots, including the man thought to have steered the plane, the thirty-three-year-old Egyptian Mohammed Atta. Atta, their leader, had bought his ticket to martyrdom on-line and sat in Flight

AA11's seat 8D. Three days before the attacks he had been on a last night out in Florida. Although less than seventy-two hours away from death, he had none the less complained to bar staff that his drinks and meals were too expensive.

Atta's now familiar mug-shot is a chilling picture of a man for whom his life's end has become the point of his existence. Later it was reported that the FBI recovered a handwritten letter in Arabic written to or from Atta. This reputedly said:

> Purify your heart and forget something called life, for the time of play is gone and the time of truth has come. God will absolve you of your sins, and be assured that it will only be moments and then you will attain the ultimate and greatest reward. Check your bag, your clothes, knives, tools, ID, passport, all your papers. Inspect all your weapons before departure. Let each find his blade for the prey to be slaughtered. As soon as you put your feet in and before you enter [the plane] start praying and realize that this is a battle for the sake of God, and when you sit down in your seat say your prayers as we have mentioned before. When the plane starts moving, then you are travelling towards God and what a blessing that travel is.

The CIA and the FBI were convinced of bin Laden's involvement. But where was this mysterious, iconic figure? Bin Laden was thought to be in Afghanistan, under Taliban protection, having established a close relationship with its leader, Mullah Omar. The latter declined the Americans' request to hand over the fugitive and told his people to prepare for *jihad*: holy war against the American 'infidels'.

With a $10 billion annual anti-terrorist budget, the capital was there to pay for the extermination of Al Qaeda's war council, but not the intelligence. The first CIA snatch bid against bin Laden had been scrapped in 1997 because the Agency did not have the necessary contacts in Afghanistan. A year later, in response to the attacks on the US embassies in Nairobi and Dar es Salaam which killed 224 people, seventy US cruise missiles struck Al Qaeda training camps near Khost and Jalalabad, killing around forty Afghans, Pakistanis, Yemenis and Saudi nationals. The United States put a $5 million bounty on Osama bin Laden's head.

President Clinton had been unimpressed with the CIA's efforts, complaining in one memo: 'We've got to do better, this is unsatisfactory.'

Middle East television station *Al Jazeera's* interview with Kuwaiti Khalid Sheikh Mohammed, a key planner of 9/11, would later give an insight into the hijackers' mindset. From a 'secret' location in Pakistan he revealed: 'The attacks were designed to cause as many deaths as possible and havoc and to be a big slap for America on American soil. We were never short of potential martyrs. Indeed we have a department called the Department of Martyrs. We have scores of volunteers. Our problem at the time was to select suitable people who are familiar with the West.'

Mohammed, the head of Al Qaeda's military committee, was arrested in a well-heeled suburb of Rawalpindi, Pakistan, in February 2003 at the home of Jamaat-e-Islami politician Ahmed Abdul Qadoos. Mohammed was the highest-ranking Al Qaeda chief at large, with the exception of bin Laden and one of the FBI's twenty-two 'Most Wanted' terrorists, with a $25 million bounty on his head.

On 'Holy Tuesday', 11 September 2001, Al Qaeda pulled off history's most audacious and destructive terrorist attack. Osama bin Laden's guerrilla force had demonstrated that it would be a worthy foe for the SAS. Its potency was one reason why the Regiment's forthcoming battle would be among its most dangerous.

4. 'ON MY ORDERS'

On 6 October 2001, a confident President Bush declared: 'The Taliban has been given the opportunity to surrender all the terrorists in Afghanistan and time is running out.' The world held its breath.

Bush's forces would have to fight hard enough to ensure the defeat of the Taliban and the capture or death of Osama bin Laden, while preventing the bloodthirsty alliance of Afghan forces from repeating the worst atrocities of the regime they sought to depose. At the same time, the fact that America was the richest country in the world was not lost in either Washington or Kabul. The American view was encapsulated by retired US diplomat and Afghan expert Edmund McWilliams, who said: 'Afghan commanders naturally respond to money. They can be bought off. That is the way things work in Afghanistan.'

When your potential allies were so fickle, however, accustomed to changing sides during a conflict and demanding large sums of money in return for giving information, co-operation was conditional on yours being the largest bid. America would need to use bribes and bullets, as General Hamid Gul, former chief of the Pakistani ISI, warned: 'They say you can always rent an Afghan. But you can never be sure you own them.'

Teaming up with the ISI was risky for the CIA after its perceived failure to prevent the attacks of 9/11. Its agents had little means of assessing the accuracy of ISI-supplied intelligence on Al Qaeda and Osama bin Laden, or preventing details they shared being fed to the Kabul regime. The CIA was not in a strong bargaining position, as Robert C. 'Bud' McFarlane, Ronald Reagan's former Security Advisor, explained: 'The CIA has failed miserably. There's an appalling lack of intelligence skills. I have not found one Dari speaker in the agency – or anyone who speaks any other Afghan dialect, for that matter; or any analyst with real knowledge of Afghanistan's history, its tribal cultures, the networks that exist there.'

CENTCOM employed its technological advantage to build an intelligence picture, not Special Forces units at its disposal such as the SAS. Although intelligence-gathering remains at the core of the Regiment's *raison d'être*, such work is increasingly carried out by camera-equipped drones and robots. A fleet of UAVs (Unmanned Aerial Vehicles), controlled with joysticks by ground-based operators at CIA HQ, Langley, Virginia, beamed back live footage of Afghanistan via satellite.

During Gulf War I, when UAVs were much less advanced, they still flew 500 sorties, lasting over 1,600 hours. Five Iraqi soldiers even surrendered to a drone. UAVs were also used in Kosovo.

As a Defense Department spokeswoman said on 10 October 2001, 'The value of UAVs is in saving lives – they give you a sense of the battlefield without putting your airmen in danger.' Another advantage was that they were cheaper to build than manned aircraft and could be deployed over enemy territory in greater numbers.

While the likes of Donald Rumsfeld, Colin Powell and Tony Blair were globetrotting in their bids to win support for military action, the world's media was feasting on predictions of how the war might be fought. In Britain, the *Sun* urged Blair to 'Kick ass, Tony', while in America Ann

Coulter, a columnist on the *National Review* magazine, said of the Afghans: 'Kill their leaders and convert them to Christianity.' In the wake of the most devastating terrorist attack in history, these sentiments, which led to Coulter's dismissal from the publication, were echoed by many.

On 7 October 2001, twenty-six days after Al Qaeda brought Armageddon to New York and Washington, the United States hit back. Waves of aerial attacks struck key AQT (Al Qaeda/ Taliban) targets across Afghanistan. Just thirty minutes after the first target was destroyed, President Bush addressed the American people from the Treaty Room at the White House. It was 1 p.m. Eastern District Time and 9 p.m. in Kabul. The war had begun.

US and British Tomahawk missiles hit thirty targets including unoccupied terrorist training camps, military airfields, a garrison and air defence sites. On that night and during the raids on successive nights, the US Air Force used fifteen land-based bomber aircraft, twenty-five strike aircraft from its US Navy carriers and B-1, B-2 and B-52 long-range bombers which flew from the British island of Diego Garcia in the Indian Ocean and Whiteman Air Force Base, Missouri.

In his address to the nation the President said: 'Good afternoon. On my orders, the United States military has begun strikes against Al Qaeda terrorist training camps and military installations of the Taliban regime in Afghanistan. Those carefully targeted actions are designed to disrupt the use of Afghanistan as a terrorist base of operations, and to attack the military capability of the Taliban regime.

'We are joined in this operation by our staunch friend, Great Britain. Other close friends, including Canada, Australia, Germany and France have pledged forces as the operation unfolds. More than forty countries in the Middle

East, Africa, Europe and across Asia have granted air transit or landing rights. Many more have shared intelligence. We are supported by the collective will of the world.

'More than two weeks ago, I gave Taliban leaders a series of clear and specific demands: close terrorist camps, hand over leaders of the Al Qaeda network and return all foreign nationals, including American citizens, unjustly detained in your country. None of these demands was met and the Taliban will pay a price. By destroying camps and disrupting communications, we will make it more difficult for the terror network to train new recruits and co-ordinate their evil plans.

'Initially, the terrorists may burrow deeper into caves and other entrenched hiding places. Our military action is designed to clear the way for sustained, comprehensive and relentless operations to drive them out and bring them to justice. At the same time, the oppressed people of Afghanistan will know the generosity of America and our allies. As we strike military targets, we'll also drop food, medicine and supplies to the starving and suffering men and women and children of Afghanistan.

'We did not ask for this mission, but we will fulfil it. The name of today's military operation is Enduring Freedom. We defend not only our precious freedoms but also the freedom of people everywhere to live and raise their children free of fear. To all the men and women in our military – every sailor, every soldier, every airman, every coastguardsman, every Marine – I say this: Your mission is defined; your objectives are clear; your goal is just. You have my full confidence, and you will have every tool you need to carry out your duty.

'The battle is now joined on many fronts. We will not waver; we will not tire; we will not falter; and we will not fail. Peace and freedom will prevail. Thank you. May God continue to bless America.'

The majority of the missiles fired were precision-guided, but not all. In Gulf War I, 10 per cent of munitions were precision-guided, that figure had now risen to 90 per cent. These were known as JDAMs (Joint Direct Attack Munitions) equipped with GPS (Global Positioning System) for navigation. Taliban leader Mullah Omar's office was struck with pinpoint accuracy – he left the building in Kandahar only fifteen minutes before the missiles struck, according to his aides – and a few days later US military sources claimed jets had hit the Taliban leader's Chevrolet Suburban vehicle, but he was not in it. Three of the first night targets were around Kabul, four close to other large settlements and the remaining twenty-three in remote areas, the MOD announced.

The US Air Force also dropped 37,500 MRE (Meals Ready to Eat) packets and medicines to refugees near the Pakistan border as part of President Bush's $320 million humanitarian aid programme. Aid organizations feared that isolated villages in Afghanistan could lose around 30 per cent of their populations due to starvation unless food arrived quickly.

America's military action received widespread support in Europe, Russia and Israel and a guarded response in many sections of the Muslim world. But the first night's action was a fraction of the size of the United States' initial aerial bombardment of Kosovo in 1998 or Iraq during Operation DESERT STORM in 1990. Former US Air Force chief of staff General Merrill McPeak said: 'This was very limited, very deliberate. We do much bigger exercises than this in peacetime. We fired more Tomahawks at bin Laden following the attacks on the African embassies three years ago than we have so far. This has been a very restrained response. The attacks so far and into the future are pretty easy, straightforward stuff.'

In Whitehall, the smooth-talking and tasselled-loafer-wearing Secretary of State for Defence, Geoff Hoon MP, and his more studious sidekick, the CDS Admiral Sir Michael Boyce, explained Britain's role. At least one of the three Royal Navy nuclear submarines in theatre, HMS *Superb*, HMS *Trafalgar* or HMS *Triumph* – the MoD would not say which – fired Tomahawk missiles at an Al Qaeda terrorist camp target near Kandahar. It was the first mission of Operation VERITAS, the name given to UK military operations in Afghanistan.

Hoon justified the Allied aerial attacks as acts of 'legitimate self-defence' under the United Nations' charter as the Taliban had refused to comply with 'tireless diplomatic efforts'. The United States and Britain, he claimed, struck back to protect its citizens from further Al Qaeda attacks. He was also quick to deny Taliban reports that the first night caused heavy civilian casualties.

The regime claimed twenty-five dead in Kabul, with the Taliban's ambassador in Pakistan, Abdul Salam Zaeff, saying: 'The brave people of Afghanistan will never be intimidated by these fears. By sacrificing their lives, they will defend the faith, Islam. The attacks were meaningless, unprincipled and illegal. If the Americans irrationally believe they can benefit from spilling the blood of innocent Afghans then they are wrong. There was no difference made between civilian and military targets.'

Geoff Hoon insisted: 'I know there have been military reports that bombs and missiles have fallen near civilian areas. Detonations at nearby targets and anti-aircraft fire can easily give the impression, particularly at night, that civilian areas are under attack. I can assure you that this was not the case. Neither the Afghan civilian population nor their homes and property have been targeted.'

In a foretaste of how the United States would direct the ground war, it became clear that Britain's air role would be limited to reconnaissance and support, despite RAF Tornado and Harrier strike aircraft being available. Meanwhile, the NATO Standing Force Mediterranean fleet of battle ships, including a Royal Navy vessel, was poised to provide force protection for the US ships, if required.

Admiral Boyce said: 'These deployments show we are committed to the long haul. Last night was not a single strike. We know that defeating international terrorism and its supporters can be neither easy nor quick. The Armed Forces are ready for a long haul and they are resolved to make their full contribution to the victory which I am sure, I am confident in fact, we will have at the end of the day.'

The second wave of air strikes, on 8 October, targeted the Taliban's strategic and tactical resources, with cruise missiles fired from US ships and warplanes at terrorist camps and air defence sites dotted around Afghanistan. Defense Secretary Donald Rumsfeld was satisfied: 'We believe we have made progress toward eliminating the air defence sites and made an impact on the military airfields. Every target was a military target.' After a third successive night of bombing, Chairman of the US Joint Chiefs of Staff, General Richard Myers declared: 'Essentially we have air supremacy over Afghanistan.'

Destroying the Taliban's static anti-aircraft guns was relatively easy. More elusive were its portable surface-to-air missiles, the US-made Stingers that were thrown on to the back of a pick-up truck and driven to a cave hideaway whenever US planes were about. After providing the *Mujahideen* with Stinger missiles in the 1980s, the United States tried, with limited success, to buy them back at $1 million each when the Russians left. It learnt the hard way how thrifty Afghans can be; some were kept and fell into Taliban hands, others sold to America's arch-enemy, Iran.

Phase One focused predominantly on 'balance-sheet' targets, such as military installations. Future air strikes would pinpoint more human targets, such as Osama bin

Laden's possible hideouts. A Taliban spokesman declared that bin Laden and regime leader Mullah Omar survived the opening attacks. The Al Qaeda leader cleverly timed the release of his latest propaganda bulletin, by *Al-Jazeera*, which had become his mouthpiece. It was broadcast just two hours after the air strikes.

Bin Laden was filmed holding a microphone and sitting in front of a rock face beside his closest Al Qaeda ally, Ayman Al-Zawahiri. He had a Kalashnikov rifle next to him. He issued a defiant message, inciting *jihad* against 'infidels', but again said nothing to link him directly to the 9/11 attacks.

'To America I swear by God the great. America will never taste security and safety unless we feel security and safety in our lands and in Palestine. America was hit by God in one of its softest spots. America is full of fear from its north to its south, from its west to its east. Thank God for that. Millions of innocent children are being killed in Iraq and in Palestine and we don't hear a word from the infidels. We don't hear a voice. When the sword falls on the United States, they cry for their children and they cry for their people. The least you can say about these people is that they are sinners. They have helped evil triumph over good. These events have split the world into two camps – belief and disbelief. Every Muslim should support his religion.'

Among the audience of hundreds of millions worldwide was esteemed US geologist Jack Shroder, from the University of Nebraska at Omaha. The sixty-two-year-old, who in 1977 went to Afghanistan to map the country, turned to his wife and said: 'I know where he is.'

Shroder, who was expelled in 1978 after accusations of spying, told US intelligence that the type of sedimentary rock seen on the film behind bin Laden could only be found in two areas of eastern Afghanistan, Paktia and Paktika.

Word of Shroder's information must have got back to bin Laden as he always appeared in front of a man-made background in his later broadcasts.

As the air strikes continued, the link-up with the Northern Alliance continued to cause diplomatic problems, with General Pervez Musharraf accusing its members of taking advantage of Afghanistan's problems in a bid to seize power. After Musharraf said he feared the country would return to 'anarchy and atrocity and criminal killing' under the Northern Alliance and that the group 'must be kept in check', US Secretary of State Colin Powell was dispatched to Pakistan to placate its premier. The United States also lifted economic sanctions against Pakistan, imposed against it and India in 1998 after both nations conducted nuclear tests, and promised $50 million of aid for refugees.

Less than a week into the Allied bombing campaign, the United States demonstrated its aerial dominance by carrying out unopposed daylight raids. American jets flew in at will, dropping cluster-bombs and laser-guided missiles. Senior naval officers on the giant aircraft carrier, USS *Carl Vinson*, from which numerous strikes were launched, explained it was no longer necessary to use 'stand-off' weapons which could be dropped from safe altitude. The jets could come in low over Afghanistan. But laser-guided or otherwise, missiles do not always hit their intended target, and rockets intended for Taliban helicopters at Kabul airport strayed into a civilian area nearby.

Over the first ten days of bombing the tally of civilian casualties grew steadily, but two incidents in particular caused America most diplomatic embarrassment. These were the deaths of four UN Security guards in Kabul on Tuesday, 9 October, and the bombing of a Red Cross warehouse in Kabul on 16 October. The four UN civilians were asleep on the ground floor of the Afghan Technical

Consultancy (ATC), the country's biggest mine-clearing agency. The US missiles struck despite the ATC giving satellite co-ordinates of its position to its headquarters to be passed on to the Americans.

Phase One was none the less completed without major problems, much to the Commander-in-Chief's relief. A confident Bush rode high in the polls. War seemed to suit the President, being something you kept as simple as possible. The battle was proving considerably easier than the exhaustive diplomatic push in the final hours before the war when, with Bush's patience running out, Tony Blair delivered to a jittery Pakistan Government a twenty-one-page document containing US intelligence reports linking bin Laden directly 9/11. Blair also went to India to get Prime Minister Atal Behari's support and to Russia to keep Vladimir Putin on board. Meanwhile, Defense Secretary Rumsfeld toured 'wobbling' states in the Middle East to firm up their offers of tangible support.

President Bush was in aggressive mood after the opening salvoes of the War against Terrorism. Holding a prime-time news conference on 11 October, exactly a month after the attacks on New York and Washington, he promised the American people that US forces would hunt down their target: 'We are dismantling their military, disrupting their communications, severing their ability to defend themselves. And slowly, but surely, we're smoking Al Qaeda out of their caves so we can bring them to justice.'

The President continued: 'My focus is bringing Al Qaeda to justice and saying to the host government, "You had your chance to deliver." Actually, I will say it again, if you cough him up and his people, today, that we'll reconsider what we are doing to your country. You still have a second chance. Bring him in, and bring his leaders and lieutenants and other thugs and criminals with him.'

A small number of well-planned and superbly executed

search-and-destroy missions might accelerate this process of bringing the Al Qaeda leaders to justice. Two spectacular Special Operations missions on 19 October were intended to kick start the war's second phase and prove that US forces could be as dominant on the ground as they were in the air.

The 'daring' night-time raids by some of the world's best-trained soldiers would maintain Operation ENDURING FREEDOM's thus far breathtaking momentum. American bombers and strike aircraft had been knocking out Al Qaeda targets virtually at will for a fortnight. It was time for the Army's 'hard-arse' elite forces to, as they put it, 'get down and dirty'.

If they were very lucky, the US Rangers and Delta Force teams might snare Taliban leader Mullah Mohammed Omar or Osama bin Laden. Failing that, the hit-and-run missions would still gain vital enemy intelligence, serve as a demonstration of their combat capabilities and give their own morale a substantial boost. They would also show the world that America had cleared that post-Vietnam psychological barrier; that it was again willing to put its troops in dangerous situations when the law of averages dictated they would not all survive.

To counter bin Laden's skilful televised propaganda, for the first time in military history one of the operations would also be filmed, with pictures beamed across the world. Not only Al Qaeda would see what US Special Forces were capable of achieving. After hundreds of Hollywood war movies, this was a case of life imitating art. America would be able to watch the real thing just hours after it happened; or so it was told.

The Start Line for the operations was drawn in the Arabian Gulf where the troops would be airlifted from US ships to forward-operating bases inside Pakistan. From these locations US troops would be flown to both target zones and infiltrate by parachute and helicopter before surrounding and outgunning their startled opposition. They had millions of dollars' worth of firepower: helicopter gun-ships, space-age navigational and night-vision aids; combat fatigues that kept the soldiers cool when it was hot and warm when it was cold, and the most lethal weaponry developed by man.

As if this was not enough, the element of surprise and cover of darkness would also be on their side. Extensive top cover would be provided for both missions by a fleet of one of the world's most destructive aircraft, the AC-130 Spectre gun-ship, whose flying arsenal included a 25-mm Gatling gun firing 1,800 rounds per minute and the even bigger 105-mm howitzer. Each AC-130 cost $46 million and was capable of inflicting withering cannon fire assaults on anything or anyone in its range.

Attack One would be on Mullah Omar's compound, just north of Kandahar in south-west Afghanistan. Approximately 100 US Rangers would secure the ground and cordon it, allowing Delta Force troops to pick off Al Qaeda soldiers and capture Tier One Personalities for interrogation. After the fire fight helicopters would sweep down and collect all US personnel and captured enemy. The proposed target of the second attack, on the same night, was a dry-lake airstrip around 200 kilometres south-west of Kandahar. This was an area of low strategic value and enemy resistance, enabling the US Rangers to practise the key infantry skill of seizing and holding ground. They would take out any Al Qaeda and issue a 'come and get us' challenge to the enemy by virtue of their presence.

Issuing such an invitation to attack, provided they could withstand any retaliation, would, it was hoped, land a hefty psychological blow, as ex-US Army Colonel Mitch Mitchell, quoted by the *Observer* on 21 October 2001, described: '[The

Taliban] said, "Come on in with 100,000 troops and face us on the ground." Well, we're going in with 100 or 200 Rangers and they should be sufficient to do the job.'

The missions were to be undertaken on the assumption that two weeks of constant aerial bombardment of Al Qaeda military installations, equipment and ground forces had significantly weakened its morale. Prior to the US Spec Ops raids the Pentagon and the MOD suggested optimistically that chinks had begun to appear in the enemy's armour, and the Afghan wartime custom of defection to the side looking most likely to win had begun.

19 October was to be the soldiers' night, when their bravery stole centre-stage from the coldly effective remote control Predator drones, equipped with high-magnification cameras and satellite-guided missiles. It was also by a huge margin the most risky phase of Operation ENDURING FREEDOM so far. President Bush had ordered the air war to start on 7 October, knowing his Air Force and Navy pilots were dropping munitions from a safe altitude and the Taliban's anti-aircraft capability was minimal – significantly less than that of Iraq, over which the United States flew hundreds of sorties in far more dangerous circumstances. Aerial bombardment was what the US military did best. This was, if you will, the war in arcade game format, in which every technological advantage would tell, and the enemy, being the Taliban, would make for a ridiculously one-sided contest.

America was going toe to toe on the ground, albeit in NVGs (Night Vision Goggles) and full body armour, and armed with rifles the Afghans would kill for; but still this would almost certainly lead to casualties. Bush, Cheney, Rumsfeld and Powell knew that the sight of body bags turned stomachs in America like nowhere else.

Successful ground attacks would provide evidence that the much-talked-of primary war objective of snaring the world's most wanted man 'dead or alive' was exactly that and not just tough talk. Bush, like the American people, wanted bin Laden brought to justice. But Afghanistan offered a million or more hiding places, and too many mud huts, caves, fox holes and tunnels to be destroyed from the skies. The US military had to prove that when a golden nugget of intelligence was received, and bin Laden or Mullah Omar had been located, it could swoop down and either kill or capture them.

The flip-side was the high price of failure. What if the missions were not the glorious success everyone hoped? Every war has its pivotal times; moments when impetus changes hands and events assume significance beyond the here and now. What if the combination of bad luck, technical mishaps and poor intelligence which seem to plague US Spec Ops teams – cases in point being Operation EAGLE CLAW and the 'Black Hawk Down' mission in Mogadishu, Somalia – again came into play?

To 'get' bin Laden – and for all the talk about deposing the Taliban, dismantling Al Qaeda and establishing a pro-Western government in Afghanistan, he was and remains the real prize – the United States could not afford to have its guns spiked at this or any other point. Given the method by which CENTCOM directed Operation ENDURING FREEDOM after this mission, it is arguable that the moment at which the US Special Forces assembled on USS *Kitty Hawk* late on Thursday, 18 October was the start of a seventy-two-hour period that dictated the pattern of US war in Afghanistan thereafter.

A fleet of helicopters carried the troops from USS *Kitty Hawk*, anchored off Pakistan's southern coast, north over hundreds of kilometres of mountainous terrain and barren desert to an airstrip at Dalbandin, just south of the Afghanistan border. This was 200 kilometres from Kandahar and close to Pakistan's underground nuclear test site, which

America had opposed. From this point it becomes unclear which version of events one is to believe: the official line put out by the Pentagon or that suggested by critics such as Seymour Hersh who wrote a damning appraisal of the missions published by the well-regarded *New Yorker* magazine.

At some point on 19 October two US servicemen were killed during a helicopter crash inside Pakistan. The Taliban's claim that it shot down the helicopter was strenuously denied by the Pentagon, and this is one of the few aspects of the mission which is not contentious.

Both the official and the unofficial versions of events which were presented were short on hard information. The Pentagon released very little on the raids, in particular the attack on Mullah Omar's compound in Kandahar. Afterwards it was determined to play down its significance, despite it being the first ground battle involving US forces and on such a potentially critical target, which was peculiar to say the least, and a number of questions remain unanswered.

Chief of the Defense Staff General Richard Myers confirmed on 20 October that Omar's home had not been bombed during the fortnight of aerial bombardment that preceded the Delta Force/US Rangers mission to strike that location. This is a key fact. Based on this assertion, logic suggests that the compound had been avoided in order to lull Omar into thinking it was a safe area, thus increasing the chance of him being there when the troops landed. Otherwise, why not bomb it? The United States had already hit the Taliban leader's car and office in Kandahar, proving that he was a high-priority target, second only perhaps to bin Laden, and there was a dearth of static enemy targets left to hit. Furthermore, there was a good chance that bin Laden would be staying close to Omar to guarantee his protection, so two terrorists might be hit with one stone.

One must also consider the extent of the firepower brought down around the compound prior to Delta Force's intended strike on the target; according to Seymour Hersh 'sixteen AC-130 gun-ships' were used. General Myers, asked at the 20 October media briefing about the planes on the mission, would neither confirm nor deny the use of AC-130s, or how many.

This was a very important target for the US, and the timing of the attack was equally significant. *TIME* magazine reported Pakistani intelligence sources, in its 22 October edition, saying Mullah Omar had arrived in Kandahar on Friday the 19th, just hours before the attack. The US is likely to have known this. Was General Myers being truthful when he said: 'We had very low expectations that any senior Taliban or Al Qaeda leadership would be involved in these particular targets.' Or was he instead trying to draw a veil over an operation he was keen to forget?

Hersh says the crack Delta Force units were forced to pull out when they came under heavy fire, including from Al Qaeda's weapon of choice: the RPG (Rocket Propelled Grenade). Were the US Rangers and Delta Force really able to operate on the ground 'without significant interference from Taliban forces'? Was enemy resistance 'light' as the General suggested? He quickly attempted to qualify these assertions by adding: 'That's probably easy for us to say here in this room. For those experiencing it, of course, it was probably not light. And there were casualties on the other side, the exact number we do not know yet.'

According to Hersh's article, Delta's problems started when they reached Mullah Omar's compound, which consisted of one brick house, thatched huts and a potholed road. From that point, *The New Yorker* and *TIME* reported, the operation went wrong. Firstly, he was not there; the place was unoccupied and this was not the intelligence cache they hoped; there was nothing worth taking with them. Then as the Delta Force troops bugged out, the Al Qaeda in the surrounding area, awoken by the fire from the AC-130s, rushed to the scene and opened fire.

The New Yorker said: 'As soon as they came out of the house the shit hit the fan. It was like an ambush. The Taliban were firing light arms and either RPGs or mortars.' The Delta team found itself in a 'tactical fire fight and the Taliban had the advantage.' *TIME* reported the Taliban's version of that night, with one of its troops, Abdu Rahman, saying that two US helicopters had arrived near Kandahar just before dawn on Saturday 20th. The Taliban were ready and waiting: 'We were ordered to wait until the Americans came closer. But nobody listened. We were all firing.' He added that the US soldiers 'flew off like sparrows.'

The ferocity of the Taliban's response apparently 'scared the crap out of everyone', *The New Yorker* reported. A bitter row later ensued between Delta Force officers and Defense Department officials over the timing of the use of the AC-130s and its lack of coordination with the insertion of the Special Forces teams.

This appears to have been a case of the Americans not using the huge firepower at their disposal to its best advantage. The air strike was apparently so loud 'it would wake the dead' wrote Hersh. It drew attention to the impending arrival of Delta Force, waking up Al Qaeda like an alarm clock and summoning them all to Omar's compound. The LZ (landing zone) into which the Delta teams were dropping from the helicopters suddenly became very hot indeed.

Delta was forced to evacuate the area with all elements heading for a pre-arranged ERV (Emergency Rendezvous) point where helicopters picked them up. The soldiers were fuming about the military planners: 'They think we can perform fucking magic. We can't. Don't put us in an environment we weren't prepared for. Next time we are going to lose a company.' General Franks was reportedly labelled 'clueless' by one of the Delta Force troops. Hersh's article reported that twelve Delta Force soldiers had been wounded and that one had lost a foot.

TIME also reported the mood of US troops when they arrived back in Pakistan after the action in Kandahar: 'American servicemen who returned safely to Dalbandin were so jittery that they refused to brief Pakistani military officers unless the officers removed their gun holsters before approaching the helicopters.'

The Pentagon's official line post-operation was vague and nondescript. General Myers said: 'Under the direction of the President and the Secretary of Defense and under the command of US Central Command, General Tom Franks, Special Operations Forces, including US Army Rangers, deployed to Afghanistan. They attacked and destroyed targets associated with terrorist activity and Taliban command and control. US forces were able to deploy, manoeuvre and operate inside Afghanistan without significant interference from Taliban forces. They are now refitting and repositioning for potential future operations against terrorist targets in other areas known to harbour terrorists.'

The Pentagon slipped into the easy routine of heaping praise on the troops, which was no doubt deserved, without giving away what they were doing; a clever tactic in the propaganda war as it makes any kind of objectivity or questioning of the mission seem unsupportive of the soldiers, and, in the circumstances of war, unpatriotic. General Myers added: 'We accomplished our objectives. To those in uniform who accomplished it, let me just make a real general statement. The credibility of Dick Myers, or the Secretary of Defense, or any of our senior leadership in the services rests really with the professionalism in the way our young armed forces members conduct themselves day in day out. They have never let us down and yesterday was no exception. We are very, very proud of their abilities and their dedication and their courage.'

This had been the case in the United States since 9/11, where there had been little self-examination or questioning about why the attacks took place. Most Americans knew and know little about their country's foreign policy in the Middle East. General Myers was right on at least one point: it is hardly, if ever, the case that US or British soldiers let down the governments that send them into battle. What General Myers did not say was that it is more often the other way around.

Secretary of State Colin Powell seemed reluctant to discuss these 'successful' missions which General Myers said 'accomplished our objectives'. Powell, interviewed on CBS's *Face the Nation* on 21 October, said: 'I think it is better you get a straight answer from the Pentagon; but just so I don't duck it entirely, I think they were looking at a compound where some information might have been available. And I believe they did come back with some documents and other items that might be useful, and they were scouting another facility. But I'll stop there and let the Pentagon deal with that one.'

The inside story of the US Rangers mission at the airstrip also came to light. The troops, the vast majority of whom had never seen combat before and were fresh out of high school, only parachuted on to the airfield after a US Army Pathfinder team arrived there first and confirmed there was no enemy in the area. The mission was little more than an exercise for the television audience. And according to one of Hersh's sources for the *New Yorker*, the presence of the cameras had not gone down well on what was essentially a 'confidence-building' exercise: 'It was a television show. The Rangers were not the first in. Why would you film it? I am a big fan of keeping things secret and this was being driven by public opinion.' Two Rangers were also injured on the parachute jump, neither severely.

Much was made of the footage shot by a US Army cameraman. Just as the Pentagon would have hoped, stills from the film made the front pages of newspapers around the world, including, on 21 October, Britain's highest-selling Sunday newspaper, the *News of the World*. It looked to everyone as if this was indeed the start of a new war, no longer just fought from the air, and that now the United States had got its boots on. After Delta Force's Kandahar mission, however, the boots were taken off again as quickly as they had been put on.

There was no footage of the contact between Al Qaeda and Delta Force at Mullah Omar's compound; only of the US Rangers' mission, with shots of them loading equipment on to transport aircraft, taking off for the trip into Afghanistan, and the US Rangers parachuting from the MC-130. This was followed by film of the troops clearing the airfield, building by building – a task the Pathfinder team would have completed before the US Rangers jumped – so this too was a TV stunt. The closest they came to any Taliban was finding a small weapons cache: RPGs, a machine-gun and ammunition which the Pentagon announced were destroyed.

Typically, Rumsfeld went on the offensive, suggesting the media should be grateful for the film as it was 'the first time, to my knowledge, that such footage has been provided'. When it comes to analysing such operations, the military machine always has the upper hand. As General Myers added, 'In terms of ongoing, perhaps ongoing ground action, we simply can't talk about this right now. Like we said Saturday, some things are going to be visible, some invisible.'

*

The failure to capture or kill Mullah Omar, the stronger than anticipated Taliban resistance, the row between Delta and the Defence Department and the so-called rethink on the use of SOCOM forces in its aftermath, need not have impacted upon the SAS. The critical point for the Regiment and the potency of the Allied ground effort in Afghanistan in late 2001 was that it did so. Did the Americans not want the SAS to follow up with a gloriously successful mission after its US equivalent, Delta Force, had again come unstuck? Such is their calibre that Delta Force's men deserved a second chance on a properly planned operation, for their own benefit and for the sake of Operation ENDURING FREEDOM; and the SAS deserved any opportunity at all.

Based on the US military's response to this mission, in that it went back to safety-first operations and used the Northern Alliance forces as a spearhead, one wonders how CENTCOM would have reacted if the night raid on Kandahar had really been, as it was described in the *New Yorker*, a 'total goat fuck' – US military slang for an operation when everything goes wrong – and if they had lost a lot of men in a fire fight. Would the Pentagon have pulled out the few hundred troops it had on the ground? No wonder some of the Delta Force soldiers were, as that publication described them, 'outraged'. At least they had been given an opportunity, albeit an unsuitable one, so early into the ground war and hence could moan about it: 'This is the same M.O. [*modus operandi*] they have been using for ten years. I don't know where the adult supervision for these operations is.' The SAS had to wait in the wings, its soldiers becoming increasingly frustrated.

Whatever the politicians hoped and expected of the military, Operation ENDURING FREEDOM started with, at best, a slim chance of catching Osama bin Laden. The odds lengthened considerably from late October when the United

States went back into its shell. If, as General Myers said on 20 October, the troops who performed on that mission were 'refitting and repositioning for potential future operations against terrorist targets', no one ever got to hear about it, and very little about US operations remains secret for long. If, after this bungled raid, US Special Operations scored a big hit, the Pentagon would have told the world. Compared to the MOD, the Pentagon is not anti-disclosure regarding its Special Forces, as Donald Rumsfeld – not Tony Blair, Geoff Hoon or Admiral Boyce – proved when he announced that the SAS was operating in Afghanistan.

Having more Special Forces on the ground, so long as they were used, made military sense if the War against Terrorism was going to be won. The future was not looking bright, however; the confidence that had characterized the first fortnight of the campaign had been lost in Kandahar. Unless there were dramatic changes, a long war of attrition loomed.

This was the view of the Generals and of the independent military experts such as the editor of *Jane's World Armies*, Charles Heyman who, on 5 November 2001, reported on janes.com: 'A long campaign will require considerable manpower. Troops operating in this environment could tire quickly and units will have to be rotated between operations and rest. If the Taliban fail to "crack" under the pressure of the air campaign and the overall campaign continues through the winter and into next summer, the Allies may well need every soldier they have, Special Forces, Raiders and light infantry.'

5. OPERATION DETERMINE

Jason, Jock and the other A Squadron guys spent late September and early October on Exercise Barren Land in the Sultanate of Oman while G Squadron's troops, having carried out a similar desert warfare training programme there earlier in the year, remained in Hereford 'sitting on their bergens', waiting and preparing for the Afghanistan infil. Smoke clouds from small arms and machine-guns drifted in slow motion through the still country air at Pontrilas as Gordon and Phil conducted live firing exercises. The sound of thousands of rounds being expended echoed through the valley, 10 miles west of 'H'; the bigger explosions scattered the sheep and horses in surrounding fields but the villagers were so accustomed to their cottages being shaken, windows rattling and huge plumes of brightly coloured smoke canisters going off that they hardly noticed.

Gordon's neighbours were surprised to see him arriving home on the bright autumnal evenings: as one said, 'I thought you'd be in the desert by now?' To which the grumbling Geordie replied, 'Howay, man, I've only just come back from there.' The man next door meant Afghanistan, not Oman, though.

Although the call from CENTCOM to join 'America's Party' was yet to come, the media assumed the SAS was already 'in theatre', with one Sunday broadsheet predicting that the Regiment would be 'dropped in by helicopter to seal off and lay waste to at least six sites' believed to be terrorist training facilities. If only, Gordon thought. Just how severely US reluctance to deploy ground forces in combat had impacted upon his unit had come as an unpleasant surprise.

A Squadron's Exercise Barren Land training schedule was geared towards optimum versatility; the ability, once inside Afghanistan, to carry out any CENTCOM-instructed operation. The troops were cross-trained on all the support weapons, GPMGs, .50s (Browning machine-guns), MK rocket launchers, mortars and Milan missile launchers; this in addition to the 'Troop Training', with Air Troop doing their parachuting and the Mountain Troop guys their rope work. It was a crucial time for Mobility Troop as well. There was great pressure on the specialist drivers and the Pinkies – the long-wheelbase Land Rovers customized for desert and mountainous terrain – to perform. These would be the Regiment's main mode of transport in Afghanistan. Exercise Barren Land was the final chance to polish driving skills and ensure the wagons were in excellent working order.

The Sultanate of Oman occupied a key strategic position on the southern tip of the Arabian Gulf, bordering Yemen, Saudi Arabia and the United Arab Emirates. Hence its Royal Family was courted by Britain, with whom it signed a friendship treaty in 1951, and the United States. In the 1950s the Soviet Union targeted Oman as being vulnerable to a Communist revolution. Moscow sought to finance and arm tribesmen to overthrow the pro-Western Sultan, Said bin Taimur, whose repressive policies made his rule unpopular. To counter this threat, D Squadron transferred from the Malayan jungle to Oman in 1958 – the Regiment's first deployment there and the beginning of an operational commitment its sabre squadrons would share until 1976. The SAS fought a battle for the hearts and minds of the Omani people against the Communist rebels; not only training villagers for military operations but providing them with medical assistance and treating their animals. In 1970, Royal Military Academy Sandhurst scholar Sultan Qaboos bin Said replaced his father, who was flown out of Oman on an RAF VC-10, and a long-overdue modernization programme was implemented.

Oman was a rich combat environment. Every SAS tour was fraught with danger and there were plenty of contacts with the *Adoo* (enemy). The turning point militarily was the Battle of Mirbat in July 1972 when nine SAS soldiers, led by Captain Mike Kealy,* repelled 250 rebels. The effort won Kealy a DSO (Distinguished Service Order), Fijian SAS legend Labalaba a posthumous MID (Mention in Dispatches) (see pp. 240–2) and broke the spirit of the Communists. The rebels saw that no matter how great they were in number and where and when they attacked, they would not be able to topple the Sultan as long as the Regiment remained in Oman.

While A Squadron was in Oman, Rumsfeld secured permission for the US Air Force to launch bombing raids from Masirah, an island 225 miles off Oman's southern coast. Oman, which has a population of 2.5 million, of which some 500,000 are foreign nationals, had signed an access agreement with the United States in 1981. Unlike the leaders of

---

* Captain Mike Kealy DSO died seven years later, aged thirty-three. Rejoining the Regiment as a squadron commander, following a period working in an administrative capacity, he volunteered to retake SAS Selection's forty-mile endurance march. One macho stipulation in the 1970s was that only 'wimps' took waterproofs with them on the Brecon Beacons. At 02.00 hrs on 1 February 1979, in driving rain, Kealy set off without them. Higher on the mountain, rain turned to sleet. At 10.00 hrs he was discovered unconscious and covered in snow. The hero of the Battle of Mirbat died, quite unnecessarily, of hypothermia.

its neighbouring states, the Sultan was at liberty to accede to the United States as the majority of his people belonged to a non-radical Islamic sect.

Whereas the Wahhabi in Saudi Arabia shared bin Laden's hatred of the West, the Ibadi were less puritanical. British industry had also benefited from this openness, the United Kingdom being Oman's third largest provider of imported goods (behind the United Arab Emirates and Japan), much of which was UK military hardware. Although Oman became a major exporter of oil in 1967, its economy still relied on sugar, banana, date and camel exports.

If CENTCOM determined that Operation ENDURING FREEDOM required just one SAS squadron, A Squadron would have been selected on the basis of its location; perhaps with any G Squadron personnel who were fluent Arabic speakers. A Squadron's troops were not the only British forces in Oman hoping to be sent into Afghanistan as Exercise Barren Land ran adjacent to Exercise *Saif Sareea* II, the two-month £90.3 million deployment of 22,000 British troops co-ordinated by the MOD's PJHQ (Permanent Joint Headquarters) at Northwood, Middlesex.

Although to the outside world it seemed otherwise, what was three years in the planning, and then the biggest movement overseas by UK forces since the Gulf War and the biggest UK services exercise anywhere since 1984, was merely coincidental; the Exercise was not intended as build-up training for the battle against Al Qaeda but more as a dry run for British involvement in Gulf War II and a test of the United Kingdom's tri-service strategic task force. Fortuitously, from the perspective of pressurizing the Taliban regime, Exercise *Saif Sareea* II – which translates from Arabic as 'swift sword' – did put seventeen Royal Navy vessels, two nuclear submarines and more than 100 aircraft and helicopters within striking distance of Osama bin Laden. Unfortunately for the UK servicemen and women, the

United States showed no inclination to take advantage of the British firepower amassed in and around Oman – early evidence of the United Kingdom's for the most part symbolic role in Operation ENDURING FREEDOM. A media guessing game over which UK units would break off from Exercise *Saif Sareea* II overshadowed the Exercise none the less; and inevitably its importance appeared to diminish, as the British Army spokesman Lieutenant Colonel Angus Taverner conceded: 'At the moment we are pressing ahead with our original plans. But we are obviously aware of what is happening elsewhere in the world.'

The National Audit Office's review of Exercise *Saif Sareea* II put the best spin on the Afghanistan factor: 'The conduct of the Exercise at the time of preparation for operations in Afghanistan, while coincidental, provided advantages, although it limited some of the training aspects of the Exercise.' 'Concurrent operations did, however, impact on the command and control structure, logistics and elements of air, maritime and Special Forces training.'

The tension mounted after Exercise Barren Land. Most of A Squadron returned to United Kingdom by the same route they had headed out, aboard an RAF Hercules – also known as a C-130 – with a pit-stop at RAF Akrotiri on Cyprus's WSBA (Western Sovereign Base Area). They touched down at RAF Lyneham, Wiltshire, and were driven back to Hereford in a fleet of military coaches, while a few guys stayed in Oman to watch the kit. It had been an extremely intense and tiring month. Jason and Jock returned looking tanned, or in the latter's case even more red, and in need of a beer or ten. The men knew the clock was ticking fast if Osama bin Laden was going to be caught. A month after 9/11 the Regiment did not have a presence inside Afghanistan and CENTCOM appeared to be in no hurry to rectify this. As Jock told a fellow NCO on the 'Crab Air' (Army slang for the RAF) bus back to 'H', it was not just the troops who thought that odd: 'I can see it now; ma wife's going to give me some strange looks when I get back.'

'Oh yeah, why's that? What's up with 'er?'

'She wasnae expectin' ta se me again this side a Christmas, y'know. Think she was looking forward to it an' all ... A wee break for her and the bairns,' he added, smiling.

'She'll be like,' Jock raised the pitch of his voice to imitate his wife's and rocked his head from side to side: ' "What a ye doin' back here? I thought youse was gonnae catch that bin Laden fella?" ' Jock's mate laughed at his impression as he reverted back to normal speech: 'Am telling ye, youse don't know half the shite am going ta get. It nivvah stops.

'She knows, ye know, oh aye. That we havnae much time ta get 'im. He's hardly gonnae hang around too long, is he?'

'Well, yeah, Jock. I reckon she's right on that score, for sure. He can't stay in a fucking cave there for ever. Eventually the Yanks will have blown everything up. Afghanistan will just be one big pile of rubble. It's a fucking shithole anyhow; maybe no one will notice the difference.'

'Oh aye, you'd be right there.'

They hardly had time for those beers. A Squadron would return to Oman, this time with G Squadron in tow. Hopefully both squadrons would infil to Afghanistan from there. The 'young 'uns', the likes of Jason and Phil, felt a tingling of excitement at the news as Afghanistan would be their first SAS operational deployment and it was finally getting closer. While A and G Squadrons were driven in coaches back to RAF Lyneham, their personal weapons and light support arms were moved covertly from Hereford to the RAF base under armed escort, with the relevant local police force, the West Mercia Constabulary, tipped off about the move. The journeys were made under cover of darkness.

At the WSBA the troops went into isolation for the first time, away from non-SAS personnel, prior to the first briefings about the tasks ahead. Isolation is also intended, not that it was needed, to help the soldiers 'switch on' to the tasks to come. If and when they did come into contact with non-SAS troops they would not discuss any operationally sensitive information. The men were given a 'brief orders' and billeted in spare accommodation, sixteen men per room with the 'Ruperts' (slang name used by troops for the officers) in with them. They stayed on the airbase throughout their twenty-four-hour stopover in Cyprus and as they both sat on the grass outside the barrack room Gordon asked Phil: 'What are you going to do with yerself while we're here?'

'Not much, mate, go for a run, get my head down, I suppose. Fuck knows how much kip we'll get after this. It's going to be an interesting few months, a real challenge, I hope. Other than that, I dunno; kit checks, that kind of thing. You?'

Gordon the grumbler was more fastidious, and liking everything to be perfect he was on the hunt for some little luxuries. 'I'll join you for a run, Phil, but I'm also after an extra bum roll [the thin sponge strip used as a mattress under a sleeping bag], mate. I'm gonna make some elbow and knee pads out of it and sew 'em into me combat gear, like.'

Phil was surprised, but then his joints were younger than the Geordie's, and provided he found his bum roll a happy Gordon meant a happy everyone else as he was less likely to moan. Phil humoured him, and scoffed about what a wimp Gordon was becoming. 'Good for you, Gordon, you shouldn't have any trouble picking another one of them up here. You must be getting old.'

'Hey, if we're diving into the shit to dodge enemy fire

I'll be glad of 'em. I don't want fucked-up knees. You should think about getting some of 'em too. You're a runner, you should be careful with yer knees.'

Some rather more important purchases than Gordon's extra bum roll were made: in particular the SSMs (Squadron Sergeant Majors) of A and G Squadrons liberated water-bags from local British units. The folding canvas material bags would be distributed among the Pinkie crews once they were in Oman. Jock seemed to have his ear permanently glued to his short-wave radio. BBC World Service reports told him the Americans had air superiority in Afghanistan but there was no sign yet of the enemy capitulating. As he wanted the Regiment to have a shot at the glory, he was relieved the Americans had not caught bin Laden. The SAS had no chance of competing for that prize while its nearest troops to Afghanistan remained in Cyprus. Addressing no one in particular in what had already become a smelly and sweaty barrack room, Jock opened up, his voice like a rifle on automatic fire.

'Fa fuck's sake! What the fuck are we doin' here? Tell me, I don't understand, y'know? The Americans have been bombing Afghanistan ta fuck forra week now, right, and there's fuck all left to hit, the Taliban havnae got a single fuckin' plane, yet we're all still sitting here, pickin' our arses. When the fuck are we gonna move?'

'Dunno, Jock,' came one reply.

'That fuckin' "Bin Liner" shitehead has been on the telly givin' it what not, can they not pick up where the fuck it's coming from? Have the Yanks forgotten how to dominate ground, I ask ye? Ye need men on the fuckin' ground, you stupid twats.'

'They've never known how to dominate ground,' was another reply from the throng.

'And ye cannae rely on the Northern Alliance or what

that fuck they're called,' added Jock. 'What is that, a fuckin' building society? Fuckin' sounds like one. They're fuckin' twats an' all.'

The following morning the troops' personal kit was loaded on a 20-tonne capacity C-130 – only one was needed as most of the gear was in Oman – as news came through that the transit would be via Bahrain. The SAS had had an LO (Liaison Officer) stationed there since September to organize such pit-stops, the tiny Gulf state being one of the countries seduced to join Operation ENDURING FREEDOM by Donald Rumsfeld. The planes would refuel on the runway at Bahrain's military airfield and the ramps dropped to let the men stretch their legs – and get rid of some of the stench – before completing the journey to the Omani Air Force base, RAFO Thumrait, 75 kilometres north of Port Salalah and 100 kilometres east of the border with Al Qaeda-infested Yemen.

The guys touched down on a warm, humid desert evening, the moist, suffocating closeness of the air sticking to their faces as they slung their bergens over their shoulders and jumped off the back of the Herc. Rifles in hand they trekked, a little gingerly, off the tarmac. Gordon and Phil walked together, the older man shaking his head at how Phil managed to sleep throughout the journey from Bahrain.

'Fuckin' Rip Van Winkle you are, aren't you?' he said enviously. 'You could sleep on a fuckin' knife edge. You'd better not drop off, man, when you're drivin' the wagon, Rip.'

Gordon's goading did not bother Phil, who liked the fact that his sleeping ability wound him up. 'Well, you know, mate, it's good to get some shut-eye.' And a break from your company, he thought.

They joined advance parties of A and G Squadrons who had flown ahead to sort out logistics and were told they would remain at Thumrait for at least two days, the call from CENTCOM to infil into Afghanistan could come as quickly as that or it could be another fortnight. They simply did not know when they would be, as they say, 'tasked-on'. The guys would sleep in dormitory accommodation in a two-storey concrete block on the airfield, twenty men per room. There were solar-powered showers and traditional Muslim squat toilets.

There is a permanent British presence at Thumrait, made up of RAF staff, and even in peacetime the SAS is in and out of Oman all year around. Isolation procedures were stepped up. But pretty much by choice, as well as strict order, there would be no talking to non-SAS personnel with the infil to the war zone possibly just forty-eight hours away.

The Regiment had some meaty military hardware to test on the firing range running parallel to Thumrait's runway. The GPMG, known as the Gimpy, had been in service for forty years and its design had scarcely changed in that time. In the sustained-fire role it ripped apart anything in its way – rock faces, masonry, armour and of course, human beings. The belt-fed GPMG fired between 750 and 1,000 rounds of 7.62-mm calibre ammunition per minute and was known for its stopping power and accuracy over a range up to 1.8 kilometres. The .50 Browning machine-gun, known to the men as 'the 50 Cal', was an SAS favourite. Also belt-fed, it could penetrate 40 mm of armour and fired 575 rounds per minute. It was fired either from a tripod or from a Pinkie. The Milan, the wire-guided anti-armour missile, came into service in the 1970s and was fired by a two-man team. Firing 1.3-kilogram warheads over 2 kilometres, it was accurate and reliable. At 12 kilograms, it was 5 kilograms lighter than the hefty .50. There were also a few MK19 grenade launchers capable of firing 375 rounds of 40-mm grenades per minute over a 1.6-kilometre range.

All these weapons were attached to the Pinkies, two per wagon in the case of the GPMG, one facing front, the other to the rear. The SAS has used the long-wheelbase Land Rovers since the 1950s, one of the latest models being the 5.5-metre-long 110, a 4×4 vehicle with a 3.5 litre V8 petrol engine. They are customized for the Regiment's use, the troops not caring for civilian necessities such as doors or the overhead cabin.

The Pinkies – named after the colour they were once painted for desert camouflage – would have a three- or four-man crew, led by the IC (In Command) Wagon, sitting in the front passenger seat. Smoke dischargers fitted to the vehicle's front and rear bumpers were seldom used but provided instant cover in emergencies. The Pinkies were also fitted with a drop-down tailgate, communications equipment and GPS for navigation and had additional storage space for personal kit, weapons, ammunition, fuel and water, camouflage nets, poles and steel planks, used as sand ladders. The Pinkies had power-steering, supple coil-sprung suspension and low-pressure sand tyres.

The briefings came every few hours, with the troops told that the Taliban regime was withstanding the barrage of US air power and Northern Alliance artillery and that there was no intelligence to indicate Osama bin Laden's whereabouts. It was the third week in October. The United States clearly had to do more to achieve its military objectives.

After two days in Oman, the CO called the two squadrons together and gave them an Operational Order: 'We are going to conduct surveillance and reconnaissance missions in the northern part of Afghanistan, we will be working with the Northern Alliance and the Americans but we will be operating as SAS units on our own rather than as part of

US patrols.' The SAS would be flown by the US Air Force to bases in Pakistan.

'At fucking last' was Jason's reaction to the CO's brief. He had begun to fear the scrap he wanted so desperately might elude him. He had only joined the SAS the year before, passing the same Selection course as Phil, and going into theatre so soon afterwards would be a huge thrill. He was a young, mouthy trooper, not having spent enough time in Hereford for much of his Para bullshit to have rubbed off. He did not mind that his attitude wound up the likes of Phil, as he was, in Para parlance, 'a hat', short for 'craphat', as Paras refer to anyone in the Army, SAS included, who is not one of their own. Jason was twenty-five and had plenty of girlfriends but no attachments; just the way he liked it. Gaining combat experience would, he believed, make his life complete.

Phil too was excited, but shyness and good manners shrouded his desire to 'slot rag-heads'. Three years older than Jason and recently married, his life was more complicated and he thought about it more deeply. With his RE background, he was an excellent mechanic and he would also drive a Pinkie, a responsibility which was never far from his mind. He would be roasted by his oppos if anything went wrong. The thought of being attacked by Al Qaeda seemed less frightening than being stuck on a wagon he had crashed with two senior soldiers screaming abuse at him.

Gordon, the thirty-four-year-old Sergeant, would be on his Pinkie. He had been married since his late teens to his childhood sweetheart and was thought of as both a grumbler and a loner in his troop, shying away from the drinking scene and preferring nights at home with his wife and daughters. What bothered Gordon most was the infil from Oman. He tried hard to control it, but he hated flying, especially in a bone-rattling, thundering Hercules, which was why it infuriated him when the likes of Phil nodded off, seemingly oblivious to the deafening noise and the fear factor.

A fleet of US C-130s was laid on for the flights, with G Squadron leaving first. There would be a number of shuttle runs on 24 October, with the squadrons landing at different locations; both would be guarded by Pakistani forces in response to the threat of attacks by groups supportive of bin Laden. Having the squadrons in separate locations, or 'holding areas', reduced the risk of too many SAS men being together in theatre. Unfortunately the Pakistani Government only allowed use of these bases on the proviso they were not used to carry out offensive operations. The CO would co-ordinate operations from Oman with his RHQ cell, while liaising with the 2IC (Second in Command) back in Hereford and the DSF.

With the kit squeezed on to the C-130s and the Pinkies chained down – three wagons inside each plane – the men clambered around to find some comfort during the three-hour flight. The prospect of an in-flight technical problem did not bear thinking about. Any turbulence set Gordon off talking to himself. Luckily he could not be heard over the din of the engines: 'Jesus, fuckin' get me out of here, man,' he said as the plane shook and took a drop. He thought: 'If Phil's fuckin' kippin' through this I'll slap him.' He turned, and seeing his colleague's eyes closed, gave him a kick. Phil kicked him back, harder. He was not asleep.

The night infil was completed without hiccups. The men got what was for all of them their first sight of Pakistan as the sun rose. Seeing the deathly grey and brown mountains devoid of vegetation stretching for as far as his vision extended, Jock wished the sun had not bothered coming up. 'Christ Almighty,' he said, shielding his eyes from its rays and shaking his head, 'what a bloody sandy shitehole.'

The split-squadron infil was made to seem pointless when a change of plan was announced. Both squadrons would relocate to a TLZ (Tactical Landing Zone) in Northern Alliance-held territory in north-west Afghanistan, roughly 200 kilometres east of Herat and 150 kilometres south of the Turkmenistan border. The switch left the men shaking their heads, but as the combat virgins were discovering, little goe to plan in warfare, and they were also unaware of how awkward the Pakistanis were being. Gordon was among the least happy, the thought of another three hours on a Herc hardly being his idea of a good time.

It seemed that the objective of finding bin Laden 'dead or alive' had been forgotten as CENTCOM gave the SAS a specific role supporting the Allied push in the north. This was no manhunt, there was no intelligence to suggest bin Laden was in this area, and indeed it would have made no sense for him to be there, among the Tajiks and Uzbeks. A and G Squadrons received a series of briefings explaining the tasks involved in Operation DETERMINE by the head sheds, who said, 'Split up into two-, three- and four-vehicle teams.' The patrols were for 'S and R [Surveillance and Reconnaissance] only', and they were under orders: 'don't start any engagements. Your task is to observe any enemy movements and to recce possible enemy ambush points. OK?'

That this was precisely as the CO had outlined in Oman did not temper the guys' frustration at being given such a tedious job, having waited so long to deploy and considering the state of the battle. In their minds, not engaging the enemy was a key reason why the war was going nowhere fast. They could moan about it all they liked, but they had to get on with it. The most battle-hungry, like Jason and Jock, were dumbfounded; they wanted to be tested, to be tasked with missions which were crucial to Operation ENDURING FREEDOM's key aims. As a frustrated Jock told a Rupert, 'Fa Christ's sake. We want fuckin' S and D [Search and Destroy]. Not S and R. What the fuck's going on?' As the officer told him, that was all that was on offer from the Americans. They could hit an OT (Opportune Target) such as a single Taliban truck, but otherwise the guys had to keep their heads down and let the enemy pass. 'Are they takin' the piss or what?' said Jock.

Gordon and Phil's wagon was kept busy. The work was dull and it meant hundreds of kilometres of driving for the younger man. Their brief had been: 'Work as part of a team of two wagons, stay within 50 clicks [kilometres] of each other, so if one of you gets bumped the other has got a quick reaction time to get to you. You've got a number of targets. They must be carried out in specific order, the most important first.'

Fortunately Phil's driving was spot on and the Pinkie stood up to the mountainous terrain. But Gordon did not bother to hide his contempt for Operation DETERMINE when he RV'ed with another G Squadron wagon after a couple of days driving through the barren, empty valleys, 'one brown corridor of shite after another', as he called it, and with no enemy in sight.

'All right, mate, this is a bag of shite, ain't it?'

'Fuckin' too right, we didn't come out 'ere to do this crap. It's bloody pointless. What you been up to?'

Gordon was spitting feathers: 'Can't fuckin' believe it, man. Had to fuckin' check the Yanks had blown a bridge up and see if a road junction was still there. I'm fuckin' sick of it, man. You?'

'Same kind of shite; marking mines, looking at roads, tracks. It's all just shite for someone's intelligence brief. No enemy, no contacts, fuck all.'

The guys knew these were required tasks. Sending troops to examine a bombed target provided A1 human intelligence of a mission's success, enabling the US Navy and US Air Force strike aircraft to move on to other tactical and strategic targets. These were locations identified as valuable by satellite photographs and had to be ticked off. However, the SAS wanted a contact – a big one – not a test of their map-reading, driving and communications skills and to them that was all Operation DETERMINE seemed to be.

Jason and Jock looked ahead. The future, as they saw it, was not bright. It was early November and they had been living off the wagons for ten days. They were sweaty, smelly, fed up with each other's company and in very bad moods. In the back of Jock's mind was the end-of-year change-around of squadron taskings. The two squadrons left in Hereford might end up getting the contacts with Al Qaeda he and Jason wanted.

'We're gonnae miss out here, laddie. Think about it and I'm bored shiteless.'

'Yeah,' said Jason automatically. 'I know that, but what do you mean?'

'Christmas is the fuckin' cut-off point. Fuckin' "D" get off SP then and "B" will be coming out here too if there's anything for 'em to do. We'll be back in Hereford. I cannae see the Yanks wanting to get stuck in before then, the Taliban havnae fuckin' budged.'

Jason replied: 'I've hardly fuckin' seen a Yank, about one Delta prick, that's been it.'

'It's gone so fucking tits up, I cannae believe it, Jase.'

Jason continued: 'I thought we'd have had it made out 'ere, fuckin' rag-heads everywhere, and givin' them a slap. Not a bit of it. And the fuckin' no-contact rule. This is supposed to be a fuckin' war!'

Jock explained, 'Aye, but there's a bit a sense in that though. Say you hit the lead Recce patrol of an enemy brigade ... You could come across fuckin' hundreds. You just wannae to shoot and scoot, blanket of fire then fuck off.'

'But we don't even get to do that!' Jason pointed out.

'Aye, laddie, suppose you're right.'

The soldiers thought the United States was fighting a different war to the SAS and there was a distinct clash of opinions between London and Washington over how best to conduct it. The SAS squadrons were hugely disappointed not to be putting their firepower to good use. At least being on the ground in Afghanistan beat life in 'H' and they got their own feel for the climate and terrain should the chance of a contact ever arise. They all grumbled but did their jobs, filing the INTREPS (Intelligence Reports) via secure communication routes using lap-tops and SATCOMMS (Satellite Communications). Every time the IC Patrol, the senior rank among the two-, three- or four-Pinkie teams radioed in, he hoped for an order to RV at a Start Line but it never came. Instead, he would be given a new set of grid references to observe and assess.

After just a fortnight on the ground they were given the order to return to the United Kingdom. The troops were totally disillusioned. The vast majority of their gear, excluding personal kit and weapons, would stay in Oman and the Regiment hoped it would return to Afghanistan once a new role was defined. The squadrons returned to Hereford on 8 November, in time for the Remembrance Sunday shindig. With the exception of skipping Bahrain, their exfil was via the same route as the infil. The mood was sombre on the journey home; they had got themselves revved up for a battle but found a phoney war instead.

6. BLAIR GOES TO WASHINGTON

Rallied initially in anger and by their President's sense of purpose, Americans had been confident that bin Laden would be found and Al Qaeda dismantled. Their optimism was buoyed by the Pentagon's claim to have secured air supremacy just three days into the campaign. By late October, however, the United States' lack of military progress was causing alarm; bin Laden's capture no longer seemed as certain. The mighty American hammer was supposed to have cracked the Afghan nut by now.

Americans are entitled to expect results for their $377 billion annual defence outlay; they could not understand why with such military, technological and financial advantages the United States was struggling. No country had been as dominant since the Roman Empire; the United States had forces in 132 of the 190 United Nations member states and air bases or base rights in forty states worldwide. Now, the hyper-power's awesome superiority seemed to count for nothing and the United States was made to appear impotent.

The Taliban's capacity and determination to hold on to power had been underestimated; and where were the predicted defections from the regime? Rear Admiral John Stufflebeem, the Joint Chief of Staff deputy director of operations, was forced to concede: 'I am bit surprised at how doggedly they're hanging on to power. We definitely need to have patience. This is going to be a long, long campaign.' The Taliban had also impressed Rumsfeld who admitted: 'These folks are pros. They are clever. They've been around a long time. They've probably changed sides three or four times and may again.'

With the civilian casualty count rising, the harsh Afghan winter ahead and Washington under diplomatic pressure not to bomb during the Muslim holy month of Ramadan, President Bush's problems were mounting. Hawkish Senators such as Vietnam veteran and Republican John McCain questioned the United States' stomach for war and the tactics employed, leaving combat to the Northern Alliance forces while not giving them sufficient support to take Kabul before a political solution was in place.

McCain said:

> We cannot fight without casualties and we cannot fight it without risking unintended damage to humanitarian and political interests. We did not cause this war. Our enemies did and they are to blame for the loss of innocent life. We can help repair the damage of war. But to do so, we must destroy the people who started it.
>
> War is a miserable business; the lives of the nation's finest patriots are sacrificed. Innocent people suffer and die.
>
> No mountain is big enough, no cave deep enough to hide from the full force of American power. Yet our enemies harbour doubts that America will use force with a firm determination to achieve our ends. We need to persuade them otherwise, immediately. Fighting this war in half-measures will only give our enemies time and opportunity to strike us again. We cannot fight this war from the air alone.

The Taliban's rule had withstood the 'asset-driven' aerial bombing campaign; so much for the Bush Administration's pledge to put 'boots on the ground': they were not there.

General Franks was on the receiving end of some personal and professional media criticism. He was, it was claimed, failing to provide sufficient 'visible' leadership and did not appear to be shaping up as the new 'Stormin'' Norman Schwarzkopf. A decade earlier it had seemed that Schwarzkopf's sheer force of character drove the war in Kuwait. This was never the case with Franks at any point in Operation ENDURING FREEDOM or during the US invasion of Iraq in 2003, also directed by the CENTCOM CINC. The mission in Afghanistan was renamed 'Operation Enduring Frustration' by Georgia Democrat Max Cleland, a war veteran who lost both legs and an arm in Vietnam, and one of many US Senators disappointed that bin Laden had not been caught.

The self-effacing Franks admitted surprisingly: 'Tommy Franks is no Norman Schwarzkopf.' What really alarmed the American people was his view on Osama bin Laden's capture, the man his President said he wanted 'dead or alive'. As the CENTCOM chief said, 'We have not said that Osama bin Laden is a target of this effort. What we are about is the destruction of the Al Qaeda network, as well as the Taliban that provide harbour to bin Laden and Al Qaeda.'

Clearly there was a lack of harmony between the United States' political and military leaders; they were fighting separate wars with separate objectives. The US Defense Department aides attacked the Pentagon's 'old-think' strategies and Rumsfeld relieved Franks of the crucial Spec Ops brief, handing over command to the US Air Force's General Charles Holland who would report directly to the Defense Secretary and the President; it was a move which did not say much for Rumsfeld's faith in Franks.

The US military and the CIA came under fire following the death of Afghan opposition leader Abdul Haq on 26 October. The forty-three-year-old, once described by Ronald Reagan at a White House dinner in 1985 as 'one of the bravest commanders who led the Afghan freedom fighters', was executed by the Taliban at Azra barracks, near Kabul, having been accused of being a 'US agent'. Five days earlier he had entered Afghanistan on a mission to persuade Pashtun warlords to abandon the regime. Former US Ambassador Richard Holbrooke conceded that Haq's death sent a 'terrible message' to Afghan warlords weighing up their options. The United States had failed to demonstrate that it was capable of protecting 'agents' prepared to undermine the Taliban's rule; as the regime's intelligence chief Qari Ahmadullah boasted, 'Anyone who tries to enter Afghanistan will meet the same fate as Abdul Haq.'

Rumsfeld passed the buck on to the CIA, saying, '[Haq] had decided to go back in the country in a form and manner of his own choosing. He received assistance – not from the US military but another agency, from another element of Government.'

On 3 November *Al-Jazeera* broadcast another bin Laden speech. He was winning the propaganda battle hands down, inciting Muslims to launch a pan-Arabic *jihad* while opinion polls in Britain indicated that support for the war was ebbing away. He said: 'Those who refer our tragedies today to the United Nations for solutions, they are hypocrites who are deceiving God, his prophet and the believers. Are any of our tragedies not the making of the United Nations? Who issued the resolution for the division of Palestine in 1947 and surrendered the land of Islam to the Jews? All the West with rare exceptions supports this oppressive campaign, for which no evidence links what happened in the United States to the people of Afghanistan. The people of Afghanistan have nothing to do with this matter, but the campaign continues annihilating villages, women and children, without right.'

*

The United States was not making the most of its assets – the SAS being one of its most potent – and was spreading itself too thin on the ground. It fell to the Prime Minister to seek to change this. With members of the Regiment utterly frustrated and beginning their unexpected exfil from Afghanistan, Tony Blair, accompanied by chief of staff Jonathan Powell, foreign policy advisor David Manning, communications director Alastair Campbell, press secretary Godric Smith and the head of his private office Anji Hunter, chartered a British Airways Concorde on 7 November for a seven-hour visit to Washington – it cost a princely £250,000 although BA waived £500,000 from what should have been the final cost, being grateful for the huge publicity the trip attracted. Although in terms of global power Blair was a pygmy alongside Bush, the beleaguered President welcomed his advice on rethinking the mission. Bush appeared exhausted, stressed and relieved to see Blair as he said: 'We've got no better friend in the world than Great Britain. I've got no better person I would like to talk to about our mutual concerns than Tony Blair. He brings a lot of wisdom and judgement as we fight evil.'

While Blair, ever the consummate politician, appeared calm and unmoved by such gushing praise, an uncertain Bush floundered as the two men stood together in the White House lobby, the eyes of the world upon them. Bush appealed for time: 'I've told the American people many times and I've told the press corps many times that this is a struggle that is going to take a while, that it's not one of these Kodak moments. There is no moment to this; this is a long struggle and a different kind of war. We know that we are fighting evil. And the American people are patient. They've heard the call.'

Of the two men Blair seemed far the more assured, in body language and rhetoric: 'The cause is just, the strategy is there, the determination is there, and there is a complete and total commitment to making sure that this is a battle in which we will prevail. And we will; I have no doubt about that at all. We have destroyed virtually all the terrorist training camps of Al Qaeda; we have destroyed an enormous amount of the military infrastructure of the Taliban. Their air power, insofar as it exists, is completely taken out. We therefore have a very, very strong situation from which to move forward.'

Over dinner at the White House with the President and their respective sets of advisors, Blair criticized the United States' methods of war; the effort had to target Al Qaeda's troops yet was not doing so. There had to be more to the strategy than the constant bombardment of the Taliban's assets. The policy was clearly not working and as results were needed fast, changes had to be made. Who better to get into their faces than the SAS? The Prime Minister was as surprised as anyone that the Regiment was not being used to maximum effect. Blair was a big SAS fan and close friends with General Guthrie; the ex-CDS was his special envoy in Pakistan and unofficial military advisor – much to the chagrin of Admiral Boyce.* After the meal the leaders were left to talk in private.

Focusing the military effort on specific areas bore fruit when the regime's northern outpost of Mazar-i-Sharif fell on 9 November under a two-pronged attack by Northern Alliance warlords Dostum and Atta, backed by intensified

---

* The long shadow of 'Tony's General' hung over Boyce during Operation VERITAS. He announced his resignation as CDS in the spring of 2002 and is known to have felt undermined by the ex-SAS 'Whitehall Warrior's' lingering presence and closeness to the Prime Minister. The Admiral also questioned privately whether Britain should follow the American lead militarily without applying conditions on the use of UK forces under US command, which might have avoided the low-grade taskings the Regiment was given by CENTCOM on Operation DETERMINE.

US air strikes. At last the United States was concentrating its air power, with 66 per cent of it directed at Mazar in the preceding days. A huge sense of relief greeted the crucial first breakthrough, more than a month into the war. Mazar's strategic importance justified its selection. The United States now had a land bridge with Uzbekistan where its troops were stationed.

Soldiers, military supplies and humanitarian aid could now be transported south. An estimated 500 Taliban were killed by the Northern Alliance defending the key city. Although the Taliban claimed its forces were merely 'regrouping' and had sacrificed Mazar, the tide had turned; though nobody had anticipated how quickly the war would swing in the United States' favour. Conventional wisdom held that taking Kabul and Kandahar would prove much more difficult – as the capital was still defended by around 20,000 Taliban. There were fears that Dostum would kill as many Taliban as he could, whether or not they surrendered. In the battle over Mazar in 1997, his troops reportedly killed 6,000 enemy. Thankfully, with the eyes of the world watching and Northern Alliance leaders aware that human rights abuses would do their cause no good, it was a less bloody coup than expected. Nevertheless, some horrific images of isolated Taliban soldiers executed by groups of Northern Alliance troops were flashed around the globe – not the best advertisement for the men President Bush described as 'our friends'.

Bush invited the Northern Alliance to 'head south' from Mazar, 'across the Shamali Plains, but not into the city of Kabul itself', as the United States wanted the capital to be, in Secretary of State Colin Powell's words, an 'open city'. Northern Alliance Foreign Minister Abdullah Abdullah assured London and Washington that his forces would fight only 'up to the gates of the city', but nobody took this pledge for granted as he added a proviso that entering

Kabul would be justified to prevent a breakdown in law and order.

With Northern Alliance forces claiming control of Afghanistan's six Northern provinces and closing in on Herat and Kunduz, the need for an interim government was increasingly apparent, but Afghanistan had not had a stable government for twenty-two years, since the Red Army's invasion in 1979. Remarkably, just three days after fleeing from Mazar, the Taliban left Kabul. A convoy of armoured cars, pick-up trucks and mini–vans loaded with soldiers, weapons and ammunition set off under cover of darkness towards Kandahar – a hellish 600-kilometre journey along Afghanistan's A1, a rocky and sandy track with just an occasional short stretch of tarmac. They dumped eight foreign aid workers, imprisoned for supposedly promoting Christianity, in Ghazni, 100 kilometres from Kabul. The world was stunned and relieved at the pace of the Taliban's fall, as United Nations Secretary General Kofi Annan put it, 'As things are moving very fast, we need to bring the political aspects in line with the military development on the ground. We have to be nimble. We have to be able to move quickly and we have to be flexible.'

Taliban foot soldiers ignored Mullah Omar's command, from the safety of his Kandahar hideout, to 'regroup, resist and fight', insisting they should not be like 'a slaughtered chicken which falls and dies'. Perhaps nobody had told the Taliban's ambassador to Pakistan, Mullah Abdul Salam Zaeff, that the game was up, as he said, 'This news is false and baseless that the Taliban are leaving Kabul. We have decided to defend Kabul.'

The Russian Premier was in Washington when the news broke, having been a guest at the President's ranch in Crawford, Texas. He listened as a relieved Bush commented: 'President Putin and I spent a lot of time talking about the Northern Alliance and their relationship to Kabul as well as Mazar-i-Sharif and other cities that have now been liberated from the Taliban. I made it very clear to him that we would continue to work with the Northern Alliance to make sure they recognized that in order for there to be a stable Afghanistan, which is one of our objectives, after the Taliban leaves, that the country be a good neighbour, that they recognize that a future government must include a representative from all of Afghanistan.'

For once the pace of diplomacy was hectic at the United Nations. Algerian diplomat Lakhdar Brahimi, head of the UNSMA (United Nations Special Mission Afghanistan), told the Security Council he would bring together parties from all the ethnic divisions for a conference to determine the country's immediate political future, 'as early as humanly possible'.

The meeting would hopefully establish a provisional council, which in turn would select a provisional government. This government would draft proposals for Afghanistan's new constitution, to be ratified in the traditional way by a national council, or *loya jirga*. Brahimi suggested the interim government should serve a two-year term before making way for a permanent administration. Where this would take place was more contentious. The Northern Alliance, with its leaders sitting pretty in and around Kabul, wanted it held there, putting Pashtun leaders in isolated areas of the country at a huge disadvantage. Eventually the Alliance was persuaded to travel to Bonn, Germany, for the conference to convene on 27 November.

On 14 November, the United Nations Security Council passed Resolution 1378 expressing its 'Strong support for the efforts of the Afghan people to establish a new and traditional administration leading to the formation of a government, both of which should be broad-based, multi-ethnic and fully representative of all the Afghan people and committed to peace with Afghanistan's neighbours. Should respect the human rights of all Afghan people regardless of gender, ethnicity or religion, should respect Afghanistan's international obligations, including by co-operating fully in international efforts to combat terrorism and illicit drug trafficking within and from Afghanistan and should facilitate the urgent delivery of humanitarian assistance and the orderly return of refugees and internally displaced persons, when the situation permits.'

Resolution 1378 also reaffirmed the United Nations' condemnation of the Taliban for 'allowing Afghanistan to be used as a base for the export of terrorism by the Al Qaeda network and for other terrorist groups and for providing safe haven to Osama bin Laden, Al Qaeda and others associated with them'. The Resolution also backed the efforts of the Afghan people to replace the Taliban 'in this context'.

Blair's response to the Taliban's surrender was cautious. He said: 'Our job is not yet done by any means. We need urgently to put in place the next political and humanitarian moves that the changing situation now permits.' US Defense Secretary Rumsfeld was in agreement: 'I would like to caution everyone that this effort against terrorism is far from over. It is about a problem that inflicts this globe of ours, with networks and cells in dozens and dozens of countries.'

There were no celebrations in Hereford to mark the Taliban's passing. At least the troopers in A and G Squadrons discovered they would be returning to Afghanistan, but once there, what would they do? Chances of a contact seemed even slimmer with the Taliban removed from all but one of the major cities and with the United States remaining uninterested in fighting Al Qaeda on the ground. They would leave 'H' on 14 November, again from RAF

Lyneham, refuelling at RAF Akrotiri and flying via Oman. Huge disappointment and anger had followed the high hopes as they prepared for the first infil. Second time around, the mood was more sombre. The war, as they saw it, was effectively over and the chances of a big scrap seemed slim.

Blair also confirmed on the 14th that 45 Commando and 40 Commando Royal Marines and 2 PARA had been put on forty-eight-hours notice to move. The Paras would conduct the first permanent peace-keeping tour of Kabul, an unenviable and unglamorous assignment. Tony Blair said: 'We must never forget why we are engaged in this action: it is because on 11 September Al Qaeda perpetrated the worst terrorist outrage in history. It is to bring them to justice, and to eliminate them as a threat to world affairs that we are acting as we are.'

Bagram airport would be the bridgehead for the infil of British forces. Around 2,000 Royal Marines, Paras and supporting units would, the Prime Minister told a packed House of Commons, fly by Hercules from RAF Lyneham on 19 and 20 November, once the airfield had been secured and recced by an advance party of Royal Marines and SBS. He did not mention that the SAS was to be sneaked back in on the 17th. There was more good news on 16 November when the Taliban confirmed that bin Laden's number three, Muhammed Atef, had been killed in an air raid near Kabul. The Egyptian was wanted by the United States for his alleged involvement in the attacks on the US embassies in Kenya and Tanzania in 1998. Taliban spokesman Zaeff announced the following day that bin Laden and his family had left Afghanistan.

7. OPERATION BLOOD

Beneath bright blue, cloudless skies, RAF Hercules transport aircraft carrying their cargo of SAS – each man trained and armed at a cost to the British taxpayer of around £2.3 million – landed and taxied along the runway at Bagram, steering a path between bomb craters and the wreckages of abandoned Soviet aircraft which litter all Afghanistan's airports. Bagram, 40 kilometres north of Kabul, with the Paghman hills to the south-west and the Hindu Kush to the north-east, was built by the occupying Soviet Red Army in 1980. The airbase was dusty and unwelcoming in more ways than one. Around 100 SBS and Royal Marines Commandos secured the perimeter, not just from attack by Al Qaeda and Taliban but from victorious Northern Alliance troops, furious at not having been told the British were landing in territory they had fought so hard to secure.

In London, Secretary of State for Defence Geoff Hoon was putting a different spin on this. 'We have been in contact with the Northern Alliance,' he said, adding, 'and the situation on the ground is pretty chaotic at the moment. We believe that they will realize the benefit of having experts on the ground who can tell them and us what needs to be done in order to make the airstrip at Bagram usable for the kinds of humanitarian and diplomatic missions that are clearly going to be necessary.'

Bagram was critical to any strategy to control central

Afghanistan: the Taliban knew this and the Soviets before them. Just days before the airstrip had been in Taliban hands; as it was essential the Allies kept this bridgehead open and fully operational, the MOD wanted UKSF troops on the ground before the Northern Alliance could secure such a critical position. Informing them in advance of the UKSF infil, a plan they might have strenuously objected to, would have been folly. They might have attempted to block the move using force. As it was, the British relationship with the Northern Alliance survived through bartering with them over when more British troops would land.

While SBS and Royal Marines patrolled the perimeter, cleared mines and installed air traffic control equipment, Bagram's giant tin aircraft hangar, large enough to store a 747 passenger jet and riddled with thousands of bullet holes, became the SAS's operational headquarters. A and G Squadrons were allocated sections for accommodation and personal kit, and the weapons, bergens and rations were hastily bundled off the Hercules.

The first twenty-four hours saw the soldiers at their most vulnerable to attack. The situation was every bit as chaotic as Geoff Hoon described. With the military hardware unpacked and tested and security procedures in place, everyone felt safer. As the men still had the hump over how they were tasked by CENTCOM on Operation DETER-MINE, nobody was getting too excited about what lay ahead. Operation BLOOD, their redeployment in Afghanistan, had been named in hope rather than expectation of an enemy contact. It was later claimed that the fall of Mazar convinced President Bush he could tear up plans to deploy 50,000 US ground troops in mid-November. Such a deployment would almost certainly have coincided with the SAS having a more active role in the land offensive and arguably increased the chances of bin Laden's capture.

While unpacking his kit, Gordon, as usual, was moaning.

What had seemed the best chance of a punch-up in his army career had become, he thought, what is known in SAS parlance as 'a gang fuck'.

'It's got End-Ex written all over it ... and I thought we'd be quids in 'ere, didn't I?' Gordon declared to all and sundry. 'We didn't get a contact before the Taliban packed it in, so we hardly stand a better chance of one now, do we?'

Although they agreed with the sentiment and the logic, none of Gordon's troop felt the need to respond; a chinwag with the groaning Geordie was unappealing. They kept their heads buried in their bergens, searching for chocolate, while hoping he would not try to engage with them directly in conversation.

He continued, oblivious to their indifference, 'The fuckin' Northern Alliance is taking over now, the Yanks are going to carry on letting them do all the fighting. I tell you, they are not going to catch "Bin Liner" this way, he'll have bugged out by now if he's got any sense; anyhow, who's going to stop him?

'And this place has got to be the biggest shitehole on earth; look at it, for Christ's sake.'

There was just the slightest pause for breath before Gordon continued: 'They're all rag-heads to me, whichever side they're on. There's more chance of us getting a scrap against the Northern Alliance than against Al Qaeda. They've got Bagram surrounded for a start. At least it's good to see we've got the Shaky Boots boys here to man the outer perimeter. It'll make a nice change for them from polishing their canoes.'

The SAS's rivalry with the SBS being what it was, Gordon's last comment brought a smile to Phil's face. The SBS were respected but not exactly popular in Hereford; they were, at least by perception, on the whole quieter and younger than their Army equivalents. They also kept themselves to themselves. The Special Forces unit, which recruits from the Royal Marines, had a quiet Gulf War compared to the Regiment; this time, however, they had Admiral Boyce fighting their corner in Whitehall. As a Royal Navy man he was accused by some in the Army of favouring using the SBS and 3 Commando Brigade detachments over the SAS and the Paras, countering the perceived bias towards those units of Boyce's predecessor.

The SAS guys at Bagram kept their personal weapons – the most popular choice being the Diemaco automatic rifle – with them everywhere they went, including the toilet. Taliban or Northern Alliance rag-heads who thought they could scare off Bagram's new arrivals by firing a few pot-shots would quite simply be slotted; questions would be asked afterwards. The hangar's entry and exit points were manned twenty-four hours a day. Everyone, be they badged SAS, SAS-attached, SBS or a USLO (United States Liaison Officer), was vetted and searched on entry.

All movement outside the hangar was restricted: the Regiment did not want anyone, friendly or unfriendly forces, or the international media, to see anything, or to be able to identify who they were. They were helped by the fact that the newspaper and television reports focused on the SBS's presence. The broadcast and print media were unaware that the SAS had left Afghanistan and so assumed the Regiment was still tasked in the north of the country. At night the men slept on the concrete hangar floor in their sleeping bags and on their 'bum rolls' with their weapons beside them. By day the bombed-out hangar provided welcome shade but by night it was windy and cold. The squadrons had brought their cooks along to provide decent food and field shower units supplied hot water for ablutions. Predictably, however, it was not long before the hangar began to smell pretty rough. The stench of sweaty men and big grisly machines such as the Regiment's fleet of huge Acmat lorries, known as 'mother ships', was potent at close quarters.

Duty rosters were written and cleaning tasks divided between officers and men. Everyone, as the SAS say, 'did their stag' mucking in, regardless of rank. It was essential that personal kit such as desert fatigues were kept clean, vehicles ran smoothly and weapons, from personal rifles to support weapons such as the GPMGs and mortars, worked perfectly. These essentials formed part of the Regiment's SOPs (Standard Operating Procedures) – what each man does to ensure he is prepared for battle. He has to be ready to respond immediately to whatever is required of him, be it off-loading supplies from a Hercules or returning enemy fire. An SAS man's life, indeed that of every soldier, involves a lot of hanging around: repetition of mundane tasks, hours turning into days on stag duty, the whiling away of time and snatching sleep, which is not very often. This was the case at Bagram for the first few days. The men spent much of their time tuning into the BBC World Service and absorbing the top secret military intelligence reports coming into the Int Cell which had been set up in a corner of the hangar.

The Int Cell was manned by the SAS's RIC detachment – men referred to as the 'Green Slime', a nickname shared with the Royal Marines due to the colour of their berets. INTREPS confirmed media dispatches that A and G Squadrons would not, after all, be joined at Bagram by more Royal Marines or Paras. There were some very angry RMs, and 'Maroon Machine' stood down again after a 'prolonged period of readiness', but Downing Street had to tread carefully with the Afghans after sneaking the Regiment back in unannounced. There was also a thirty-strong RHQ Cell, including the CO, 22 SAS's Ops (Operations) Officer, the

RSM, QM (Quartermaster) who, working with A and G's SQMS (Squadron Quartermaster Stores), was responsible for logistics, admin clerks, 264 (SAS) Signal Squadron and US liaison officers.

Phil was as keen and professional as any of the younger troopers. None of the senior soldiers in his troop looked at him and questioned how he had made it through Selection; he was clever and extremely fit. What impressed the older guys most was that, unlike some of the 'gobshites', he knew when to shut up and listen to those with operational experience. Phil kept his head down, hoping 'talent would out'. He just wanted to do his job properly; the senior NCOs would either like him or not.

On the way back to his basha after grabbing a scoff he overheard OC G Squadron chatting to the CO. The boss, RSM and the DSF were pushing hard for a proper mission this time around; until then it looked like the two squadrons would be stuck out on a limb again, this time in southern Afghanistan doing hearts and minds jobs. With his wide-eyed enthusiasm for all things SAS, Phil did not question the head sheds' decisions as much as some, but he knew Gordon and the rest of the troop would be pissed off. Being the messenger meant he would be the one they shot at.

'Bad news, guys.'

'Yeah, what?' said one.

'There's hearts and minds jobs coming up.'

'Oh, that's a fuckin' surprise!' the same man replied.

'We're going to be fluffing up the natives and it's down south this time. Hardly what we came for, is it?'

Gordon kicked off: 'I can see this going really tits up. If we're not going to get a scrap we might as well piss off back to "H". I don't know why we bothered coming back in the first place. We should be pushing these Al Qaeda fuckers around a bit, they've only got AK47s and RPGs and we're armed to fuck. The head sheds had better sort this out, all this hassle and we could go home empty-handed. The Yanks are controlling everything. We're stuffed.'

Hearts and minds was a regimental speciality dating back to the Regiment's deployment in the Malayan jungle in 1952. Far more often than is recognized, the SAS's way is to persuade, not to threaten or kill. SAS medics have conducted mini-doctor's surgeries in the jungle and the desert, providing basic medical check-ups, extracting decaying teeth and giving injections against common diseases. A village full of scared and reticent natives responds better to offers of food and medical care than to gung-ho infantrymen pushing them around, as the Americans would later discover to their cost, with US Special Forces and the 82nd Airborne falling out over this matter.

With enemy intelligence a key priority and bin Laden's whereabouts being the jackpot, time had to be spent persuading Afghans who only wanted peace to give up what they knew. The world's most wanted man was not going to be found from an aircraft cockpit at 22,000 feet. It was not as if the United States had better troops at its disposal; and the desert had always been a happy hunting ground for the SAS – from the Regiment's formation in Northern Africa during the Second World War to operations in Oman and the Gulf War – all reasons why the men, perhaps naively, expected to be at Operation ENDURING FREEDOM's cutting edge.

The mood was brightened by the rumour that Tony Blair had been attempting personally to secure the SAS a more offensive role while visiting President Bush in Washington.

A signal arrived by secure communications from the DSF into the Int Cell. Perhaps thanks to Blair's pressure, the United States had surrendered a key Al Qaeda target and appeared ready to support an SAS ground assault on an enemy position. The Regiment was going to be blooded in

the first combat mission since it rescued British Army
hostages in Sierra Leone, and what would turn out to be its
biggest and most destructive battle since the Second World
War was suddenly just days away.

It arrived in scrambled burst and was written along
these lines in clear, basic English, rather than code:

TOP SECRET, CO 22 SAS EYES ONLY
    FM DSF (From Director Special Forces)
    DTG (Date, Time Group): MOD CLEARANCE
OBTAINED FOR OP TRENT. POTENTIAL TARGET. AQ
OPIUM STORAGE PLANT. APPROX 60–100 ENEMY
DUG IN DEFENSIVE POSITIONS.

The signal then gave Al Qaeda's base position:

LAT 29' 33m.
LONG 63' 40m.

The CO and the RSM were hugely relieved: at last they had
a task their men would relish. Jock spotted his squadron
OC, heading for the CO's corner of the hangar. The two
officers went into deep conversation. Then he saw OC G
Squadron heading in the same direction. 'Look out, some-
thin' might be up here,' he said, nodding in the direction of
what was now a three-man huddle.

Jason took note; some handily placed G Squadron boys,
including Phil, were also aware of developments.

'What do you reckon, Jock?' said Jason hungrily.

'Och, I dunno, but I ain't doin' any cockstands right
now,' said Jock. 'Our tasks have been shite so far, I'll believe
its fa real when we're on the Start Line, ready to rock and
roll.'

'Whatever it is, I hope we get put on it,' said Jason.

'Why's he got both OCs in, for fuck's sake? We've got to get the nod over G, Jock. If it's a contact it's bound to be small. Fuck, man, we'd better be tasked.'

The CO had given OC A Squadron and OC G Squadron a Warning Order – a military instruction to prepare for a specific task – in this case along the lines of the signal. More intelligence and briefings would follow.

A huge intelligence-gathering operation began immediately, the Int Cell tasked to provide an up-to-the-minute, past, present and future intelligence assessment of the specific target, its surrounding area and the enemy's air defence systems. The CO needed a wealth of bespoke INTREPS to plan any attack. Relevant information would include: enemy activity at the site and in the area over the past few months, Allied air activity: current and planned Allied operations; all information possible – aerial photographs, maps, defences, morale, state of readiness, etc. All sources of intelligence would be called upon in this process, including US/UK strategic and tactical sources. No stone would be left unturned to gather the information needed to ensure the thorough preparation and planning so essential to successful Special Forces operations – at least, that was what was supposed to happen.

News of the mission had spread rapidly among the men before any formal briefings, also known as 'O' groups. Jason watched as Phil's OC trotted back to his squadron's end of the hangar, his hurried pace denoting a sense of urgency. The OC passed brief instructions to some of his NCOs as he passed. He felt sure Phil would have overheard what was said, and jogged over to talk to him. He hoped his Selection buddy would fill him in, and had forgotten all the grief he had given him.

'Hey, Phil, what's the score?'

'I don't know, Jase, could be a two-squadron job by all

accounts. Opium plant or something. Bunch of druggies! It's virtually in Pakistan, mate, fuckin' miles away.'

Jason felt a little more in the know. Turning to walk back to his Pinkie, however, he saw Jock had cornered a troop commander. So he too would know what little there was to know. Jason's opportunity of getting one up on the old fox had passed.

With the RHQ and both squadrons living in such close confines, numerous conversations between 'head sheds' were overheard and the whispers passed on. The OCs were at last able to tell their men officially that something big was in the offing, but until more intelligence was available they should 'wait out'. The bosses met frequently in private to assess the scope and the scale of the operation, methods of infil and exfil being primary planning considerations. The CO had to know what air assets the Americans would provide – to get the SAS from A to B, he needed TAT (Tactical Air Transport) and as 'top cover', also known as CAS (Close Air Support), once on target. All other planning factors stemmed from that information. The distance from SAS HQ Bagram to target was 850 kilometres; driving all the way was a non-starter. It would take a fleet of transport aircraft or helicopters to get the squadrons within striking distance of the opium plant. INT REPS and aerial photographs indicated the enemy was dug in. The SAS wanted, if possible, US F-14s or F/A-18s for CAS. The USLOs – permanently attached to RHQ while the Regiment was in Afghanistan – were tasked with finding out what planes CENTCOM would provide and when.

The men needed to ensure they had all the kit they needed. Jock remembered how in the Gulf War the squadrons were short of ammunition and due to a shortage of Pinkies the men had to strip down Land Rovers to make them as much like the genuine article as possible. As he told

Jason, 'I'll be damned if I'm on the end of another kit cock-up, laddie.'

With a battle looming, Jock wanted a surplus of everything: 'Right, Jason, what the fuck are we diffy [deficient] of?' And he pointed at his colleague. 'If there's anythin' missin' we've got to sort it now. Understand? Check and check again. If we're short of anythin' and the QM won't play ball, you'll have to nick it. I've waited a while for this an' I don't want anythin' going wrong. Got it?'

'Sure, Jock.'

'An' another thing,' Jock added. 'You reckon this Pinkie's up to it?'

Jason shrugged. He was neither a mechanic nor a regular Pinkie driver.

This time there were enough Pinkies but they were showing their age. Common complaints included poor steering, bad suspension, a lack of power and pieces snapping off the chassis. This was no reflection on the design: the Pinkies were genuine off-road vehicles, bouncing non-stop up and down tracks, driving through rivers and up and down sand dunes, the Omani sand penetrating the engine and eating into the rubber-covered oil seals and grommets. Four to five years of that routine had simply taken its toll. The ageing Pinkies had to be patched up for one last drive; they could not be replaced until the SAS returned to Britain.

It was as if someone had turned a key in Jock's back. Having reluctantly toed the line during Operation DETERMINE, the genuine prospect of a scrap seemed to have transformed him. He was eager, in control, the total professional. As one of the SAS rat pack – the old sweats who had been there, seen it and done it – he knew all the tricks: hiding the best pieces of kit, pinching bits and pieces, where to stash his extra rations on the Pinkie, and the more obvious places where Jason was likely to hide his. Experience had also taught him to be wary of false alarms; the hurry-up-and-wait scenarios when everyone scampered around only to be stood down by the Ruperts at the last minute. This could still be one of those. In case it was not, he wanted enough ammo on board his wagon to tear Al Qaeda to shreds – that meant keeping an eye on every tin box.

Jock gave Jason a stare that meant business. 'Hey, Jay, get this. Ye don't let any bastard near our kit, ye hear me? The bastards will have it away before you know it if you're not switched on. Just in case this doesnae all turn to shite and it's fa real, I don't want to be short of ammo, fuel, water or any other shite. I'll fuckin' blame ye if we are.'

Jason, for once, said nothing. He knew the pecking order and his place in it: the bottom. For all his bravado, he was 'the Tom'. The way Jock addressed him at times like these left him in no doubt that the bottom was where he would stay unless he did the business on this operation. Jason would rather die than make a serious mistake in such company.

It was up to the RHQ cell to carry out an appreciation of the various options open to the Regiment to carry out the task and to develop these into a plan. A and G Squadrons' OCs tasked their troop commanders with analysing key issues critical to the operation's success. For example, both mobility troops had to assess the amount of fuel, water and spare parts the vehicles would require as they drove across Afghanistan. The length of that journey would be determined by the USLOs' report. It contained good news, and some which stunned the men and the head sheds. Air assets would be provided: a fleet of six C-130s to transport men and kit, four F/A-18 Hornets and two F-14 Tomcats on target. So far, so good.

The bad news concerned the time and duration of top cover: one set hour on a preset day and that time was

11.00 hrs (local). Should the SAS accept the mission to destroy the Al Qaeda opium base, recover potentially price-less intelligence and 'slot rag-heads', they would have to do so under sunny skies: a reversal of military logic and common sense and contrary to the Regiment's SOPs.

Whoever the enemy, they have a lesser chance of killing you if they cannot see you. The British Army prefers to launch its offensives before first light, under cover of dark-ness, when the human senses are at their least acute. This contact would start six hours too late and in broad daylight. The highly motivated and skilled Al Qaeda would spot the SAS coming across the desert plain from several kilometres away as the convoy kicked up clouds of dust. The element of surprise, so important to the attacking force, would be non-existent. But what was the CO to do? His men were already agitated and they would become even more restless the longer they were denied combat. Significant pressure had been placed on the US Government at many levels to get the SAS properly involved. The Regiment was not going to turn down what would probably be its only chance of a contact.

The hour of attack is usually the commander on the ground's prerogative, not that of a senior-ranking officer sitting thousands of miles away in Florida. Why was CENT-COM being so inflexible? It smacked of reluctance, a lack of approval: to them, every target was the same; there to be bombed only. The SAS would only get planes from the US Navy, which were aboard aircraft carriers south of Pakistan, when CENTCOM was willing to direct them away from bombing runs.

With an old head on his shoulders, Jock realized the United States was going out of its way to get the SAS involved. As he told some of the younger guys, 'Ye gotta remember this whole business here, it's America's party, not ours. This is a revenge mission for them. Just be glad they've given in it at last. It might not have happened at all if it wasnae for the CO's and the Government's persistence by all accounts. We've been thrown a chicken leg from the table, just be grateful for it.'

Other NCOs also took it in their stride, seeing the funny side amid the cock-ups. As one said, 'Fuckin' hell, Jock, it's gonna to be like the charge of the Light Brigade when we come over that last sand dune!'

Jason was more disillusioned. He said, 'I don't get it. It's like they are saying, "You wanted a battle so fuckin' much? Well, here it is, now don't fuck up, else it might put us off other business." Thanks very much.'

The Regiment was on the wrong end of a double booking. If the SAS did not like it, it could turn down the mission. There was no way the CO was going to do that. Putting aside the higher than necessary level of risk, at least the CO could now plan the mission. With between sixty and a hundred Al Qaeda defending the plant, he knew it would take all of his men and firepower to remove them, bearing in mind their strength in numbers relative to the SAS and the unfortunate 'H-hour', 11.00 hrs (local), the time the operation would start, coinciding with the availability of combat aircraft. Both squadrons would attack together, a full frontal assault, the first in the SAS's post-Second World War history. If this mission went wrong, the British Army would lose large numbers of its most prized, even priceless asset; the one facet of its forces that the colossal US military machine envied. Any failure would surely also lead to a major fallout between London and Washington, and potentially bring Operation ENDURING FREEDOM grinding to a halt.

Each troop in A and G Squadrons carried out its own O Group, with all the men, from the troop commander, who in most cases was a Captain, to the NCOs and troopers involved in problem-solving and the initiation of ideas.

Everyone had their say in how various parts of the operation would be carried out. The system, known in the Regiment as a Chinese Parliament, is not democratic – the bosses still give the orders and have the final say, but only after every soldier has contributed. Contrary to public perception, the Regiment's missions, no matter how big or small, are not worked out on the back of a cigarette packet. The SAS is obsessed with planning and detail.

The tension was mounting. Jock watched Jason check his rifle, strip it, put it back together again, and repeat the whole process. Then he pulled his bergen apart and stuffed everything back inside again, in the same order it was in before he repacked it. Jock had seen enough. 'Hey, Jase, fa fuck's sake, son, don't be a dickhead. I can tell you're shiting yourself, but stop fuckin' checkin' your weapon and your kit, eh? Fa Christ's sake. It's all there; you've cleaned it, so just leave it. Have a wank or something, eh?'

Jason was embarrassed. 'Yeah, all right, Jock, I just want to be sure, you know? I don't want a stoppage.' His behaviour was obsessive, the repeated weapon-cleaning a nervous reaction. Others wrapped increasing amounts of masking tape around their rifles, making them feel a little safer. Masking tape had a number of practical uses in battle: sealing homemade demolitions, and loose bandages and stopping a magazine from dropping off the stock of a weapon when the soldiers dived for cover.

The CO balanced tactical requirements against logistics. He had to find a TLZ for the C-130s to drop him, his 120 men and around 250 tonnes of equipment within striking distance of the target. The shorter the distance the forty-vehicle convoy had to travel across south-west Afghanistan, the better. The timing at each stage along the 850 kilometres route had to be worked out by backtracking from H-hour. The SAS had to be there, ready and waiting to dovetail their attack with the passes of the F/A-18s. The CO alone was responsible for the plan and he had to ensure those in the chain of command understood his instructions. By this time he had just another twenty-four hours to work everything out.

8. OPERATION TRENT

Needing a TLZ meant putting an SAS advance party on the ground to select a suitable area. The CO decided to deploy an eight-man HALO (High Altitude Low Opening) parachute team from G Squadron's Air Troop. They would be jumping into the unknown where there were no friendly forces with whom to link up on the ground. If compromised, they would have to fight for their lives. If the Regiment lost men, the CO was ultimately responsible.

He and the RSM trusted the men to execute a well-thought-out and clearly explained set of Battle Orders. This operation, however, was not out of the SAS textbook. Regular infantry units, not Special Forces, carried out full-frontal attacks. The Regiment's four sabre squadrons had bayonet strength of around 240 men, excluding attachments. The CO was proposing to lead half of them into a hail of small-arms fire and RPGs fired by hardcore Al Qaeda troops from a well-fortified position – not a decision he took lightly.

The British Army considers a 3:1 ratio the minimum manpower for advantage for an attack. As Al Qaeda were estimated at sixty to a hundred in strength, the SAS would have at best a 2:1 advantage. The late start time, the opium plant's fortress-like defences and natural surroundings were against the CO who was working with sketchy intelligence, and against the clock. There would be no time for a CTR (Close Target Reconnaissance) or to set up OPs (Observation

Posts) from where the enemy are usually watched at close quarters.

The CTRs and OPs were important for four reasons. First, an assessment of the area would allow the SAS to make optimum use of its weapons systems, knowing where best to situate the .50s, GPMGs and Milan rocket launchers. It would also ensure the appropriate taskings, groupings and concentration of forces, pinpointing where those who would lay down covering fire and where those who would advance on foot would position themselves before the attack. Third, the CTR would highlight areas of dead ground – locations which would be safe from enemy fire and view and positions where troops and the Regiment's assets could be concealed. Lastly, advance parties of SAS would have assessed 'the going', the nature of the terrain under foot and wheel; a crucial consideration when it came to calculating speed of movement, the tempo of the attack and basic factors such as how long it would take the convoy, fourteen Pinkies in A, and fifteen to eighteen vehicles in G, to reach the target.

The only maps were on a scale of 1:1,500,000, and these did not even show the target, or offer the usual intelligence about the nature of the ground, escape routes or the local population. If things went seriously wrong, the 'grunts' would be left to act on their own initiative. The area of the proposed TLZ, for example, was simply a blank space.

It was to overcome such seemingly insurmountable obstacles that the SAS bred its men to be the world's most highly trained, skilled and resilient soldiers. The SAS man sought alternative solutions to problems and thought laterally in peace as in war, where little or nothing went according to plan. This was what would determine the success or failure of this operation.

The CO, like other COs before him, believed that, despite the difficulties posed by the enemy, the logistics and, as it

turned out, by CENTCOM, his men would triumph. As for
death and the possibility of the same . . . this was an integral
part of the SAS man's make-up, CO included. If the question
of whether or not the SAS would take casualties or fatalities
determined its operations the Regiment would never leave
Hereford.

As long as the SAS wanted to be at the front of the
pecking order, danger was part of the job, but the rescue
and, if necessary, the body recovery procedures are always
in place. Bodies are taken back to Stirling Lines, even if the
SAS has to fight to get them back. That is part of SAS
folklore and dates back to the deep shame and embarrassment felt after *Adoo* in Yemen in April 1964 decapitated two
SAS soldiers killed in action and displayed their heads on
top of wooden stakes in the village of Taiz. Al Qaeda would
undoubtedly do the same, and reap a bountiful publicity
coup given half the chance.

The sheer size of the operation, the logistical com-
plexities involved, the number of personnel and the amount
of kit that had to be shifted across Afghanistan impressed
the men – and not just those new to the Regiment – as well
as presenting a number of significant logistical challenges.
Putting aside inter-squadron rivalries, the thought of everyone going into battle together united the men and gave the
operation a unique feel.

Jason was revved up, ultra-confident, convinced his
Regiment could wipe the floor with Al Qaeda whatever the
disadvantages. His excitement bubbling over, for once he
resisted the temptation to take the mickey out of Phil for
being a 'hat', when he bumped into him.

'Hey, mate, we're gonna be slotting some rag-heads after
all!'

'Looks like it, yeah.'

'I ain't fuckin' around, Phil. This is it. They don't stand
a chance against us.'

'Guess not.'

'I don't care how many of them there are compared to us. Fuck the three-to-one rule, that's bullshit. You never get a three-to-one advantage, everyone knows that.'

Phil was a little less gung-ho by nature. He would keep his aggression under wraps until they were on the Start Line.

'Yeah, maybe you will slot a few, mate. It's good both squadrons will be going in. Basic strength in numbers, two being better than one.'

Jason butted in. 'What? We don't even need G Squadron, mate. Your lot are probably just coming along for the ride. You might as well have just stayed in Hereford. A are going to clear up.'

Phil shook his head: typical Para arrogance, he thought. 'Strength in numbers is common sense. Common fuckin' sense, twat.'

Another interruption: 'Let's just get down there and see which squadron takes out the most enemy. They ain't gonna know what hit them by the time A Squadron have finished.'

Phil was riled. 'Oh yeah? I've heard there ain't gonna be a CTR or anything, don't you think about shit like that? Or the piss-poor maps. Doesn't that bother you?

'Yeah, yeah, fuck that,' said Jason, adding, 'The old sweats say the Arabs are shite fighters anyway. It will be a turkey shoot.'

Phil had heard enough. 'You're one cocky fucker. I'm here for the same reason as you, mate, and just as good as you. I just don't shout my mouth off about it. Now fuck off.'

Jason replied: 'I wonder why you bothered joining, mate.' With that closing remark he smirked and walked off, his Para-induced prejudices about 'hats' confirmed.

Back at his wagon, Jason said to Jock: 'What are they

like in G, eh? That Phil and his oppo Gordon? Thank fuck
I'm not with them.'

Jock agreed. 'Aye, but what did ye expect, they're a pair
of fuckin' hats.' He added: 'Thought ye went through
Selection with that laddie, what's his name . . . Phil?'

Phil had helped him get through some of the longer tabs
through the Brecon Beacons, but Jason did not want to
admit it now. 'Yeah . . . I didn't talk to 'im much, though.'

Jock enjoyed a wind-up, so he continued: 'Ye sure about
that? Little birdie told me he was dragging you along when
ye were on your chinstrap, eh? Fitter than youse, isn't he,
Jase? And being a hat as well . . . dear oh dear. What's
happened to the Paras since I left? It was nivvah the case in
ma day.'

Jason was fuming. 'What? 'Im? Nah, nah, you gotta be
jokin', Jock.'

'No? Ye sure about that? That's strange, y'know. Most
guys think that laddie's got the edge on ye.'

The CO finalized his plans and called in his OCs. It was
time for the battle plans to filter down the chain of command. Though they were heavily involved in the planning
process, as were all the soldiers, it was critical that A and G
Squadrons' bosses understood the CO's final instructions
perfectly in order to brief their men. These briefings needed
to be precise, covering every aspect of the operation thoroughly – infil, battle, exfil, tactics, 'what ifs' and emergency
procedures. When the squadrons left Bagram every man
had to absolutely sure of his role; once A and G were in Al
Qaeda territory there would be little time or opportunity for
reassessment.

Members of both squadrons were pensive as they were
called into the hangar for separate briefings. At one end,
Jock and Jason, still wound up, sat in anticipation on the
bonnet of their Pinkie, which seemed to have more kit

packed on to it than either man had seen before. Gordon and Phil were at the other end of the giant tin hut, waiting for OC G's brief.

To ensure co-ordination, regimental SOPs dictated that both squadrons would be briefed on each other's roles as well as their own and that these meetings would take place at the same time. The latter was a rumour-control procedure – the OCs liked to brief their men before they heard the tactics through the grapevine.

The wind rattled through the roof and helicopters buzzed overhead as the OCs spoke up to make sure they could be heard.

'A and G are to mount a joint attack on an Al Qaeda base, 250 kilometres south-west of Kandahar. As this is drug-smuggling country, the whole area, not just the target, is to be considered "most hostile".'

The OCs, with input from Ops and Int officers, gave the Battle Orders in a structured sequence familiar to the men who wrote down the details in their *aide-mémoire* notebooks, usually carried in a thigh pocket in their DPMs. The briefings would be followed by further O Groups at troop level. The sheer quantity of the timings, facts and figures which they had to assimilate and the fact that there could be no margin for error meant every effort had to be made to keep the instructions clear and simple. The target was a huge opium storage facility, one of Afghanistan's largest. The quantity of opium in storage had an estimated street value of £50 million. Some of Al Qaeda's best infantry troops had been selected to guard it. The men were told that the enemy personnel were 'hardcore Al Qaeda'.

Opium was traditionally Afghanistan's most popular cash crop. Although the Taliban had supposedly destroyed two opium laboratories in Helmand province, where the SAS had been tasked a year earlier, many labs were now relocating from Pakistan to Afghanistan. One reason on paper for the SAS's mission was to destabilize the drug industry.

The OCs used aerial photography to show how the enemy position was roughly 20 kilometres north of the Pakistan border and dominated by a single massive geographic feature: Spot Height 2213, its height in metres. The SAS referred to such isolated points as 'pimples'. This did not do Spot Height 2213 justice: it had an imposing presence overlooking the target and surrounding area. There were no friendly forces in the vicinity. The men were also told of possible minefields, potential ERVs and LUPs (Laying-up Positions) between the TLZ and the opium plant. No one knew if there were any 'bad radio areas' where signals could not be sent or received *en route*.

The ground would be undulating, sandy and craggy. There were few cultivated areas in the target's immediate vicinity but mines were assumed to be a factor. Afghanistan had the world's largest collection of landmines, at least fifty different types. It was estimated it would take ten years to get rid of them all, assuming hundreds of millions of dollars were made available. Around 8,000 people, mainly Afghans, were killed or injured every year this way. It was impossible to tell whether they would be *en route* or on the target, but as there were hundreds in Bagram's vicinity there was every chance of encountering them. The advice was simple: 'Don't step on any.'

The Meteorological Report, provided by the Met Office's mobile unit stationed at Bagram, predicted that the weather over the next few days there, *en route* to the target and at the target itself would be sunny and bright. The enemy's location was given as the opium plant's grid reference. Both the target and the surrounding area were regarded as a 'total hostile environment' but there was no evidence from the satellite pictures, no 'ground truth' to establish whether there were enemy patrols. It would take an OP or CTR to prove that.

According to the intelligence brief, the enemy were the elite, likely to have been trained at one of bin Laden's camps. They were well equipped, disciplined and highly motivated. The prospect of death held no fear for them. Again, because of the lack of an OP or CTR, little was known about their routine, what they did on a daily and nightly basis.

The briefing continued covering the following areas based on intelligence from satellite pictures and friendly Afghan sources:

Routes and transport links to and from the target: A single track running east to west used by lorries to transport the opium.

Sentries: Unknown.

Trip flares, mines, fixed lines and booby traps: Unknown.

Strength, dress, weapons and equipment: Estimated between sixty and a hundred, dressed in traditional Afghan attire, well armed with AK47s and RPGs. Known to have stockpiled ammunition.

Morale: Very high, buoyed by the fact that no Allied troops have dared take them on.

Defences: Trenches and bunkers surround the opium plant. Expect them to be manned by Al Qaeda.

Likely ambush positions: Every rock around the fortification is a potential hazard position. The threat could come from anywhere and everywhere, from TLZ to target. An Al Qaeda guerrilla could hide behind any fold in the ground.

Enemy intentions: Unclear. Assume they will intend to hold and protect what they have got – likely to put up stiff resistance.

Installations and camps: A large, heavily fortified camp secured on all sides, with all-around defence, bunkers, trenches, natural protecting features in the form of the spot height to the north, slow, undulating, rocky and sandy terrain to the east, west and south and a small river to the south of the camp parallel to the track running east to west. Camp boundaries are difficult to define, as there are no fences or walls. Towards the south of the camp appear to be two large, single-storey warehouses, 150×60 feet, of brick construction, and single-storey buildings on the west and south-west sides of the camp. One of these buildings is the enemy's headquarters. The camp is illuminated by a series of basic lights run by a generator.

Reinforcements: Expect Al Qaeda to be able to call on reinforcements. Intelligence reports have picked up Al Qaeda heading south from Kandahar, which is coming under increasing pressure from US aerial bombardment and the Northern Alliance.

Friendly forces: US CH-47 for 'casevac' (casualty evacuation). CAS from four US Navy F/A-18 Hornets and two F-14 Tomcats.

Civilian population: Nomadic tribes of Pashtun and Baluchi descent.

Dress and customs: The enemy will look pretty much like all the Afghans you've come into contact with and Arabs.

Attachments (*Guides, interpreters and specialists whom the Regiment might bring along for assistance*): None.

The Ops officers then moved on to the most important part of the brief, starting with the definition of the mission.

Objective: To destroy the enemy, the opium, recover any intelligence at the target and establish a presence in Al Qaeda territory.

*

The execution of the battle plan was broken down into five phases:

Phase 1: The move by elements of G Squadron's Air Troop to create a TLZ at a location south of Kandahar.

Phase 2: The infil of the main SAS party from HQ Bagram to the TLZ.

Phase 3: Main party and the HALO team move from the TLZ to a FUP [Forming Up Point].

This would be the last scheduled stop before attacking the target. The CO's order was that the convoy should drive from TLZ to FUP before first light, stopping there for an hour before the final approach. The FUP would be recced by a motorbike detachment to ensure it was clear of enemy and to check out at least one bug-out route in case of attack.

Phase 4: The assault on the opium plant by A and G Squadrons. A would get as close to the target as they could on the Pinkies before de-busing and advancing to contact on foot. G Squadron would provide a FSB (Fire Support Base) laying down a blanket of heavy fire to protect the advancing troops. The RHQ, including the CO and the RSM, would assess the progress of the attack from the flank. Once the target was secured, it would be searched for any enemy intelligence.

Phase 5: Withdrawal.

Both OCs then continued in detail about the exact route in and out; the specific groups, formations and the all-important order of march. There would be nothing random about which vehicle took up which position in the convoy. It was all planned to coincide with the vehicles' positions on target.

The target itself was then discussed in more detail. Where would each squadron form up in relation to it? What were 'Actions On' the target and would deception be employed? What were the signals to fire? What would

happen if a patrol got lost? What were 'Actions On' in the
event of ambush, downed aircraft or, heaven forbid, a 'blue
on blue'? (On US and British maps and battle plans
'friendly' forces are shown in blue and enemy forces in red.
When the enemy attacks friendly forces it is a 'red and
blue', when friendly forces attack friendly troops it is therefore a 'blue on blue'.) Would prisoners of war be taken?
Would Al Qaeda casualties be taken, and what would be
done if members of the roaming local civilian population
were engaged?

Jason had been scribbling furiously, trying to get most
of the information down; Jock less so, more confident he
would remember all he needed. Jason had not fully understood everything but did not want to make himself look
stupid before the whole of A Squadron by asking a silly
question, which slowed the briefing down.

The troops were also told of the estimated times of
departure, when they were expected to return to Bagram
and when a post-operational de-brief would take place.
Lastly, they were given the frequencies for communications
and synchronized watches.

H – 47.00 hrs

By now the air inside the hangar was thick with sweat,
engine oil and anticipation. After years, and in some cases
decades, of flexing muscles in preparation and simulation,
this was for real. This was an opportunity to be squeezed
by the throat.

Some were angrier and more intense than others, but to
a man their focus was razor-sharp. Jock gave one or two of
the younger lads a piece of advice about fear: 'If ye bum is
twitchin', don't fa fuck's sake let on. Just get on with it, nae

fuckin' drama.' He was right, and keeping busy steadied the nerves. Some could not keep still, whistling and drumming their fingers. A few, such as Jock, managed to carry off with apparent ease the 'I just get on with it, whatever the operation' attitude. Some had to work harder to block out natural human emotions.

Luckily the CO and RSM oozed calm assurance and confidence in the men, which lifted them. They trusted both men's decision-making ability.

Phil toyed with the prospect of his wagon being part of the FSB. Whichever way he looked at it, that was not what he wanted. He would have preferred to be advancing to contact with Jason and Jock as part of A Squadron. As he cleaned the GPMG a sense of envy rose in him. The two-squadron tasking did not mean he would not get a sight of the enemy; just that Al Qaeda might be far away. Going through the weapons routines in the hangar, it was hard to visualize the FSB's position, whereas he could see Jason and Jock going eyeball to eyeball with the rag-heads; and deep down that was what he wanted to do. Phil would never be the big drinking and fighting SAS man, and with a young wife he had other priorities beyond the Regiment, whereas Jason just seemed to live for it. But that did not mean he did not want to experience combat. He also wanted to test himself, physically and psychologically, to the limit; and that meant closing with the enemy.

Although he would not show it, Gordon did not share Phil's sense of disappointment. He had at most two or three years left in the Regiment, and while he would never let anyone down, he would not be the first to volunteer to run towards the enemy and risk his life either. He was delighted just to be getting a contact after all these years. He could not help it that at times like these his thoughts turned to his wife and daughters. He felt the responsibilities of a husband

and father, not just of an SAS soldier to the Regiment, and more than most he was determined to return to Hereford in one piece.

Phil had gone pretty quiet; he wanted to be at the heart of the operation, tasked with a role which was central. That had not happened, and not being in Air Troop meant he was not going to be considered for the HALO jump either. Gordon attempted to gee him up.

'What's up with you, Rip? Feelin' tired? You're not sayin' much.'

'Just wish I was on the jump, that's all.'

Gordon could barely believe what he was hearing, like most of the guys he thought the Air Troop guys had a screw loose. 'Yer jokin, aren't ye? Those guys are gonna get what's comin' to 'em tomorrow, Rip.'

'What do you mean?' said Phil curiously.

'Well, those "sun gods" spend the whole fuckin' year poncing about in America practising their freefall, right? Odds are there'll be one jump when something goes wrong. They can fuckin' keep it, man, and I know most people would agree with me. Freefallin' over Kandahar? They can keep it, mate. Parachuting scares the crap out of me.'

'Yeah, that ain't saying much, Gordon, flying shits you up, for fuck's sake.'

As for once he had been genuinely trying to give Phil a lift rather than winding him up, Gordon did not appreciate getting grief back. He was incensed.

'Fuck off, Phil, you'd probably fall asleep anyway and they'd have to leave you on the plane.'

'Shut up, twat.'

'Even when you jumped you'd probably nod off and forget to pull the cord.'

'Piss off, Gordon, you creaking old git.'

*

The potential TLZ site was selected in the wilderness of sand, dust and clay south of Kandahar, an area known as Registan, which translates from the Persian as 'country of sand'. Registan was Afghanistan's largest desert; an unforgiving and uninviting environment, barren, devoid of vegetation, with sand ridges and dunes climbing to 30 metres. The enemy could be found roaming anywhere, as could unknown numbers of nomads, who led their herds of underfed goats, sheep and camels across the desert plain in search of food and water. Registan was their winter pasture.

This was where eight SAS men would land by parachute, unsupported and isolated. The Regiment's prospective TLZ was virgin territory for Allied troops and situated at least 100 kilometres from friendly forces – the United States was setting up its FOB (Forward Operating Base), Camp Rhino, in the north of Registan. The team was tasked to hold its territory for twenty-four hours, working by night to test the ground and hiding by day. Every minute spent on the ground left them vulnerable to attack. They would leave Bagram as soon as possible after last light in order to give themselves the maximum time to recce the TLZ. They wanted to be safely hidden in their LUP and OP before daybreak.

9. HALO

H – 40.30 hrs

Air Troop had waited for the sun to disappear over the mountains. Ground preparations were finished and the CO, RSM and OC G had wished them good luck. They would be making history: the first SAS operational HALO jump of its kind into enemy territory.

They had packed their parachutes and tightened and taped up bergen straps, making sure there was nothing loose to catch on the inside of the RAF Hercules that had been refitted specially for the descent. Now the team was driven from the hangar to the aircraft where the Loadmaster and the PJI (Parachute Jump Instructor) were to meet them. Both members of the air crew were from the RAF's Special Forces Flight at RAF Lyneham and worked frequently with the Regiment. The PJI was looking at his watch. His would be the last friendly face they would see before shuffling off the ramp and dropping 28,000 feet in five minutes into Al Qaeda's back yard.

Each man carried up to 180 pounds of personal kit: ammunition, weapons, two parachutes, main and reserve, and chest webbing, which contained spare magazines, a survival kit, a TACBE (Tactical Beacon) to assist in event of a search-and-rescue operation, chocolate, field dressings and a multitude of potentially life-saving gadgets and equipment such as GPS. Their dog tags hung around their necks with two cylinders of morphine, the painkiller stored in 2-inch glass phials and protected by masking tape. Some men tied one of the tags to a boot.

The RAF crew had flown in from Oman specially for the jump. Although the men were keen to get on, it was good to be among people they knew at such a dangerous and nerve-racking time. They stepped inside the plane, past the huge oxygen console which would provide them and the crew with air above 12,000 feet. It had been secured to the aircraft floor and was protected against buffeting by a metal cage. For the last twenty minutes of the flight and the jump, the team would switch oxygen supplies from the console to their 'walk-around' bottles, which contained a thirty-minute supply. These were miniature versions identical in shape to divers' oxygen tanks and were strapped to the soldiers' stomachs.

The purpose of a HALO jump was the fastest possible covert insertion of SAS troops. Intelligence suggested Al Qaeda did not have radar, and in any case if they had, this would not have picked them up. The men would shoot down towards the TLZ at speeds of up to 140 mph, falling around 25,000 feet in under three minutes before deploying chutes and floating to the ground. The air temperature would be as low as −60 degrees in the higher climes, causing ice to form on their wrist-held altimeters. The freezing air would only be bearable because they were travelling so fast, and were wearing up to four layers of lightweight, thermally insulated clothing.

The deployment of steerable TAPs (Tactical Assault Parachutes), at 360 square feet almost twice as large as sports parachute canopies, was controlled by an AOD (Automatic Opening Device) which responded to barometric pressure, pre-set to launch when the men dropped to 3,500 feet. The reserve parachutes sat piggy-back on top of the main chutes, an advance in parachute technology which came as a major blessing. The SAS men hated the old-style front-mounted reserves, which, strapped to their chests, frequently caused bad 'body attitude' in the air, obstructed ground vision before landing and stopped them wearing chest webbing.

The guys sat down inside the dark and sweaty interior of the Hercules, the air thick with the smell of aviation fuel. They faced inwards, towards each other, backs to the walls of the aircraft. Everyone knew what was expected of them; little was said. The final pre-take-off briefing had covered 'Actions On' in emergencies, such as SAM attack (Surface to Air Missile), the likelihood of which was at its highest immediately after take-off. The troops knew that the pilot would attempt a safe landing but there was little chance of it succeeding. If the missile hit later rather than sooner and the navigational equipment failed, leaving the Hercules' exact whereabouts unknown, the team leader would have to decide whether or not to jump and then TAB (Tactical Advance to Battle) to the TLZ.

The roar of the engines was so loud as they started up that it silenced any words, if not thoughts. The men focused on the priorities; stable body position during freefall and being lucky. This was no time for a malfunction, partial or otherwise. The clocks tick fast at 3,500 feet; they would have just seconds to save their lives.

A fatality or severe injury to one of the Air Troop would probably cause the operation's postponement or cancellation. Everyone knew the story of Lance Corporal 'Rip' Reddy, who had died after his rigging lines became tangled following G Squadron's 10,000-foot drop into northern Oman in 1970. Reddy's death had been a severe blow, not only as the loss of a good man, but because, as the SAS made a point of returning bodies to the UK whenever possible, the squadron's operational cover was blown by the helicopter flying in to collect him. This time members of the Regiment were dropping into enemy territory from a further 18,000 feet up.

The men sat down with their bergens in front of them, parachutes and weapons to one side. Falling to earth, they would balance their bergens on the backs of their legs, a most unnatural position in which to carry weight.

H – 40.00 hrs

The Hercules seemed to take off in slow motion, lumbering through the first few hundred feet of its climb; a sitting duck for any Al Qaeda hidden near Bagram with a Stinger. The knowledge that Al Qaeda did not have any military aircraft was scant consolation. Once out of SAM range, Operation TRENT would finally be underway.

The PJI held up the first instruction sign: 'Fit parachutes'. The lack of light made this tricky, with the line of infra-reds on the floor of the Hercules providing the only meagre illumination. The PJI checked every man's waistcoat, and tightened chest and leg straps. Once all this was done, the parachutists sat down, stepping through the shoulder straps of the bergens in front of them.

At 10,000 feet the PJI gave his second order, for the Air Troop to plug in to the Hercules' oxygen console. They did this via a pipe connected to their helmets; the same pipe would shortly connect them to their 'walk-arounds'. Everyone checked off and the PJI reported to the pilot by radio that all was well.

Trapped inside their Darth Vader-style oxygen masks, the thunder of the Herc's engines in their ears, weighed down with kit, time passed terribly slowly. The men exchanged occasional nods and winks but that was all. It required enormous mental discipline; they had to remain switched on for every second of the journey.

At last came the 'P minus 20' sign: they were just twenty minutes away from jumping and twenty-five from the ground. Cruising at 27,000 feet – 5 miles high – they began the switch from oxygen console to 'walk-around'. Their bodies twitched in nervous anticipation of what was to come. An error now would kill them or leave them severely brain-damaged. They had thirty to forty-five seconds to change over; any longer without oxygen and they would be vegetables.

The plane rocked up and down as they fumbled with the pipes. Teamwork in the form of the SAS 'buddy-buddy' system was essential. Time spent in decompression chambers had taught them to recognize the first signs of hypoxia. They stared at each other, looking for the initial symptoms, 'wide eyes' and any hint of drowsiness. The suffering and risk levels endured on exercise ensured they stayed alive at times like these. It took years to be this good.

'P minus 10' and then 'P minus 5' passed. Their minds screamed: 'Think body shape and emergency procedures.' The other voice, just as loud screamed: 'Just get me out of here.' They were eager to jump, to feel the exhilaration of descent, to experience freefall's precious sense of freedom; to dive towards earth and hear the air roar. But below them was a war-torn conflict zone where potential danger lurked behind every rock and fold in the ground. Would they land on a hot DZ (Drop Zone)? Was the intelligence right? Would luck be on their side or Al Qaeda's? If the main canopy failed they would rip it away and deploy the reserve. At 3,000 feet, travelling at 130 feet per second, it would take the reserve another 1,000 feet to deploy fully; there was precious little room for manoeuvre.

The rear of the Hercules opened, the giant aircraft swallowing a huge gulp of icy-cold air which pinned the men back against its walls. The PJI confirmed to the pilot that the ramp had locked out. The men groped at their masks, ensuring oxygen pipes were securely in place, and followed them down from their helmets to their walk-around bottles. Nervously, they tugged on every strap they could see.

Last-minute check: weapon, chest webbing, bergen and parachutes tightly in place. Finally the critical procedures of putting on their goggles and snapping on their cyalume stick lights, the little plastic tubes attached to the backs of their helmets. Squeezing them hard caused the luminous green liquid inside to glow. The bright cyalume stick was their best chance of seeing one another in the night sky. They wanted to be close enough to assist in mid-air if required but far enough away not to cause problems.

Two lights, either side of the ramp and just above head height, would signal when it was time to jump: 'RED ON' for prepare, 'GREEN ON' for go. There was no room for hesitation. Once on the ground they had seven hours to recce the TLZ and locate OP and LUP positions before daybreak. They then had to stay hidden for fifteen hours before guiding in the C-130s.

If compromised and outnumbered they would 'shoot and scoot', firing as much lead as possible in the enemy's direction before splitting up and regrouping at a pre-arranged ERV (Emergency Rendezvous).

Each man had the large-scale 1:1,150,000 Escape and Evasion map. This had a panel in the top left-hand corner on which was written in a variety of languages, including Dari, Urdu and Persian, instructions which the SAS would show to a local if he thought the stranger could help him.

It read:

I am British and I do not speak your language. I will not harm you! I bear no malice towards your people. My friend, please provide me with food, water, shelter, cloth-ing and necessary medical attention. Also, please provide safe passage to the nearest friendly forces of any country

supporting the British and their Allies. You will be
rewarded for assisting me when you present this number
and my name to British authorities.

They knew the order to jump; base man first. As he
carried heavier kit, he had reduced air mobility and was
less able to track across the skies. He would be the mid-air
target for the others to aim at. Like a pregnant penguin the
base man shuffled forward; in a few seconds he would 'frog
off' backwards into the dark depths below. The PJI, hooked
up by safety strop and wearing a parachute, stood back
from the ramp and checked off the base man's gear. The
Loadie, standing furthest inside, saw no problems with the
rear man. The men were ready and the PJI – his unit's motto
'knowledge dispels fear' – radioed the OK to the pilot.

'RED ON': The base man inched backwards, immediately behind him 28,000 feet of open space, with Al Qaeda
possibly waiting to welcome him. He put his goggles on.

'GREEN ON': Over he went, tumbling down into the
abyss, buffeted by the aircraft's slipstream. He rocketed
towards the ground, travelling faster by the second,
approaching terminal velocity – 0 to 120 mph in ten seconds.

The rest of Air Troop followed as the PJI watched
anxiously over the ramp edge for the heavily laden figures
to fade away. All he could see now was their cyalume stick
lights, until the moment came when he could see nothing at
all. It was time for the aircraft to return to Bagram and for
the pilot to radio back to base to inform the CO – 'TASK
COMPLETE'.

H – 38.00 hrs

All eight men shot through the night skies above Afghanistan, falling through the first thousands of feet. Their gog-

gles immediately misted up in the cold air, making freefalling like driving a speeding car blindfolded. They wiped them to see where they were going. Crashing into another parachutist would send them both spinning out of control and possibly kill both of them. The penalty for being directly above anyone at chute deployment time would be a faceful of rock-hard canopy. The patrol would lose two men, 25 per cent of its strength, before they had even reached the ground.

Desperate to close in on the base man, they hunted for green lights below. They wanted to be between 10 and 20 feet apart; this required precision accuracy, hard enough by day and extremely difficult at night when carrying 200 pounds of kit. Falling towards Afghanistan, they were roughly in a diagonal line between the ground and the aircraft heading away. At 5,000 feet, it would be time to 'bomb burst' and track to a safe space. At 3,500 feet, the AODs would kick in; if the devices were late, just a marginal error of a couple of seconds would prove fatal if mismanaged.

Tracking is the fastest form of freefalling. The parachutist adopts his most streamlined stance, pulling his arms down from the star-like delta position – when the arms are above the head as if surrendering – until they are tightly by his sides, as he clutches his weapon and legs tightly together. For a few precious moments they were human bullets, racing at 140 mph. But this was only for a short time; they did not want to be tracking when the AOD functioned at around 3,500 feet.

One by one they switched to the 'flare up' position, an exaggerated form of the delta which produced the greatest resistance to fall. This was to avoid a partial 'mal'. If the canopy deployed when they were tracking, it would shoot out of the pack at the wrong angle. Tracking had to stop at 4,000 feet.

The AODs jolted into life and pulled open Air Troop's main parachute packs. They had been falling for a little over two minutes and had a similar time to go before they hit the ground. First, a 3-foot compressed spring designed to take with it the parachute's rigging lines flew out, followed by the canopy, which opened with a crump sound. There were no malfunctions, partial or otherwise. They felt a huge jolt – a drag factor at last – and reached above their shoulders for the steering lines. Fastened by Velcro ties to the main risers, these were the parachute's four central rigging lines. They took off their masks. Lifting their goggles, they saw the sandy, rocky ground coming up to meet them. All-around observation confirmed that everyone was safely apart and safely together.

At around 200 feet they turned into the wind. It was the job of the lowest man to assess its direction. They were getting ready to hit the deck, coming in on half brakes, and they wanted to land into the wind. At 100 feet they released their bergens and pushed down on the metal hooks on their left and right thighs. Weapons were loosened as the bergens were kicked down and dangled beneath them on a thick cord. The sounds of them smacking into the ground would be their final warning before impact. They pulled both steering lines simultaneously. If they got it right, touching down would be like stepping off a kerb on to a road; if they got it wrong, the impact would be like jumping on to the road from a second-storey window. A broken femur was not recommended at this stage of the operation.

All eight men landed safely. Quickly, and in total silence, they collapsed canopies, undid parachute harnesses and dragged them from the DZ. It was imperative that they oriented themselves with their surroundings as quickly as possible. Their rifles were undamaged, the first round in the magazine was still in the firing position and the safety catches were switched on.

They breathed in the dusty night air and took in the undulating, craggy and unwelcoming environment that stretched as far as the eye could see. Under the bright ambient starlight the sandy ground seemed almost like an alpine scene. Everything was still. The men huddled together, bergens on the ground, listening and watching. They were in the all-around defensive position covering 360 degrees for every possible angle of attack. With the adrenalin still pumping through them after the jump and the sensation of thundering towards earth, it felt strange to be so motionless.

They looked for unnatural lights, beams from trucks, fires and any uniformly shaped outlines. A thumbs down signal would indicate suspected enemy presence. They remembered the phrase from basic infantry training: 'Shape, Shine, Shadow, Silhouette, Movement, Noise and Smell'. Shapes such as straight lines or regular patterns would give them away to the enemy, and vice versa. They spent fifteen minutes surveying their new surroundings, thinking about where their nearest hide might be, and the closest escape route. As silently as possible, the parachutes were packed away and a compass bearing was taken. They were on 'hard routine' – no hot drinks, no hot food, no cigarettes and the only talking permitted was a whisper to exchange operational details.

H – 37.30 hrs

Thoughts turned to the TLZ recce. A SITREP (Situation Report) signal was sent back to HQ Bagram: 'SAFE LANDING CONFIRMED'. The first stage of the TLZ recce was to test the firmness of the ground, which would have to cope with twelve Hercules landings that evening. They pressed a device shaped like an American football with a metal spike on the bottom into the ground. The machine then gave a reading of the ground's resistance. They needed to test an area 900 × 40 feet: just wide enough for the plane's wheel span and long enough for the Hercules to land and take off safely again.

They tested the ground, pushing the device's metal spike into the dusty earth. The area was marked out and the wind direction calculated: pilots preferred landing into the wind. At the end of the process there were six marked-out points: the border of a 900 × 40-foot runway. By the time of the last flight, the area would probably resemble a ploughed field, but all that mattered was that the planes were able to land safely and take off again.

H − 31.30 hrs

The men now set off from the TLZ to find OP and LUP sites. The OP had to be big enough for at least two soldiers at once to lie still in a position where both could see the TLZ and the surrounding area. The LUP had to be big enough for eight, providing cover from enemy fire and view. Both the LUP and the OP needed at least one bug-out route and to be close enough to each other and to the TLZ to keep all movement between sites to a minimum. The LUP was the base camp facility where they would eat, sleep and clean their weapons. It had to be able to protect its flank and rear, so a natural ground feature was preferable, from where they could look down on the TLZ. The greater the degree of natural fortification and camouflage for both positions the better. The men would leave as little trace of their presence as possible at either location when they left.

The men were gripped by the desert's eerie stillness before dawn. It was freezing cold and uncomfortable, a layer of dust covering them and their kit. Silently, in two groups of four, they moved from the TLZ to the OP and LUP spots. This was a tactical move, unhurried, weapons at the ready, the men constantly on the lookout. The point man looked ahead for enemy, mines and booby traps. The rear man looked behind; those in the middle left and right. Every few minutes both groups stopped to listen for artificial sounds and look for unnatural lights. Two men were put on OP watch; another pair on guard duty, and the remaining four rested, cleaned their weapons and ate cold rations.

H – 29.30 hrs

When the sun rose Air Troop saw Registan's stark, desolate landscape stretching before them for what seemed like hundreds of miles. This was a horrible place to be, but most importantly there was no sign of any enemy or nomadic herdsmen. The area was uncultivated and as empty as it had seemed by night. It was warmer now and they were well camouflaged and ready to respond to any attack. It was difficult to sleep during the day, in the knowledge that tomorrow was the day of the battle, and that at a moment's notice their present location could be compromised. However ready and confident they felt, they still feared the unknown and the unexpected. They were relieved the jump had gone well, that the TLZ was ready and that they had found secure areas to rest until night fell again. The Air Troop could be satisfied but it remained a job half done.

10. START YOUR ENGINES

Fourteen years separated them, yet Jason and Jock had much in common, contempt for REMFS and 'hats', hunger for combat and an unconditional love of the SAS being just three shared attitudes. Another similarity was that neither man would admit the trepidation he felt as they made their final preparations to leave Bagram. The prospect of two hours trapped inside a sweaty and smelly Hercules, susceptible to Stinger missile attack on take-off and landing, filled both men with dread. As control freaks – a trait SAS training exaggerated – they hated their fate being out of their hands and would feel better seeing the enemy in front of them, when their next moves would be up to them; anything beat being stuck in a potential metal coffin, particularly during take-off and landing.

For the two Falklands War veterans there were also the memories of the greatest single loss of life in 22 SAS's history, on 19 May 1982, to contend with. On that freezing night in the South Atlantic a Royal Navy helicopter carrying thirty passengers and crew crashed into the icy waters on transit between HMS *Hermes* and HMS *Intrepid*. All but two of the twenty-two victims were members of D and G Squadrons. The overloaded Sea King plunged into the sea after an albatross or giant petrel flew into its engine air vent. The bodies of the dead were never recovered. Among them were members of D Squadron's Mountain Troop who just days before had destroyed eleven Argentine aircraft at Pebble Island in the most daring operation of the war.

As they loaded the Pinkies in the Bagram hangar hardly anyone spoke. It was a time to shut out the outside world. Jason could only imagine war's brutality; he had not witnessed the horrors of flesh torn from bones, although anyone who had seen him spear a hessian sack with his bayonet during basic Para training at Aldershot knew he had the aptitude for it. But how would he react emotionally if and when his comrades fell in agony beside him? Could he cut it when the bullets were whizzing past his ears?

Jock knew Operation TRENT would be the acid test for the virgins. If they were found wanting he did not want to have to take a bullet for them. He also wondered whether his own luck might run out, as he had successfully dodged enemy fire before. There was also the chance that someone untried in combat, such as Jason, would freeze at the crucial moment. A split second lost in hesitation could be the difference between life and death – cool, instant reactions would be required to shoot back at the enemy and rob him of any opportunity to win the fire fight. If there was a tragedy, be it on the Herc, during the overland journey or during the contact, he and his 'oppos' would just have to get on with it: the show would go on no matter how many good men might fall. For Jason, as he contemplated his first time in combat, there was something hugely comforting about being part of such an elite force. The worry was that he might screw up – not that he would ever admit to such a fear. Like everyone else involved on Operation TRENT he would have to be 100 per cent reliable. There was no room for passengers, or those whose fears would overcome them.

The Regiment's view was that such an attitude towards death set it apart from Delta Force, who in the aftermath of some of its unsuccessful operations had bleated on about dreams being lost on the battlefield and the nightmares that followed. Body bags would give Operation TRENT credibility in Hereford, where fatalities, though regrettable, are viewed as the price the Regiment pays for its success.

H – 28.00 hrs

The moment for which Jason had joined the SAS was within touching distance. Jock, although he had been in this position before, was equally excited, if less obviously so. Having a cup of tea and a cigarette for breakfast, he sat hunched against the driver's side of the Pinkie, his weapon leaning against the wheel arch. He took a long drag, as he watched Jason walk towards him carrying a massive sack.

'What the fuck's that, Jase?'

'Rice,' Jason replied.

'Rice? We've got tonnes of that already, laddie.'

'Yeah, I know, but the boss says it's for the locals once we get down south. The wagon is going to fuckin' creak under all this shite.'

'Aye, too right, son. If you ask me, some twat in Group [term for UKSF, which replaced Special Forces Group] has got his priorities wrong.'

'Yeah,' said Jason, adding, 'I joined the Regiment, not the Red Cross. I'm not 'ere to feed refugees.'

'Ah well, it's the hearts and minds stuff, laddie, we all have to do it. I know where we'll stuff 'em, behind the front seats, they'll do as a frag catcher. I'm counting on your bergen as a bullet stop too. You may be thankful for it if we go over a mine, there's fuckin' millions of the bastards round here.'

'Fuck 'em, Jock. If the Pinkie's overloaded and we're in the shite, the first thing I'd sling is the rice. The friendlies will have to starve; I'd rather carry an extra half-shaft and more PE4 [Plastic Explosive].'

Jason's outburst concealed his real fear, not of Al Qaeda, but of doing anything to knock the operation off course, even something like overloading the Pinkie, which already had eighteen jerry cans of fuel and six of water on board and enough rations to feed three men for ten days. If he performed well he would earn the respect of Jock and the other seasoned NCOs who ruled the roost in A Squadron. If he showed fear, or was tentative, his life in the Regiment would become considerably more difficult. The bitching at his expense would start as soon as the sound of gunfire subsided.

The sense of urgency was greater at G Squadron's end of the hangar as its troops would be leaving from around 18.00 hrs, five hours before A. The planes would perform a rolling drop-off of G's men and kit at the TLZ before turning around to collect A Squadron. The CO wanted everyone at the TLZ as soon as possible after 01.00 hrs and crucially for the squadrons to arrive in what would be their order at the FUP – which was why G Squadron was leaving first. Its Pinkies would become the FSB and were weighed down with GPMGs, .50s and Milans.

Gordon and Phil's Pinkie had twin GPMGs and would be near the front of the order of march. Gordon gazed across the cavernous hangar and the hundreds of tonnes of kit that would have to be crammed on to the planes and driven across 150 kilometres of desert. He was confident that the convoy was sufficiently armed to see off any terrorist ambush.

He turned to Phil, the younger soldier looking for acceptance in a squadron less gung-ho than the ex-Para-dominated

A. As a body, G's troopers were quieter but just as professional. They had not spoken since the spat over Gordon's fear of flying.

'This is gonna be some infil, man. Hope the scrap is worth this hassle, eh, Rip?'

'Fingers crossed.'

'Air Troop better not have fucked up. I don't fancy our chances landing in a sand dune with all this weight on board.'

'Yes, Gordon,' said Phil, humouring him again.

'You flown with the Yanks before?'

'Yeah, laid back, aren't they? Unlike the Crabs [RAF].'

Gordon smiled. 'For sure, and I'm glad we are on the ground first because that TLZ is going to be pretty ripped up when the Hercs drop A off. If there's any rag-heads around we'll take them apart with the twin GPMGs. Thank fuck there's no more of that non-engagement crap like we had on Operation DETERMINE.'

In addition to the Pinkies, both squadrons' motorcycles, eight in total, would be packed on to the early flights and used to patrol the TLZ and recce the ground ahead *en route* to the target. The CO would be among the first to leave Bagram as he wanted to lead from the front. By contrast, the RSM, the designated 'Tail End Charlie', would be among the last to go.

As the SAS would not be able to take the enemy by surprise – impossible given the bright sunshine at 11 a.m. and the huge dust cloud signalling the Regiment's arrival – speed of movement was even more crucial. A rolling drop-off would save time at the TLZ. The SAS men, sitting on the motorcycles and wagons would drive down the aircraft ramps as they taxied along at 10 mph over the bumpy air strip. As the vehicles drove off to the side, the Hercs would turn around and take off in the opposite direction, with a following wind. Such organization would increase speed and time.

The Hercules, the workhorse transport aircraft in both the USAF and the RAF, was chosen for Operation TRENT for its ability to operate from rough dirt strips and carry up to 44,552 kilograms of kit or up to ninety-two combat troops. The four turbo-prop engines could reach 384 mph and had a maximum range of 2,536 miles when carrying a full cargo. The planes would not need to refuel during the four-leg trip. Having got up at the crack of dawn to get everything sorted, A and G Squadrons had the day to get through, waiting for darkness to fall once more and the infil to begin.

H – 19.00 hrs

The six-strong US C-130 fleet was set a tactical distance apart on Bagram's runway – far enough apart to ensure that if a mortar, RPG or Stinger missile struck one, the engine fire would not spread to another. The Pinkies would be 'locked down' inside the aircraft with metal chains secured around the front and rear axles. It would take around thirty minutes to load up each plane. Once loaded, they would leave at five-minute intervals.

The Hercs would take either three Pinkies or two and an Acmat lorry on each journey. It would be a tight fit on board for each vehicle's three-man crew; roughly 2 feet of spare room either side. The men would have to clamber over vehicles to get anywhere – at least the Hercules' high ceilings prevented claustrophobia. There were no significant differences between RAF and US Air Force Hercules aircraft.

Although the kit was distributed evenly, the Pinkies were dangerously overweight, scaling 3.5 tonnes each, a

tonne above the advised maximum weight. As the terrain
would be hard going, this added to the troops' concerns.
Everyone kept their belt order – chest and waist webbing
storing personal ammunition and grenades – on their person. Each man had around 80 pounds of personal kit,
substantially less than if he was on a foot patrol; on this
occasion water supplies were kept to a minimum. Most
Pinkies carried a spare half-shaft, which connected the front
wheels to the engine, and at least one spare tyre. These were
the most likely parts to give way in Registan and Helmand
– otherwise all other spares were carried on the 'mother
ships'. Because Gordon was worried about Phil's driving, as
IC Wagon he made sure he took an extra half-shaft.

H – 18.00 hrs

The CO's last act at Bagram was a final pep-talk, telling the
guys to have a good flight and that he would 'see them on
the ground'; this was what they called a 'back-slapping
tour', with the CO talking to them in small groups, briefly
and informally. The Colonel would leave on the second
Herc.

Troop by troop, G Squadron's Pinkies made their way
slowly towards the US transport aircraft. Phil was behind
the wheel of his, with Gordon on board, both men dressed
in desert DPMs, Arab scarves around their necks and moto-
cross goggles in their smock pockets. They would be put on
minutes before leaving the Herc to stop them swallowing
mouthfuls of dust as they span off the makeshift runway.

While the US aircrews were a bit more easy-going than
the RAF, they would be just as pissed off as the 'Crabs'
if a moment's indiscipline or carelessness damaged their
precious aircraft and rendered it unserviceable. Until the

On 'the day of infamy', a fire fighter looks on helplessly
as one of the towers collapses and Manhattan is draped in a
blanket of dust. In total 343 of this man's FDNY colleagues died
on September 11th, 225 of them when the South Tower fell.
In addition, 37 Port Authority officers and 23 NYPD
were killed.

A two-man team test fire the Milan anti-tank / anti-armour missile system.

The weapon system, part of the FSB on Op TRENT, fires 1.3kg warheads accurately over a range of up to 2km. Milan has been in service since the 1970s.

The C-130, made by US aircraft manufacturer Lockheed, is the United States Air Force and the RAF's transport workhorse, and is used to deploy HALO and static-line parachutists, or transport men and equipment. The Regiment squeezed three Pinkies into each 'Herc' for the journey from HQ Bagram to the TLZ.

On this formation HALO descent, the soldiers carry Armalite rifles. Note the bergen strapped on top of the legs of the parachutist left, and the AOD attached to the main chute on his back. The parachutist centre checks his wrist-mounted altimeter. The team disperse before deploying chutes.

The battle took place in the shadow of Spot Height 2213.
The TLZ was approximately where 'Registan' appears, south of
Kandahar. Al Qaeda could have called on reinforcements from the
nearby town of Malah do Kand, less than an hour's drive away. No
allied troops had ventured this far south on the ground. Note the
proximity to Afghanistan's southern border with Pakistan.

There has been much speculation that Osama bin Laden has been, or is still, hiding in this corridor. The 1:1,150,000 scale Escape and Evasion maps rendered the landscape effectively featureless when it came to planning an emergency ex-fil from the target area, as it is depicted merely as blank space. The Dasht-i-Margo, or 'Desert of Death', lies immediately to the north.

At least 12 Al Qaeda guerrillas were 'slotted' using the Barrett semi-automatic .50 calibre long-range sniper rifle. Against such a deadly weapon any fleeing 'rag heads' became 'guaranteed kills'. Fired here by a Royal Marine in Afghanistan in 2002, it is an SAS favourite and has been in service for a decade. The 12kg Barrett has armour-piercing capability up to a range of 2km. Note the muzzle brake fitted to the end of the barrel to reduce the kickback effect after firing.

This Pinkie carries a fraction of the equipment that the vehicles hauled across Afghanistan on Ops DETERMINE and TRENT. Scaling approximately 3.5 tonnes each (a tonne over the advised weight ceiling), they experienced terrible problems in the soft sand despite their power steering, supple coil-sprung suspension and low-pressure tyres. The drop-down tailgate is used to good effect here. Front- and rear-mounted GPMGs provide the best form of defence and attack, immediate and rapid fire for a 'shoot and scoot'. In its various forms, the Pinkie has been the Regiment's vehicle of choice for over half a century.

The Boy Stirling is mad. Quite, quite mad. However in war there is often a place for mad people. – Field Marshal Bernard Montgomery of Lieutenant Colonel Sir David Stirling, founder of 'L' Detachment, SAS Brigade, in July 1941. Under his leadership the SAS destroyed 250 aircraft and hundreds of enemy vehicles in North Africa. The 'warrior spirit' of the 6ft 5in Cambridge-educated Scots Guardsman lives on. Revered by all those privileged to have worn the sandy beret, Stirling was imprisoned by the Nazis at Colditz. He was knighted in 1990 and died later that year aged seventy-four.

CONSPICUOUS GALLANTRY CROSS

Two CGCs were awarded for extreme bravery on Op TRENT. The medal is second only to the VC in the order of gallantry awards. Instituted in October 1993 and first awarded in 1995 to Corporal Wayne Mills of the Duke of Wellington's Regiment in Bosnia, it replaced the Conspicuous Gallantry Medal (CGM) and Distinguished Conduct Medal (DCM). No consideration is given to rank when awarding the CGC, which is open to 'officers and men' alike.

MILITARY CROSS

For leading their troops into Al Qaeda fire, two of the participants in Op TRENT were awarded the Military Cross. The MC was first instituted in 1914 as a bravery award for junior officers. 'Ranks' would receive the Military Medal. The Royal warrant has since been amended to remove the rank distinction for bravery awards.

DISTINGUISHED SERVICE ORDER

The DSO was won by one of Op TRENT's officers for his leadership under fire. The DSO is awarded in recognition of command in the face of the enemy rather than for a single act of bravery. A high percentage of SAS COs have been awarded the DSO.

Loadie gave him the appropriate hand signal, Phil was not going to approach within 30 metres of the plane.

Phil was in a file of more than a dozen Pinkies crossing the bumpy Bagram tarmac shortly after sundown. It was a balmy, humid and still evening; best not to think of this as being the start of the biggest operation in 22 SAS's history. If Phil pranged his Pinkie and put it, and worse still one of the Hercs as well, out of action, Operation TRENT's precise timescale would be thrown into disarray. Their wings and propellers were worryingly easy to hit in the descending darkness and it was essential that every plane left on time.

After waiting what seemed like an eternity for the Pinkie in front to be swallowed up, the Loadie beckoned Phil towards him and Gordon slapped him on the back: 'Don't crash, Rip,' he said as he jumped off, allowing Phil a clear view over 360 degrees as he performed the tricky task of reversing over 3 tonnes of machinery and kit inch by inch up the ramp. He balanced the Pinkie on the clutch as the US aircrew ushered him inside. There was only a matter of inches to spare on either side. He drove back at dead slow speed, clearing the left side of the aircraft interior by a whisker.

'Fuckin' hell, it's going to be hot in here,' he thought, a rush of heat smacking him in the face and the sickly smell of aviation fuel turning his stomach. Having piled on the revs to get up the ramp, he felt queasy after a whiff of the toxic fumes. The air would get even thicker after take-off.

Feeling claustrophobic, he de-bused, leaving the keys in the ignition. He dared not put them in a 'safe place', as not being able to remember where that safe place was was not even worth thinking about. At best he would be facing a huge cash donation to the end-of-operation piss-up; at worst an official charge. The vehicle was left in first gear and secured to the aircraft floor.

Gordon joined him. Soon it would be too loud for conversation – much to Phil's relief. He would be spending enough time in confined spaces with Gordon in the days ahead. The Herc engines started with a roar as they watched the aircrew tug on the safety strops which connected their Pinkie to the floor; again, they did not want their vehicle to be the one that caused a pile-up because it was not properly secured – guaranteeing a hefty donation to the Squadron beer fund. The ramp went up and the blackness closed in. 'Bye bye, Bagram,' thought Phil.

The next two hours would be spent in the giant bumble-bee of an aircraft as it flew in a convoy over central Afghanistan. Phil reckoned the most dangerous part of the journey was as the plane taxied along the runway and gradually climbed into the sky. The SAS men had seen how hostile Bagram's surrounding area was. If the Taliban and Al Qaeda were lingering, armed with a Stinger, they were in deep trouble.

The danger of the infil and of having so many members of the Regiment in a hazardous environment concerned some senior officers in UKSF. The blokes' view was that this so-called fear was born of envy. As Phil thought, 'They just wished they were on the ground doing it themselves, not stuck behind a desk in London. Fuck 'em, they've had their turn, this is ours.'

To a man, the guys respected the CO's decision to go for it, having weighed up the risk factor against the benefits of the operation and what the Regiment would achieve – the damage to Al Qaeda, and getting so many men blooded. The CO knew that failure would have dire consequences but the fear of it weighed lightly on his broad shoulders. He was a gentle, charming man but also one who readily accepted challenges and risks.

*

H – 17.00 hrs

Engine power increasing, the Herc lurched forward, making grumbling Gordon feel sick. His fear of flying came flooding back. 'Christ, man, is this plane going fast enough to take off?' he thought. 'It feels like we're only doing 30 mph.' In fact the speed was rising towards 180 mph, it just did not feel like it to those inside. Much to Gordon's relief, the plane finally levelled out and the guys clambered over the Pinkies to get a cup of water, some of them sneaking a cigarette, which was banned on board. They had to be wary; a moment of turbulence could send them falling off a wagon and returning to Bagram as a medevac case.

H – 15.30 hrs

The day had passed with painful slowness at the TLZ. Everyone took their turn to stag-on in the OP and get some shut-eye. The HALO guys were at the hub of the mission and their most important task was yet to come – guiding in the C-130s, by shining infra-red lights into the night sky. These signals would be picked up on the pilots' Forward-Looking Infra-Red shields. Each HALO team member was aware of his individual task responsibilities and all the relevant 'Actions On'.

Two men were on the centre points of the TLZ, left and right of the C-130 on landing and half-way along the airstrip. These were the scariest positions – any mistake by the pilot with the angle of approach and the men would be killed instantly. The Herc's propellers would be around 15 feet from their heads.

The order of march to the TLZ had been determined by the distance each of them had to trek to their designated point on the landing grid; the man with the longest walk

went first. The lead man had checked the ground ahead for
obstacles and any signs of enemy. If bumped by Al Qaeda
in these last few minutes before the aircraft arrived they
would try to fight their way out of the contact and head for
the ERV, following the same procedure in response to
ambush as was in place when they had landed twenty-four
hours earlier. The C-130s would abort the landing. The last
task before getting on to the TLZ had been to send a signal
back to HQ Bagram: 'IN PLACE'.

P Minus 5: They switched on the infra-red torches. This
coincided with the front chains being taken off the Pinkies
inside the nearest C-130. The men were ready to start their
engines and stared ahead at the plane's ramp, waiting for it
to inch downwards.

P Minus 2: The HALO team could now see the Herc,
which seemed to cover the whole sky, as if about to land on
them.

Onboard the Loadie screamed in the ears of the front
Pinkie's crew: 'Start your engine.' There was a cacophony
of noise, the aircraft engines and the vehicles competing to
pierce the eardrums. As the ramp dropped, a welcome blast
of cold air was sucked inside. There below them was enemy
territory; Registan, everyone's favourite holiday destination.

In the chilly stillness of the desert night the six HALO
soldiers stood exposed on the grid, crouching into the
smallest positions their bodies could adopt. With the Herc's
lights off, they had heard the plane long before they saw
it. What began as a gentle humming sound rose to ear-
shattering crescendo as the C-130 sped past, but they
resisted every instinct to inch back from its path. They
tensed their bodies and closed their eyes, trusting in the
skill of the US pilots and crew.

The lead Hercs had held off in-flight, ensuring they
would land in formation at the TLZ, a couple of minutes
apart. With the aircraft ramp descending, Phil and the other

drivers were ready, engines running for their Grand Prix start. Gordon gestured a 'thumbs up' and Phil nodded sharply back. The noise from the Pinkies and the Herc engines 'turning and burning' was incredible. Both men put on their goggles.

H – 15.00 hrs

The plane banked left and right in the last seconds of flight. The Pinkie's engine gave a reassuring roar as Phil stepped on the gas. 'For fuck's sake don't stall on me now,' he thought.

The Herc landed with a thump, flashing past the HALO team stationed on points Alpha, Bravo, Charlie and Delta. Phil stared intently at the US Loadie man: 'Come on, man, raise your thumb, will you!' he shouted – not that the man could hear him. Then the signal came, and with the plane doing 10 mph, Phil, Gordon and the other crew member shot down the ramp, dropped a foot on to the barren earth and skidded right to clear the air strip. The Pinkie was even harder to control than usual as it was being driven against the aircraft's momentum. Behind them the plane carried on; any second now it would turn and prepare for take-off back to Bagram.

It took about ten seconds to empty each of the Hercs and within thirty minutes of the first plane landing, all of G Squadron's firepower was on the ground. The men and vehicles went into all-around defensive mode, silent and with their vehicles pointing out from the TLZ to repel any attack. Gordon's senses were acute as he took in the Registan desert by night. The dense and muggy night air, thick with sand, buffeted him as he bounced along in the front of the Pinkie. Illuminated under the ambient light, the landscape was white. The rush of the dramatic landing was replaced by a sense of foreboding stillness. As someone who hated flying, however, he was hugely relieved to be on the ground and off the Herc.

H – 14.00 hrs

The SAS corporal looked down the barrel of his weapon, surveying the snow-like scene for the slightest artificial noise or movement. The formidable force of which he was part stood motionless and silent. After the Hercules departed it was now so quiet that the men could hear one another breathe. Phil felt beads of sweat drizzle down his lower back, as much from the tension as the heat – he had not been on the ground long enough for the chill of the desert night to kick in. They communicated in low voices and with hand signals. The SAS did not want to give away any further indication of their dramatic infil.

The CO was conscious that while the Taliban and Al Qaeda did not have any sophisticated comms, the neighbouring Russians, Pakistanis and Iranians did. All comms were made on secure frequencies. After the listening watch, recce parties were sent out from the TLZ to ensure the surrounding area was clear of enemy. The Pinkies were formed into a giant circular fortress, stretching as far as a kilometre from the runway, ground permitting.

H – 10.00 hrs

Finally the second set of six Hercs landed with a bump at the TLZ but nobody was injured. Time would tell whether burning off the back of the aircraft ramps had had any adverse affect on the wagons. The men were all too aware that the vehicles were severely over their weight limits and not as powerful as they once were.

By 01.30 hrs the full complement of A Squadron had joined G. Both squadrons were ready to start the 150-kilometre drive to their common target. The area had been saturated with movement for more than twenty-four hours and they were eager to press on. The longer they stayed, the more vulnerable they were to attack. The next eight hours would be spent bouncing up and down on the Pinkies across Registan, Kandahar province, and into southern Helmand. Their maximum speed over such arduous ground was 25 mph. The SAS's plan was to reach an LUP, lie up and move on again before first light. The HALO team in particular would welcome a cat-nap.

H – 9.00 hrs

A and G Squadrons' last instructions at the TLZ were 'Go to Hotel' the 'H' point on the landing grid being where the CO was waiting and where the wagons would be checked off. The roll was called: all present and correct. The forty-vehicle convoy led by a Pinkie armed with twin GPMGs set off. The more vulnerable Acmats were kept in the middle of the convoy, which stretched over 2 kilometres, a rumbling swarm of firepower behind a huge cloud of sand. The vehicles were between 50 and 200 metres apart. All the Pinkie crews carried out their own manual navigation by compass, leaving the TLZ on a bearing of due south. The plan for G Squadron to head off first was scrapped as most of A's vehicles were already at the 'H' point. The order would change later in the journey.

After twenty minutes the squadrons stopped for a listening watch. This also allowed the crews to carry out a 'Dead

Reckoning fix' – an assessment of the ETA at the LUP, based on the distance covered so far. The GPS systems on each wagon were only for backup; the soldiers preferred to use their compasses and maps as this was what they were accustomed to. The column headed south-west.

A Squadron's boys were chuffed to be the assault force, leading from the front. G Squadron would be static during the fire fight, standing off the enemy. The guys in both squadrons knew the mission's importance and the risks involved. None of them had been on anything larger than a single-squadron operation, even on exercise.

Gordon was a bossy IC Wagon, watching Phil's driving intently from the front passenger seat: 'Mind that rock, Rip,' 'Bump ahead,' 'No nodding off, Phil, eyes open.' By now Phil was convinced Gordon got a kick out of antagonizing him.

'Leave it out, Gordon, for fuck's sake,' he said, pulling his scarf down from over his mouth where it was stopping him swallowing sand as he drove through the clouds kicked up by the wagon in front. Driving conditions were hellish. At just 20 mph Phil could barely see the path ahead and took every opportunity to wipe his goggles clean. He added: 'We haven't had a crash or a near-miss. Just keep your eye on your compass will you?'

'All right, Rip, lighten up,' replied Gordon.

The LUP was map-predicted at HQ Bagram and its position included in each OC's set of orders. If the convoy was attacked *en route* and had to retreat – albeit unlikely, given its awesome firepower – it would split up before re-forming at a pre-designated ERV. Unlike the LUP, the ERV sites were selected on the ground and recced by motorbike riders.

They were confident, whatever the hype about Al

Qaeda, the *Mujahideen*'s supposed defeat of the Red Army
and the ferocity of the Taliban. There was a huge difference
between being an elite SAS soldier and a rag-head living in
the hills with a gun. The guys had little respect for Al Qaeda
beyond that afforded to them as fellow combatants willing
to put their lives on the line for their cause.

The CO was at the centre of the file and the RSM at the
back. Like worker ants protecting their queen, eight motorcycles floated around the column, two out front, two at the
rear and two on either flank. The men at the front were
particularly vulnerable; the bikes' infra-red lights barely
illuminated their path. If Al Qaeda were waiting behind
rocks on route they would have had little chance of survival
or of returning fire while riding. There was no end of
potential ambush sites. The Pinkie drivers relied on their
oppos in the front passenger seats looking ahead with their
NVGs.

H – 6.45 hrs

The drive to the LUP passed without incident. Half an hour
before the two squadrons arrived the motorcycles went
forward to recce the area. This had to be roughly the size of
ten football pitches, big enough for about forty vehicles to
stand a tactical distance apart in circular formation. Though
it was impossible to hide so many vehicles on a desert plain,
even at night, any cover by way of folds in the ground or
rocks would be utilized.

A Squadron arrived first, fading right from the LUP
entry point, manned by a motorcycle outrider. G faded left;
when both squadrons' vehicles had come to a standstill they
were shaped like a bull's horns, protecting the Acmats and
the CO's party in the middle. The LUP stop was a welcome
break after two hours of sand kicking into their faces,

getting in to their mouths, noses and ears. They were also constantly wiping their goggles on their smock sleeves. After weeks of waiting, combat was less than seven hours away. The vehicles were covered in camouflage nets and the men talked to each other only in whispers.

A simple mistake, an Al Qaeda bullet, and it would all be over. No more SAS, no more family or life. Looking around them at the GPMGs, .50s and Milans buoyed their confidence. Given the ridiculous H-hour, how many lives would be lost in winning the battle? Killing at least sixty Al Qaeda without sustaining a single loss was a big task.

The danger at this stage of the infil was a suicide attack. All the Pinkie crews were vulnerable to ambush, especially as the guerrillas were unafraid of death. They took greater risks and were prepared to make bigger sacrifices than conventional opponents, as 9/11 had shown.

Were a Pinkie crew to be taken out by a mine or an ambush, the squadrons would continue the mission. No time would be wasted; the SAS would take any dead bodies with them and head to the target. The main concern would be whether or not any deaths reduced fighting capability. With that in mind, the LUP was no picnic.

On the CO's orders a signal was sent back to London reporting the convoy's progress. The men kept up the incessant routine of personal weapon-cleaning and kit checks. Driving through the sandstorm, gravel and sand penetrated everywhere. Taking a swig from a water bottle they swallowed bits of sand, and it penetrated their rations. 'I could murder a brew,' said Gordon quietly. He knew he would not be having a cup of tea for a while, though. Hard routine rules applied.

One hundred kilometres of desert, rock and clay lay between them and the opium plant. The terrain would become more arduous and undulating further south, near the Pakistan border.

They had less than one hour of darkness left. First light increased the danger of being spotted. After the motorcycle recce teams had surveyed the first few kilometres, the wagons rolled out through the LUP exit point, where each vehicle was counted and the men asked whether there were any problems. 'None so far, boss, only Gordon,' was Phil's reply.

H – 5.30 hrs

As ambient light gave way to the sun inching above the craggy outcrops, the risk of driving through the desert in daylight became obvious and the whispered effing and blinding increased. Everyone on Operation TRENT knew that 11.00 hrs was a crazy time to attack any target, let alone a well-fortified one manned by hardcore Al Qaeda. In the early morning sunlight the convoy would be seen from 10 kilometres away. They could be forgiven for turning the air blue, albeit quietly.

In military terms this was a high-threat enemy target, as described in the OCs' orders. Operation TRENT was intended to gather intelligence and break Al Qaeda's morale; even so, what was the harm in sticking to a few basic infantry attack principles, such as using the cover of darkness? These were the questions the troops asked themselves. It seemed perverse that while US generals overestimated the threat to their troops and hence deployed so few of them, the SAS was to attack a heavily guarded Al Qaeda target in the middle of the day.

The sunshine helped Jock feel less groggy. He was switched on and calm. Scanning the horizon, he smiled and gave Jason a kick, saying, 'Hey, laddie, take in this beautiful scenery, why don't you, now it's light. It's a fuckin' lovely place, eh, Afghanistan? Bring ya kids when you've got

some. All this lovely sand. They'll love it.' Jason and the
driver burst out laughing. Humour helped everyone handle
the stress.

Some of the slower vehicles were beginning to feel the
pace and the Pinkies groaned as they climbed towards
higher ground. In the distance lay Afghanistan's fortifica-
tions: the mountain range on the Pakistan border which for
centuries had scared off armies that lay in its shadow.

H – 4.00 hrs

By now the soldiers' thoughts were, as they put it, 'very
closed in' – entirely focused on the remainder of the drive
and the attack. The terrain became more hilly, the climbs
steeper, the descents more precarious. Handling the Pinkies
was a battle in itself: the steering wheel had to be squeezed
while the engines snarled their disapproval at the sheer
weight they were forced to carry over such tough ground.
Every jolt and bump sent driver and passengers off their
seats and crashing down on the Pinkies' metal frames, while
the wheels squealed like piglets, skidding off rocks.

The men gripped their weapons more tightly and looked
back at where their bergens were stored, visualizing them
flying off the back of the wagon.

H – 2.00 hrs

Suddenly the SAS's good fortune came to a halt. Roughly 8
kilometres from the target, a Pinkie broke down; one of the
twelve armed with GPMGs. As it was clear that Operation
TRENT required all the CO's assets, losing just one was a
blow. The convoy came to a halt as in desperation the three-
man crew tried to restart it. Anger set in as a plume of light

grey smoke rose from its V8 engine. It was the fault of neither crew nor vehicle that its best years were behind it, as with so many wagons both squadrons were using.

The clock was ticking down. The convoy had made good time over the 140 kilometres, but the SAS could not afford to wait while repairs were attempted. Absurd as it sounded, the Regiment was less than two hours away from attacking a target it had never seen before in broad daylight in territory that had not been recced, and Al Qaeda would see it coming from miles away.

The head sheds went into a huddle. They did not want to lose a Pinkie but there was not enough time to fix it and no guarantee it could be.

A hard decision had to be made and the result of the mini-conference was the one the crew dreaded – they were to be left in the sand while the convoy carried on as planned. The men looked at one another in silence. They would be close enough to the opium plant to be collected once the fighting was over. Meanwhile, they would just have to sit there hoping that no Al Qaeda ran in their direction. If they got 'bumped' they had the Pinkie's twin GPMGs and their personal weapons. Had the broken-down Pinkie been carrying a rocket launcher, hardly ideal for immediate return of fire, the situation would have been more dangerous.

This was absolutely no consolation to the crew, having travelled half-way across the world to arguably its least attractive country and kicked their heels for a month waiting for what might be the only fire fight of their lives. The SAS being the SAS, their colleagues showed no mercy. As the other crews remounted, crude hand gestures were exchanged. The convoy disappeared over the sandy hills, leaving three very angry men staring forlornly at its trail of dust.

*

H − 1.00 hrs

Time spent tending the stricken Pinkie had taken its toll and was no longer on the Regiment's side. The terrain would only get worse. As the entered the foothills there were no tracks and the sand got deeper and deeper, clinging ever more tightly to the wheels of each vehicle. Again, the weight the wagons carried did them no favours. Cursing their slow progress, the men felt like dumping the rice sacks.

The opium plant was still out of sight, and the Regiment had no HUMINT to confirm the best approach route. The Pinkies inched forward, the CO knowing he could not allow the situation to deteriorate further. He was 3 kilometres away from what would be the FUP, with an hour to go.

Al Qaeda troops could be hiding in the rocks ahead, biding their time before an ambush. Nobody knew. Could the convoy thread its way through a labyrinth of craggy outcrops, sand dunes and ravines and emerge unscathed? It was impossible to tell what dangers lay ahead. Seldom had the often-used SAS phrase 'time spent on a recce is never wasted' seemed so apt. This hugely frustrating situation brought home just how costly it was that a CTR had not been conducted. At this juncture, − 'int' wise, the SAS was clueless and so close to the enemy position.

H − 0.45 hrs

It was the CO's responsibility to rectify the situation. The convoy came to a halt again. Using a TACBE, he contacted the US pilots poised to strike the opium plant, instructing one to fly directly over the SAS column and head off in the target's direction. The SAS would follow that line and the pilot would tell the CO if there were any Al Qaeda patrols between the convoy and the target, there were some steep climbs in between.

The downside to this quick-fix solution, as off the cuff an example of TAR (Tactical Air Reconnaissance) as anyone could wish to see, was that Al Qaeda would hear the aircraft and be alerted to the Allied presence on their turf.

With the enemy at such close quarters, the men were revved up. Battle loomed and they wondered why they had stopped again. 'What the fuck is this for?' said Jason, adding, 'Let's fuckin' get on with it.' The CO was in the middle of the SAS file, A Squadron to the rear, G Squadron in front. Jock got the wagon's 'bins' out to see if he could spot the CO's Pinkie, thinking it might give him a clue as to what was up. No such luck, the clouds of sand were so thick he could only see a few wagons ahead and the boss was not in one of those.

Hearing a rumbling behind them, Jock and Jason turned instinctively. 'Fuck, cover your ears,' said Jock as the noise grew to a thunderous roar. 'Fuckin' hell,' screamed Jason, though the F/A-18 was so loud and flying so low he could not even hear himself. The aircraft screamed over the top of the convoy, seemingly just a few metres above the wagons. The pilot's message was 'Follow my slipstream' as he veered off over the top of the lead SAS vehicle.

'What the fuck was that all about?' screamed Jason.

'I think he's showing us the way,' shouted Jock, as he laughed, 'and giving Al Qaeda an alarm call, just to let them know we're here. Wakey-wakey, rag-heads!'

The CO was now satisfied it was safe to advance north. The Pinkies lumbered up and down the sand dunes; tempers were fraught as crew members were sent hurtling into the air, the ground was the worst it had been. Gordon was livid with Phil and the feeling was mutual. 'For fuck's sake, Phil, close in on that wagon in front.' His contradictory instructions angered the trooper. 'And if you don't go slower on the down slopes I'm gonna deck you. You'll snap the fuckin' half-shaft the way you're driving.'

All the drivers were getting the same grief from their IC Wagons: 'Go left,' 'Go Right,' 'Close up,' 'Fucking hell, your driving's shite.' As the vehicle came crashing down one slope, Phil thought: 'Thank fuck for the upgraded suspension.'

H – 0.30 hrs

The CO saw how tight the schedule was getting – there was no margin for further misfortune or error. Having reached the pre-determined FUP, he ordered the convoy to halt. The squadrons had to get the angle of attack right. The thick sand had slowed them down for the past two hours. If they got stuck in sight of the enemy they would be sitting targets for Al Qaeda snipers – and dead meat. The CO told his OCs he was going forward in his Pinkie with his signaller to assess the ground ahead. It would be an emergency CTR.

As his vehicle reached the crest of the hill, the opium plant lay before him. It consisted of five buildings, one of which was the headquarters. The plant sat at the foot of the isolated spot height which looked awesome and foreboding. This was the target he and his men had travelled 850 kilometres by air and land to hit – and at huge risk. It was also the war's furthest Allied exploration into enemy territory.

It was a warm, sunny, peaceful day, more conducive to a squadron barbecue than a battle. The plan the CO had originally devised was for G Squadron to advance ahead of A from the FUP – the point where he had broken off from the convoy – to positions on the eastern side of the target, or at two o'clock as he faced north towards the plant. A Squadron would sweep behind the FSB and go further east, leaving the western flank clear for the US jets to launch missiles and strafing fire. Looking ahead, the CO's prognosis was that the terrain made these plans unworkable – he saw too much soft sand on the approach to the eastern flank and the proposed FSB site.

It was time for him to ditch the original plan and come up with a new one very quickly – exactly as he was trained to do when he completed SAS Officer Selection some fifteen years earlier.*

From their position near the front of the convoy Gordon and Phil had seen one wagon speed off ahead. 'The boss was in there, wasn't he?' said Phil.

'Aye, yer right, Phil,' replied Gordon, 'he must be checking the ground. The fuckin' enemy are only the other side of that hill!'

'We've got to get this fuckin' approach right. I'm fuckin' sick of getting stuck in this shite,' said Phil angrily.

'Aye, man, we'll be sitting fuckin' ducks if it's like this when we're closer,' added Gordon.

At this last minute, the enemy poised to defend its fortress with their lives, the answer was for the SAS to switch flanks. His mind made up, the CO hurried back to the convoy, eager to hold a brief 'O' (Orders) Group with the OCs and get the new plans passed on to the men. The attack would now be launched from the west; the US pilots would be informed. Phil revved up again, like all the drivers he was ready to whizz forward, hoping to get through the last stretch of sand as quickly as possible. Gordon shouted,

---

* SAS Officer Selection Week, which candidates must pass in addition to the tests non-officers face, is designed to weed out those who cannot think up imaginative and practical plans under times of immense stress from those who can. SAS officers must be capable of original thought, as one SAS CO told his potential officers assembled before him: 'What I am interested in is what you've got between your ears – I've got Sergeant Majors for the rest.'

'Go, fuckin' go, Phil,' as they were gestured forward with
frantic waving of arms ahead of them. Phil stuck the gears
into first, then up into second as the wheels span furiously
and kicked up a dust cloud. At last the men could make out
the target and, through pairs of binoculars, tiny dark figures
racing around – the enemy.

11. A AND G LET RIP

H – 0.15 hrs

Gordon's hands clenched around the GPMG's handle and the Pinkie's metal frame as the wagon made a sharp left, skidding through sandy earth which kicked up into his face. 'I'm getting showered in shit here,' he thought, struggling to keep his balance. The convoy headed north-west, the opium plant on its right-hand side. Phil demanded more of the Land Rover's torqued-up engine, working clutch, gear and brakes as finally it snarled and spat its way through the last of the soft sand which had plagued the SAS for so long. Each crew's relief was palpable as the ground became harder and rockier, the Pinkies' tyres leaving a trace of burning rubber. 'Could have sworn we were gonna use the eastern flank,' thought Gordon.

A shrill whistle sounded, familiar and unnerving, as Al Qaeda opened fire with RPGs, their favourite support weapon, capable of piercing 30 centimetres of conventional armour and deadly effective up to 500 metres – it seemed they had indeed been warned of the SAS's approach by the low-flying F/A-18.

'They'll never fuckin' hit us from there, man,' said Gordon dismissively, his grizzled, unshaven chin jutting forwards. But the rag-heads were not firing the usually shoulder-held weapons conventionally, on a flat trajectory.

The guerrillas found extra length launching the missiles skywards, as if they were mortar rockets. 'Keep an eye on those fuckers fallin',' Gordon added, watching the grenades fly way beyond where he had expected them to land. 'Fuck you,' Phil snapped back, as the Pinkie jumped over its thousandth pothole, 'you wanna drive?'

The extension of the RPGs' firing range meant establishing the FSB 1 kilometre out. Phil braked hard as OC G ordered his section of the huge snaking convoy to halt. Kicking up a wave of sand, Phil swerved right and north to face the target. Gordon, the wagon's senior rank, was 'number one on the gun' and fired the belt-fed GPMG secured to the vehicle's front roll bar. The 'number two on the gun', the other crew member, ripped open the ammo boxes and pulled out 200 rounds of 7.62-mm link, running the chain through his hands to check for breaks before he 'fed the beast'. As the SAS say, Gordon was rapidly turning rounds into empty cases. His fire cut through the walls of the opium plant buildings – and it felt good. At last the smell of cordite, then the reassuring thud of a '50 cal' Browning machine-gun, a 17-kilogram hulk of a weapon, pounding away from an adjacent Pinkie, testing the weapon's monopod shock absorbers as its sheer power shook the whole vehicle. The first kills soon came. Al Qaeda who had not made it into the trenches dropped to earth, their bodies riddled with lead.

The two Acmats had been left at the FUP with three Pinkies under the RSM's supervision. He was IC of the rear protection party: responsible for defending side and rear flanks as well as handling prisoners of war, guarding and co-ordinating the resupply of ammunition and attending to casualties. Soldiers of his and the CO's importance – the 'leaders of men' – would not usually be on target. Even the FUP was closer to the action than the RSM was supposed to get. Nearing the end of his SAS career and having seen combat in the Falklands, he could not feel hard done by.

The CO's group stopped at the FSB from where the commander would direct the battle's opening passages. He had to be out of range of enemy fire yet close enough to assess the progress of the assault. With his signaller at his side, the CO could play Napoleon, marshalling the forces ahead of him. Like the king on a chessboard protected by pawns, the CO was accompanied by heavily armed troopers.

Jock and Jason got a whiff of the smell of expended rounds as their wagon, near the front of the A Squadron column, swept behind G, the CO's position and through the dust clouds. They wanted to get as close as possible to the opium plant to make the advance to contact across the western flank as short as possible. The RSM was further back near the FUP and the mortar line.

Seeing Spot Height 2213 looming dramatically ahead, its gravelled slopes rising sharply towards reddish peaks resembling teeth on a dinosaur's back, Jock realized the enemy could be hiding anywhere and he reminded his driver and Jason: 'Keep fuckin' switched on, the pair of ye, these fuckers could be all over the place.'

'Sure thing, Jock,' replied Jason.

'Ye don't wannae get slotted in the back before the fun really starts, laddie,' Jock added.

'This is serious shit,' thought Jason, 'no time for a fuck up, Jock will kill me if Al Qaeda don't.'

As G Squadron's Pinkies had before, A Squadron now came under effective enemy fire from RPGs. The wagons bounced over every dip in the ground, throwing passengers into the air as Jock shouted at the driver, 'Watch those bastard rockets on the right. For fuck's sake, steady on.' Eventually the lead wagon on the fourteen-Pinkie convoy would reach a level plane of latitude with the opium plant.

The veteran Glaswegian cursed Al Qaeda's RPGs. 'This is going to be one bastard of an advance to contact,' he thought. Even though A Squadron were still 1,000 metres out, the rest of the journey would have to be made on foot, and under constant enemy fire.

Jason had gone quiet, just a momentary lapse in bravado but enough to concern his IC Wagon. He did not appear sufficiently revved up. Jock leant over and slapped him hard on the shoulder. 'Come on, Jase, fuckin' switch on, this is the easy bit,' he shouted, jabbing his forefinger at him.

'Course I'm fuckin' switched on,' Jason replied angrily, staring menacingly at Jock to make his point.

'Well, you don't fuckin' look it!' insisted the battle-hardened Scot, wanting the young soldier psyched up to the maximum.

'Fuck you, Jock,' said Jason, with eyes that killed.

'Fuck you too, laddie,' Jock hit back, determined both to rile him and have the last word.

H-hour

The men at the FUP heard what began as a gentle rumbling from the south, beneath the sound of mortars and whistling RPGs. Gradually it grew deeper, louder and angrier so even the guys firing on the FSB could hear it. Phil and some others who were not shooting turned to see the US Navy's F/A-18 Hornets and F-14 Tomcats, armed with Sidewinder, Sparrow and Maverick missiles.

'Fuck me, that's a sight and a half,' said Phil.

'A once in a lifetime,' added Gordon, momentarily taking his eyes off his GPMG's targets.

The F/A-18 Hornets gave a thunderous roar as they descended for the first bombing run. With a shrill noise they released their deadly cargo, fizzing through the air like archer's arrows into the opium plant's two single-storey concrete warehouses. There was a enormous 'Boom' and the ground shook under the force of the explosion as, lifting their noses, the planes headed away from the target in a northerly direction.

The opium plant became a volcanic backdrop for the SAS's advance; the troops gazed at the scene of brilliant devastation, mayhem and fury. Flashes of bright orange sparked between vast clouds as tens of millions of pounds' worth of opium literally went up in smoke, thick black smoke.

Jock and Jason looked over their right shoulders towards the carnage. 'Fuck me, Jock, you see that?' the young trooper said excitedly.

'Aye, I did. I hope it didnae kill all the twats in there. Better had left some for us.'

Jock need not have worried. More Al Qaeda ran screaming from the headquarters which was spared, as Operation TRENT's key objective on paper was to gather intelligence. The soldiers would have to fight their way into the command centre, search it and get out again, protecting their cache of information.

Phil could not help but be impressed by the sheer size and devastation of the explosion, the biggest he had ever seen. But it emphasized how far he was from the target itself. He wished he was on an A Squadron wagon.

Gordon, in contrast with his younger colleague, had come alive and was as close to the action as he wanted to be. 'Look at the little fuckers run,' he shouted, as, like an army of ants, the terrorists scrambled towards bunkers and the two mud huts on the plant's western side. 'Die, you bastards,' he added, pumping away on the GPMG in their direction. Right now happiness for him was a warm gun.

Phil was firing the Pinkie's other GPMG into a different

arc, laying down harassing fire into an area the SAS did not want Al Qaeda to occupy. He hoped the enemy would be stupid enough to try their luck against his weapon. Not so far.

'Come on, you rag-heads, run over here,' Phil thought, before shouting in his frustration, 'For fuck's sake, I need a target.'

The mortars had been hauled from the Acmacs, barrel and the mounting equipment weighing 16 kilograms, and the missiles 1.8 kilograms each. The bottom end of the 1.28-metre barrel slotted into a base plate dug into the ground secured with sand bags. The diagonally slanting mortar barrel rested on a pair of supporting legs known as the bi-pod. Barrel elevation, measured in degrees, was adjusted according to the range required; in this case, around 1.2 kilometres from mortar line to target. While one man secured the base plate, another opened the bi-pods and connected the tube and plate to the pods. The first two mortar rounds were removed from their protective tubes and the augmenting charges attached.

The QACs (Quick Action Commands) were screamed along the mortar line.

'Bed in Charge Six.'

'Elevation 1242.'

The recoil of the bomb striking the tube's firing pin fixed the base plate into the ground.

'Bed in Charge Two. Two rounds, fire for effect.'

While each team prepared their mortar, two senior soldiers had specific roles: the CPO (Command Post Operator) and the MFC (Mortar Fire Controller). The CPO was the senior rank stationed at the mortar line and gave the fire order. He had a radio link to the MFC, hidden closer to the opium plant in a position to see the mortars strike. His role was to calculate mortar barrel elevation and work out the bearings of the mortar line and range to the target. He signalled these to the CPO. The FAC (Forward Air Controller), part of the CO's group, was tasked with communicating with the jet pilots, informing them of the direction of mortar fire. He had listened for the pilots to signal they had reached the 'Initial Point', a preset position *en route* from which they could calculate exactly the time they reached the target.

The first mortars were fired 'for effect', so the MFC, who had a better view, could assess the fall of shot and radio over adjustments: 'Add one hundred, left fifty,' he instructed. The mortar teams also fired at secondary targets, away from the opium plant's buildings, potential danger areas from which Al Qaeda – known in mortar-speak as X-rays for enemy – might launch a counter-attack, such as from behind A Squadron. Points on the mortar dials for these targets were recorded on the CPO's palm-top computer, these areas were then said to have been 'DFed' (Direction Found). If the enemy did strike from behind A Squadron, the mortar team would be able to drop rounds down on the enemy, already knowing the direction and range of Al Qaeda's new position.

The SAS had a range of mortars rounds, HE (high explosive), smoke and white phosphorous (WP), also known as 'warm persons', the latter used to set fire to buildings or humans. The fired 'for effect' mortars were predominantly HE but combined with a few to 'smoke off' the target were known as a 'Dolly Mixture'. They immediately proved as effective as Al Qaeda's adapted RPGs, exploding on the enemy ground near the bunkers. As the US fighter pilots did, the CPO and MFC ensured the mortars did not hit the opium plant headquarters.

*

H+0.15 hrs

As the odd terrorist with spindly arms and legs sprinted for
cover dressed in baggy *shalwar kameez*, then dropped to
earth, cheers went up from the FSB as the men got stuck in.
Phil, however, knew none of his bullets were hitting anyone,
just protecting an arc. Although 'keeping heads down', as it
is known, was crucial to the support of the assault, it was
not half as enthralling.

Al Qaeda were furious at the loss of their enormously
valuable drug. Frantically they fired their AK47s. It did not
matter whether or not they did this into the air; they were
hopelessly out of range. The rifle had a killing zone of
around 600 metres, with a secondary shot area of approximately one kilometre. Amid huge clouds of dense smoke
billowing from the warehouses, they could just be made
out, squeezing into holes in the ground. With their precious
poppy crop destroyed and smouldering behind them, they
were ready to fight to the death.

Above the plant, the jets blazed a trail of piercing white
light through the blue skies dazzling in the sunlight. They
would fly in a holding pattern until their next run. The
aircraft climbed and soared like birds of prey, wings fully
outstretched, as if with their heads down, surveying the
ground below.

This was a new and painful experience for the Al
Qaeda troops, even those who had been under attack
before. Most of the US bombing of Afghanistan had been
from high altitude; not this time. They would have been
even more stunned to see those who they assumed were
Americans heading towards them, accustomed as they were
only to seeing Northern Alliance on the ground. Al Qaeda
could not have known the advancing force was British.

The sky jockeys had got Operation TRENT's Phase Four

off to a thunderous bang. The battle was in full swing, the FSB laying down waves of fire, spotting areas of enemy movement and taking out opportune targets. In theory, if not in reality, this would endure Al Qaeda were sufficiently preoccupied to let A Squadron advance from the west relatively unhindered.

Its wagons were still on the move towards the target. Every time they strayed inwards from the western flank, however, the vehicles were showered with secondary fragmentation from falling RPGs. This was effective enemy fire, with the Pinkies just a few metres from taking direct hits.

'Christ, these fucking rockets are close,' said Jason.

'Aye, we'll have to de-bus any minute. We can take cover on foot,' replied Jock.

He was right. The men would find it easier to dodge missiles away from the 3.5-tonne truck.

Most of A Squadron's Pinkies were coming into range of the Al Qaeda support weapons. Once on the ground, Jock and Jason would run, crawl and fight their way ahead, leaving the driver behind with the vehicle.

'Incoming!' Jock screamed at the top of his voice, as another Al Qaeda rocket caused the driver to take evasive action and swerve left through the sand cloud the exploding missile kicked up.

Slapping Jason again and making sure he was loud enough for the driver to hear, Jock shouted, 'Right, get ready to get the fuck off here, we're gonnae fucking de-bus now. OK?'

They could barely hear each other over the noise of the rockets and the Pinkie engine, nor see each other through the increasingly dense clouds of sand.

Time for Jason's inner man to reveal himself. Running into the hail of bullets, rockets and fragments from exploded

munitions, all his individual strengths and weaknesses
would be exposed. It was the combat virgin's ultimate test,
though he was not fighting alone, none of his mates could
stop a bullet for him. His reactions had to be lightning-fast,
his thoughts clear and his judgements precise. If pinned
behind a rock, with bullets whizzing past his ears, he would
find out how hungry he really was for action. It was going
to be a long, hot and sticky afternoon. The T-shirt under
Jason's combat smock and operational waistcoat clung to
his back with sweat, his cam cream merging with a thin
film of sand and dirt which stuck to his face.

Jock scoured the landscape immediately ahead of the
Pinkie for a suitable stopping point and pointed the way.
'Twenty metres, on your right, by that big fuck-off rock,' he
screamed, although he was sitting just inches from the
driver's left ear.

A Squadron's Pinkies bounced and wove over the last
stretch of uneven ground, a few turning right to face the
target before skidding to a halt, sending showers of dirt
high into the air. Jock did not need to worry about Jason
being sufficiently psyched up, but like all the senior NCOs,
the warhorses who bossed each wagon, he kept the pressure
up, shouting, 'Get out for fuck's sake, go, go, go.'

Jason was first off, sprinting 10 metres towards a slight
rise in the sandy ground which would provide cover. He
had smelled war, now he tasted it as he hit the deck face
down. He turned onto his side and looked back at the rest
of A Squadron, expecting them to be on his shoulder. They
were not all there yet. He would have to wait for the rear
vehicles to catch up before the advance to contact on foot
could begin.

He kept tight to the ground, making his body less of a
target while his eyes scanned the ground to his left, right
and straight ahead. Glancing behind, he saw his A Squadron mates taking cover as the fire orders boomed out across

the battle ground: 'Enemy left, 300 metres.' Jason gripped his weapon even more tightly, then checked and resecured his webbing.

Two men from each Pinkie would form the assault party: twenty-eight men in all spreading out laterally and working together. Jock did not want Jason or any of the other 'Toms' going too far ahead just yet, there was no point in becoming separated, different groups of soldiers heading off to confront Al Qaeda in twos and threes. 'Jase,' he shouted, 'fuckin' stay there.'

'Too right, Jock, I ain't fuckin' movin',' he replied. Even Jason did not want to take them on single-handed.

Waiting for the other guys allowed him another weapon check. He looked over his rifle yet again. Squeezing its body, he ran through the basics in his mind: 'For fuck's sake don't have a stoppage, check safety catch is off, got to have clean magazine changes; cover arcs.' Since joining the Paras at the age of seventeen he had practised fire and manoeuvre thousands of times, on exercise in Wales, in Northern Ireland and across the world with both the Paras and more recently the SAS. Now, for the first time, it was for real. His pulse racing, he even unclipped the magazine and took a quick peek inside, checking for rounds. Jason realized how stupid this was. Nerves were taking over. 'For fuck's sake, stay calm,' he shouted at himself. He knew the magazine was full.

The advance to contact would be done in the 'buddy-buddy' system, in pairs, which was known as pepper-potting. This was a drill British infantry units practised to perfection in the open spaces of the Brecon Beacons, though the vast majority of soldiers never do it with a live enemy in front of them.

To put real pressure on Al Qaeda, momentum had to be developed then maintained. A uniform advance would be impossible. All that mattered was that a sufficient number of troops closed with the enemy under suppressive, covering fire.

On Operation TRENT, the troops faced the longest advance to contact of their lives, roughly two and a half times further than they had 'pepper-potted' before. The advance to contact under fire, and carrying 50 pounds of webbing, helmet, weapon and ammunition, is usually too exhausting for the soldiers to go beyond 400 metres – 'No wonder the Americans did not fancy this mission,' thought Jock.

Through the dust kicked up by exploding rockets Jason could just about make out his OC issuing orders. His heart was pumping. He was so keen to get on with it that it felt as though he had been on the ground for hours.

Suddenly there was a massive explosion, 20 metres from Jason's well-covered position, as an Al Qaeda RPG went off. 'Fuckin' hell,' thought Jason as he was showered with metal splinters and rock fragments. The ringing in his ears was agony. He lifted his head up a few inches, checking the enemy had not scored a direct hit. Thankfully not.

The order Jason had been waiting for came at last. 'Right, everyone ready? OK, spread out and watch your fucking arcs. Let's go!' In the confusion of battle and the rocket attack, Jason set off with another trooper, forgetting Jock's plan for them to buddy-up, not that he could hear or see him. After the near miss with the RPG the combat virgin was desperate to find dead ground at the earliest opportunity – safe from enemy view and fire – with or without his IC Wagon in tow.

'Get fuckin' down!'
   'Watch it, watch it!'
   Shells exploded around Jock and the others with colossal

booms, spraying more metal in all directions. Taking cover
for the first time, Jock looked around him.

'Jason, where the fuck are ye?'

No reply.

Then he spotted him charging ahead and thought, 'Ah
for fuck's sake, this has gone for a bag of rats already.' He
would never admit it, but he had wanted to keep an eye
out for Jason from the start of the advance.

H+0.30 hrs

Jason and his new buddy ran forward as a pair, zigzagging
across the slope of Spot Height 2213 which fell from their
left to right and through the dust and dirt. Jason did not
waste a round, knowing the terrorists dotted around the
opium plant headquarters remained out of range. However,
A Squadron troopers were coming under more effective
enemy fire than had been anticipated. 'Fuck, where's that
coming from?' thought Jason, as bullets tore up the ground
around his feet.

He crouched into the smallest body position possible
behind a rock and looked ahead, the bullets now speeding
just a metre or two above him. Seeing two bunkers 300
metres away and higher up on the hill, he screamed, 'Hey,
enemy in bunkers! Fire, ten o'clock! Got incoming from the
front as well.'

Another guy shouted from behind him, 'Hey, can anyone get a "five-o" [Browning] to adjust on those fuckers?'

Jason did not want to wait; he had never been as revved
up in his life, insisting, 'Nah, come on, let's take these rag-
heads out.' He was being naive.

'Cool it. Just fucking wait, Jason,' snapped one NCO
aggressively.

'Just go firm, go firm,' said another.

The three men had better views than Jason of the enemy positions and saw it would be suicidal to run up the slope towards them. A better option seemed getting one of A Squadron's Pinkies to target the bunkers while the men on the ground consolidated their well-advanced position.

The wagons, which had been static, drove up behind the men and provided more supporting fire. Ideally the CO would have wanted the wagons to stay put, out of range, having parked in a 'safe' position. The vehicles had to edge east to add weight to the attack and, in particular, pressurize the positions causing A Squadron's left flank such problems.

Leaving the Pinkies unmanned was not an option, even though it would have freed the drivers to join the assault party. The battle would take on an even darker complexion if one of the guerrillas pinched an SAS vehicle: what a price a Pinkie armed to the teeth would fetch on the Kandahar black market!*

The Brownings' heavy bullets churned up the ground surrounding the top bunker, tearing through the rocks and coarse gravel, but such was the angle of strike, with the bunkers being above the Pinkies, that the fall of shot could not be directed inside the enemy positions.

The minutes seemed like hours as Jason waited impatiently. His infantry training told him to go forward. He felt guilty about not advancing, even though it would have been insane to make a dash for either bunker. The trooper would rather have died than be called a coward.

---

* Leaving vehicles in a position where they may be vulnerable to enemy capture is an absolute 'no-no' for SF and non-SF forces alike. In April 2003, during Operation IRAQI FREEDOM, the Republican Guard overran an SBS position in Northern Iraq and seized a Pinkie, Quad bike and high-tech communications equipment. The bounty was paraded on *Al-Jazeera*, a hugely embarrassing episode for UKSF.

AK47 fire whizzed either side of him, leaving strike marks on the rocks. He popped a boiled sweet into his mouth, to dilute the sickness in the pit of his stomach. The tension also caused a buildup of saliva in his palate.

To his right, Jason saw other members of A Squadron making smoother progress; they did not have the steeper ground or the Al Qaeda bunkers to contend with. The mind games continued. Jason, still hiding in the dirt, questioned his actions, or lack of them. 'I should be taking them on, that's what I was taught. Even though the guys said wait, we've gotta have a crack at the position.' He also remembered he was supposed to have 'buddied-up' with Jock: 'Where is Jock? Shit, maybe he's been hit?'

With the steep mountainside preventing attack from the north, and bunkers and trenches facing east, west and south, Al Qaeda were well set. From their well-fortified positions there was no shortage of SAS targets at which to aim. Any hopes that G Squadron's fire would be enough to keep the outgunned and outnumbered enemy busy had proved unfounded. Al Qaeda were holding firm in the face of a mighty pounding from the .50s, GPMGs and Milan rocket launchers from the FSB and the mortars. It would take longer for the Regiment's 'weight advantage' to tell.

Watching from the rear, the RSM was becoming increasingly twitchy, seeing his fellow soldiers under a barrage of fire from positions they were unable to knock out. He felt frustrated, but had to stay put. Eight kilometres away, three more frustrated SAS men had heard the US jets scream down ahead of them to show the convoy the final approach and return for the first bombing run. They had also watched the huge plumes of grey smoke wafting slowly towards the skyline. The RSM may have been feeling left out, but at least he was safe. With their broken-down Pinkie sitting helplessly in the sand, the crew were severely exposed. What if Al Qaeda's reinforcements came from behind their position? If they lived to tell the tale, it would be an incredible one.

Though in constant radio contact with his squadron OCs, the CO also needed his own, first-hand intelligence. This meant leaving his secure position close to the FSB. Heading west would have been treacherous, putting himself between A Squadron's right flank and the FSB's left arc. He tracked east, where the advance had been due to start.

Frustrated at the failure of the .50s to take out the bunkers, Jason heard furious screams that summed up his feelings: 'What the fuck are we going to do about these bunkers?'

The battle plan would have to be adjusted.

'These fucking rag-heads have got us pinned down,' screamed another guy.

Word reached the head sheds. The FSB was ordered to advance 300 metres in a line roughly 650 metres from the opium plant. Phil stopped firing his GPMG, started up the Pinkie and drove forward, while Gordon kept pumping away on his weapon. G Squadron could now put down heavier fire towards the bunker and the plant. The wagons edged forward, leaving a trail of thousands of brass cases from spent rounds behind them. Firing from a moving vehicle was more difficult and less accurate but time was precious. Though Jason was one of many cocky young troopers who wound up the 'old and bold', they did not want him to get his head blown off.

Al Qaeda were getting closer to scoring a direct hit from the bunker. Jason felt that if he moved an inch he would get a bullet in the head. He dug his feet into the gravel to stop himself slipping down the slope. Bullets with his name on them pinged off the surrounding rocks. He had to fire back. When there was a momentary lapse he would lift himself up and fire off a few rounds, then get down again, adjust his position and rattle off another burst, knowing never to fire consecutive bursts from the same spot as it increased the enemy's chances of pinpointing his position.

H+0.45 hrs

The CO got on the net and, as a last resort, called in an immediate air strike. The SAS only had use of the US aircraft for another fifteen minutes. He might as well make the most of it.

A single F/A-18 thundered in and scored a direct hit on the top bunker. The ground erupted into a huge ball of fire and smoke. Such was the devastation that it was as if the missile connected with an underground plastic explosives store. It set off a landslide, taking out the lower bunker as well. Al Qaeda guerrillas in both positions were blown to pieces.

'Right, we're back in business,' shouted Jock, desperate to make up for lost time. 'There'll be a load of dead rag-heads up there. They're sorted, but still cover 'em,' he added, viewing the hole in the hillside consumed with fire.

Recognizing his voice, a relieved Jason remarked, 'Where the fuck have you been?'

'Watchin' your slack arse, you cheeky fuck,' replied Jock, before adding, 'Now, get on with it!'

'Let's get forward,' screamed another.

'Come on, come on,' snarled Jason, consumed with aggression and confidence once more.

The F/A-18 pilots were ready for the second and last of their pre-scheduled attacks but unaware of Operation TRENT's complex developments. The first run had reduced the warehouses containing £50 million of opium to charred remains and intoxicating smoke. Their finale would target Al Qaeda's infantry with strafing fire from the planes' 20-mm Vulcan cannons.

Built into the noses of the strike jets, on the cockpit fuselage's port side, the cannons had six revolving barrels, loaded simultaneously and fired individually as they passed through the top position. They consumed vast amounts of ammunition extremely quickly. Unlike the GPMG, the onboard 20-mm cannons were fed by a linkless feed system to prevent jamming. The rounds were pressed into the gun on a hydraulically operated conveyor belt. The angles of the six barrels were adjusted for different dispersion patterns and twisted grooves built into each making the rounds spin. Increased aerodynamic efficiency led to improved stability in flight and enhanced range and accuracy.

The Vulcan cannon took 0.3 seconds to wind up to full rate of fire, and 0.5 seconds to switch off. The weapon's accuracy was believed to be at its truest as soon as it was fired. The Vulcan's cannons were air-cooled and fired at 4,000 or 6,000 rounds per minute. For ground strafing, the pilots chose HE incendiary rounds.

Having circled high in the air, biding their time, the pilots would descend any second now, dropping to around 2,000 feet to riddle the Al Qaeda positions with deadly fire.

The attack would come at a critical time. Operation TRENT was in need of a boost, with A Squadron's left flank having lost all momentum.

This would be the aircraft's last contribution. After this run, the SAS would close with Al Qaeda alone. This was, after all, 'America's Party'; while 120 British soldiers put their lives on the line to win a battle, the jets had other bombing runs to carry out.

The strike aircraft arced and turned, dropping through the skies towards the opium plant from the south-west and over the broken-down Pinkie's position. They headed on a bearing, the raucous engine noise echoing across the rugged landscape. In the distance were the mountains of Pakistan; the target now appeared in the foreground beneath a lingering plume of grey smoke, the legacy of the first bombing run, while the pilots were aware the SAS had switched flanks they had not been told about G Squadron's advance. They thought the FSB was still 1,000 metres south of the target. The huge rounds would now be fired down into the earth at the same point as the FSB's new position and then run up to the target.

Gordon, Phil and the fifty-plus other members of G Squadron heard the F/A-18s approach but kept their eyes forward as they aimed their GPMGs and Brownings.

They came in low, the lead pilot's finger on the Vulcan's electronic trigger. He squeezed: instantly, sounding like a drill bearing into concrete, the first vicious cannon opened up . . .

The hail of cannon fire screaming downwards drowned out even the machine-gun fire on the FSB. A thunderstorm of lead rained down on the G Squadron positions, drilling holes in the ground between the Pinkies – any man standing in the way would have been instantly torn limb from limb. The wave of US fire flashed through the SAS line, ripping up the earth and speeding on towards the opium plant.

Everyone in G Squadron was stunned, breathless. Surely a number of wagons had been taken out? The air was toxic with the smell of ammunition; US ammo inadvertently aimed at the SAS.

'Christ,' screamed one, 'it's a fuckin' Yank blue on blue.'

'What the fuck was that?' shouted another.

Gordon's eyes darted left and right, looking for his mates splattered all over the desert plain, their bodies riddled with holes big enough to put your fist inside.

'Fuckin' hell, man,' he said as he did an all-around observation. They had survived by luck alone. The US cannons had missed the SAS wagons by inches, going between a gap in the column.

But G Squadron was not safe from the US Navy yet; another F/A-18 was due in any moment for its strafing run. Surely the SAS's luck would not hold; cannon fire would slice through the Pinkies, not the ground between them. The CO received an emergency Sit Rep from the FSB and had just seconds to contact the pilots. He screamed down the net: 'Check fire! Check fire!' The message was received and disaster aborted.

Having escaped an instant but brutal death by a whisker, the usually placid Phil went crazy: 'Fuckin' stupid Yank twats, they fuck everything up,' he said.

It was a few minutes before anyone on the FSB regained their composure. Relieved to see everyone had survived, Gordon laughed. 'Oh well, Phil, at least you can say you've been fired at now. It might be as close to the action as you'll get.'

This comment confused the inexperienced soldier. 'Is he mad? How could he say that in the middle of a fire fight?' he thought. 'We nearly got killed by our own fuckin' side!'

This was one blue on blue that could not be pinned on the Americans. If they knew G Squadron had advanced, they would have altered the height at which they started firing, avoiding the FSB. There had been a communications breakdown.

Stunned, hugely relieved and for once a little shaken, the FSB resumed firing. The post-mortem into how so many SAS men were almost wiped out would have to wait. The SAS had a battle to win and as things stood, victory looked a long way off. The RSM was becoming increasingly frustrated; his men were taking a pounding from friendly and unfriendly forces. He could contain himself no longer. Jumping into a vehicle, he drove to the CO's new position.

*

The battle's first hour had been a frantic and frightening introduction to combat for the virgins and a shocking reminder of its unpredictability for those who had been there before. It was impossible to confirm the exact numbers of enemy on target, somewhere between sixty and a hundred, or numbers of enemy dead, thus far. Most had survived the air strikes. More were dying now from the SAS's onslaught. Although the Regiment tightened the screw by moving up the FSB, a lot of progress still had to be made on the western flank. Greater risks would have to be taken to ensure victory.

12. CLOSE IN AND KILL HIM

H+1.00 hrs

Having dived into the earth head first, Jock's already dry mouth seemed 'full of shite' and grains of sand stuck to his lips. During the infil he had stuffed every extra magazine he could into his operational waistcoat. Now it propped him up a few inches above the pitifully shallow hollow chosen out of necessity as a cover position. His body armour also added to his size. Jock wondered whether this potentially fatal elevation above the sun-baked ground was divine intervention, punishment for being so greedy about getting ammunition back at Bagram?

Either way he had to get lower to the ground. An old sweat's trick was called for. Jock undid the waistcoat's plastic toggles, releasing the front flaps so they lay either side of him on the sand. He felt fractionally lower and seized a couple of minutes' respite from the battle for his aching thighs, heart and lungs. Dead ground was at a premium at 500 metres out from the opium plant. Getting his breath back, he fastened the chest webbing and looked ahead for Jason, who had gone firm behind a rock.

'I'm moving, ready?'

'Yeah, move!'

Jock dashed forward under Jason's supporting fire, then, spotting another fold in the ground, slid into the dirt and shouted to his oppo: 'Move!' This time there was no reply.

Immediately Jock was anxious, as the whole of A Squadron were vulnerable to AK47 attack from Al Qaeda's ring of trenches surrounding the plant. A few dried-out stream beds and the occasional rock offered the only affordable cover positions.

'Where the fuck are ye?'

'Enemy left, 200 metres, ten o'clock,' came the sharply delivered response.

'OK, OK,' said Jock, a little more sympathetically now.

'Spotted!' shouted another voice just before a torrent of small-arms fire struck the enemy position which had Jason in its sights.

Neither Jason nor Jock could see whether the enemy had been slotted or not, until another friendly voice from the rear informed them: 'Jock, got two confirmed [dead] enemy in that position – hang tight.'

There were more Al Qaeda still alive in the trench. They would have to be taken out before the pair could resume their advance. Desperate to find an angle to hit them, Jock shuffled sideways across the bone-dry earth on his stomach, working knees and elbows while small-arms fire narrowly missed his head. Taking up a firing position, he saw a figure scurrying through the canopy of smoke from SAS mortars and let rip.

Jock's bullets tore through him and the figure dropped, pain etched across his weather-beaten, bearded face. 'Dead rag-head,' he thought. 'Go and meet your virgins.'

He gave Jason a hand signal to advance as his victim wriggled momentarily in the dirt then lay still. Another rag-head popped up but was quickly taken out by A Squadron troopers behind the Scot.

*

A Squadron's soldiers were now advancing close to the line of fire of the Pinkies on the FSB's left flank; making precision shooting from the wagons in the direction of the opium plant even more important.

Gordon aimed every round on the GPMG at the Al Qaeda trenches, shouting, 'Come on, ye bastards, poke your fuckin' heads out.'

Watching A Squadron's advance from the left, dangerously close to Phil's arc, a G Squadron NCO shouted, 'Phil, check fire!' Reluctantly, Phil nodded back.

The battle was not turning out as he hoped, from a personal point of view. He knew he could not risk firing into his arc as the corridor of dead ground between the forces narrowed. He wondered when, or even if, he was going to get a kill. Thus far the Americans had come closer to killing him than he felt he had to slotting any Al Qaeda.

Phil looked on enviously as somebody to his right screamed, 'Break out the Barretts' – a command for the FSB's snipers. These were the SAS's semi-automatic .50 calibre long-range sniper rifles, first used in the Gulf War, and incredibly accurate over distances of 2 kilometres or more. The rounds exploded on impact and had armour-piercing capability. Phil had fired one on the range back in Hereford but, much to his chagrin, he was not going to get his hands on one now.

Being a bit of an anorak, as many outside G Squadron thought most of its soldiers were, he knew its specifications: the Barrett weighed 12 kilograms, was 1.4 metres long, and had a ten-round magazine. The weapon would be fired from a bipod and with a muzzle brake fitted to the end of the barrel to reduce what is known as 'felt recoil' – the kickback effect after firing. 'Christ, I want one now,' thought Phil.

The Barrett had not been used in the battle's early stages when weight of suppressive fire across the enemy's positions was paramount. It fired a slow and heavy shot, and was used against single, clearly identifiable targets, i.e. individual rag-heads, and never into wide areas of ground for 'harassing fire' purposes, as Phil had aimed his GPMG.

They rummaged through each Pinkie's myriad of storage boxes and compartments where the Barretts were stored, wrapped in thick protective material. Watching the guys piecing the weapons together on the vehicles' chassis, Phil was jealous. Not being able to fire his GPMG was bad enough, but seeing his mates eyeing up virtually guaranteed human targets was worse.

'Fuckin' hell, I should be on one of them,' he thought, 'now I'm doing fuck all and there's all this fighting going on in front of me. Maybe that prick Gordon was right; the fuckin' strafing is as close to the action as I'm gonna get. What a pile of shit.'

The body count rose as the snipers found their range, and it was a quick death when the Barrett ripped through a guerrilla's vital organs; slower when it took off an arm or a leg. Then they writhed on the ground in agony, limbs oozing blood. A 'double tap' execution to the head if or when it came from a passing A Squadron soldier would be a blessing for any of the crippled terrorists.

H+1.15 hrs

The RSM arrived on the eastern flank and met the CO. A conversation ensued, the precise details of which are known only to them. It is believed the CO accepted the RSM's request to advance and he did so, taking soldiers from the CO's party with him: the driver and rear gunner from the Colonel's back-up Pinkie, the FAC and two others.

Jason and Jock felt they were being bleached dry under the sun's rays. In the dustbowl battlefield, they advanced into the teeth of Al Qaeda's resistance, spitting out mouth-fuls of dirt as they crawled towards the enemy and wiping it from their eyes with sweaty, muddy hands.

The pair found themselves lying up behind the same rock and surveyed the deathly drab panorama of greyish-brown mountains surrounding the desert plain – these were southern Afghanistan's natural defences that had kept invaders at bay for centuries. It was a moment of relative calm, but not one to switch off, just for the troops to get their heads and weapons together.

'Fuck, I'm thirsty,' said Jock, taking a water bottle from his belt webbing and unscrewing the top. The sand had encrusted around the rim. 'This shite gets everywhere,' he muttered before putting it to his lips. 'Here, laddie, have a swig.'

'Cheers, Jock.'

It was their first chance to discuss the early stages of the battle and what the troop was going to do next.

'You can see these little fuckers scurryin' everywhere through the smoke,' said Jock. 'I fuckin' took one out, clean shot; nae fuckin' bother. What about you?' This was a rhetorical question as Jock, having had a good view of his younger colleague's progress, knew he had not killed.

Jason did not know either but chose to bluff it. His initial hesitation was fatal.

'Er . . . Yeah, fuckin' took one out earlier when we was behind that rock, in front of the bunker.'

'Bollocks, laddie, no you fuckin' didnae,' Jock cut in. 'I fuckin' saw ye, ye just had your fuckin' head down.'

'Ah, fuck off, Jock, I shot one earlier and I'll kill some fuckin' more. You're so slow over the ground you won't make it back from the HQ.'

Jock laughed. 'You'll get your chance to get off the mark, there's fuckin' loads of rag-heads still there. I thought they'd have pissed off. Seems they've swallowed the crap about becoming martyrs and all that shite.'

'Looks like it,' Jason agreed.

'Make the most of this lull, Jase,' said Jock, breathing heavily. 'Check yer ammo and make sure you've got grenades ready.'

Jason nodded back.

'And fa fuck's sake watch out for mines as we close in, OK?'

This last instruction made Jason feel a little uneasy. Getting slotted was a quick job; an 'in and out' wound seemed infinitely preferable to stepping on an AP mine and looking down at shattered and splintered bones which used to be one of his legs. Such a prospect put the fear of God into Jason.

There were more trenches crammed with terrorists, surrounding the command centre.

'We've gottae take those positions ahead, Jase,' said Jock, adding, 'There's fuck-all cover, we need smoke lobbed in there first. Don't go charging off just yet, ye hear?'

'Too right, Jock.'

'Oh, and by the way, what the fuck happened to you earlier, laddie? You were supposed to team up with me, you little twat.'

'I couldn't see you, Jock.'

'Couldnae see me! I was right behind you. Anyway come on, get your arse in gear, we're off.'

H+1.30 hrs

A Squadron were 'skirmishing' – another term for advancing – feverishly, guys from all four troops, Air, Boat, Mobility and Mountain, getting forward, firing, diving into the dirt then attacking again. They were unsure sometimes as they charged forward whether they could reach their next point of cover; but if they always waited, the Regiment would be there all day.

It was an erratic advance towards the command centre, at times slow and deliberate, faster when ground and enemy fire allowed, and finding themselves sharing ground and cover, Jason and Jock teamed up with other soldiers and advanced as a four on occasion.

Suddenly the cry went up, 'Man down, man down!' A Staff Sergeant from Mobility Troop, an ex-Para, took a 7.62-mm round from an AK47 in the arm and dropped to the ground. He was thought to have been shot from a range of 200 metres. Other guys could scarcely afford to take their eyes off the Al Qaeda in front of them but could not help glancing towards him.

'I'm with him, I'm with him,' screamed the nearest man.

'Get him into dead ground,' shouted another.

Luckily there was no need for heroics. It was just a flesh wound and he was able to make his own way back to cover.

'It's only a graze. It's an in and out,' added one of the guys.

'There's a lot of fuckin' blood, twat,' screamed someone slightly more sympathetic.

The wounded man did not panic, assuring those around him he was not badly injured. This point in the battle, when the Regiment took its first casualty, was another psychological hurdle for the combat virgins. Seeing a colleague and a friend get hit, even though he was not seriously wounded, was a test. Were they strong enough mentally to prevent hesitancy or fear, as a result of witnessing the shooting, creeping into their decision-making and actions? If not, it could prove fatal.

Some members of A Squadron saw the enemy celebrating the first hit on an infidel – fists were raised from the trenches. Having lost so many themselves they seemed overjoyed. Hearing their victorious cries in Arabic and the cheering, one trooper said, 'Look at the little fuckers,' pointing it out to a mate lying close by, 'You'd fucking think they'd won, those fucking rag-heads are going to die.'

'Yeah, well, let's make sure it's the only fucking hit they get.'

Much to some of A Squadron's amusement – those sufficiently advanced to see it – Al Qaeda were goading them forwards, believing the world's finest Special Forces were suddenly for the taking.

News of the first casualty came over the radio just as the RSM's party left the CO's position. Such was the ferocity of Al Qaeda's resistance that the head sheds were relieved just to have a single man down at this stage.

Minutes later, the RSM arrived at the FSB with soldiers culled from the CO's group. Gordon was, to put it mildly, surprised to see him, saying to Phil as he pointed into the distance along the line of the FSB to where he was standing, 'Hey, what the fuck is he doing here? That twat is supposed to stay at the FUP.'

Neither Gordon nor Phil had any idea that the RSM wanted to take extra G Squadron troops with him to the front line and were too far away from his position to offer their services. There was no shortage of volunteers, as engaging with the enemy eyeball to eyeball beat the hell out of staying on the FSB. Phil had been unlucky again. Given the chance, every man in the Regiment, CO included, would have gone to the front. He could not. The Colonel's job was to conduct the orchestra, and Phil's to do nothing, at that moment.

The RSM now led a party of ten. After a quick Chinese Parliament they set off, having decided to work as two separate fire teams. They would dart forwards to link up

with A Squadron's right flank, which inevitably, in the
course of the advance, had become fractured.

'The lucky bastards,' shouted Phil at Gordon, having
found out what the RSM was doing. 'Why the fuck didn't
he [the RSM] come and fuckin' get me? I have to fuckin'
stay here and I can't even fire my fuckin' weapon.'

Gordon laughed. For once it was somebody other than
him who was grumbling. 'Shut up, man. Let them go on
their fuckin' glory run. We can't all piss off from the FSB.
You've got to have a fuckin' fire support.' Phil just scowled
back. 'You might get to fire again later,' Gordon added,
mockingly.

'Fuck off, you Geordie twat.'

At the time it was little compensation for Phil, but
Gordon was right. The GPMGs and .50s would be used
later to mop up 'runners' as the SAS refer to them, any Al
Qaeda fleeing the opium plant. Their only escape route was
north, over Spot Height 2213. If they headed south, east or
west they would be mown down by the FSB.

The RSM's party made swift progress, 'pepper-potting'
as A Squadron had before them as the snap orders – the
spontaneous commands of battle – came thick and fast.

'Cover me!'

'Enemy, one o'clock, 100 metres!'

'Grenade!'

'Move now!'

Getting closer to the enemy HQ, many of the A Squadron guys saw for the first time in their lives the reality of
war and how intense the fighting on Operation TRENT had
been already. Corpses, rags and cartridge cases littered the
dirt and gravel ahead of them. Barefooted, dusty bodies lay
lifeless, often not in one piece. The soles of the dead men's
feet looked as though they had been painted white from the
dust and their heads were tilted back. Still warm, open-

mouthed and pale, they were gaunt figures, the faces of those with their eyes shut strangely expressionless.

The hard yards were getting even harder for Jason and Jock. They were well within range of Al Qaeda's AK47s and fire poured down from the enemy's positions. They too could see the gory reality of war. Al Qaeda looked so malnourished that Jock could barely make out a body beneath the pile of bloodstained, dirty rags. 'Smelly little bastards,' he thought. They already stank from living in the inhuman conditions of southern Afghanistan, a place where only the weapons are clean. Soon the corpses would reek of death and flies would pick at them.

During another brief respite Jock saw the remaining Al Qaeda ahead of him looting dead men for weapons and magazines. 'You see that, Jase, they're fuckin' wasting their time. They're still gonna get slotted.'

The opium plant resembled an open-air mortuary. The accuracy of SAS fire reduced enemy numbers between them and the command centre, its muddy walls merging with the landscape. Jason had found a well-covered hollow and lay on his front, tilting his head over the stock of the Diemaco. He closed his left eye and focused with his right through the rifle sight. He felt confident. It was a lethal weapon in the right hands; and these were the right hands, Jason tracked the human targets as they scampered furiously across the sand, their backs hunched as they rattled off a few rounds in his direction, their headscarves flapping in the wind behind them. He could not help but smile at seeing their skinny little legs moving frantically and sticking out from beneath dusty, dress-like robes.

He fired a short burst, then followed his strike marks hitting the ground and ran them up to the targets. Jason made them leap dramatically for cover behind the command centre's walls, and jump over the mounting number of dead bodies to get into cover, screaming, *'Allah Akhbar!'* as they went.

'Fuck, missed!' shouted Jason.

Jock dived down beside him, out of breath from the exhausting advance to contact. 'You're a shite shot, laddie,' he opined.

'Fuck off, old man.'

'I'll say this for 'em,' said Jock, 'they sure are hanging around.'

Despite being confronted by such overpowering force, and surely knowing they would die, there were very few 'runners' for the FSB to take out. It was as if the manner of their death was more important to Al Qaeda's soldiers than actually avoiding it.

H+1.45 hrs

Suddenly there was a friendly shout of 'Grenade' and the earth around Jock and Jason shuddered violently. A Squadron troops from behind them were smoking off the target. Foreign voices screaming in agony confirmed a direct hit. 'Fuck me, we are far forward,' said an amazed Jock.

The numbers of Al Qaeda dead had risen to the point where the surviving enemy could use corpses as cover. In the trenches ahead it was difficult for Jason, Jock and others to see how many were alive, obscured by the bodies and the dust clouds kicked up every time the enemy moved.

Jock did not think many were left in the nearest trench. But he was not going to take any chances and storm it.

'Right, Jase. We're gonnae grenade that fuckin' trench, OK? If we take these fuckers out we can move forward again. Don't go chargin' off just yet, though.'

'OK,' Jason replied, searching for a grenade in his operational waistcoat. Fired up, Jason had to be kept on a leash by Jock. His youthful inexperience could be the death of him. Jason and Jock would pull the pins and keep hold of the priming levers.

'You go first, laddie, then me. Make sure ye spot where the fucker lands. I don't want it fuckin' bouncing back.'

Jason nodded and shouted 'Grenade' as he let fly. They watched as it landed past the Al Qaeda position before exploding.

'Got the fucker,' screamed Jason seeing an enemy head knocked back and convinced his grenade had accounted for him.

'Nah, you've just stirred 'em,' said Jock.

In truth it was impossible to tell – the man could have been slotted by any number of A Squadron troops in advanced positions. That would not stop Jason claiming the kill. Jock shouted 'Grenade' and hurled his. It landed a fraction closer.

Another voice shouted, 'Jase, Jock . . . move, I'm covering you. The bunker's clear.'

'You heard him, Jase. Go, go, go,' bellowed Jock as they picked themselves up and drove on.

They found shallow holes dug into the dusty earth, reinforced first with sandbags and, at the bitter end, the corpses of comrades. Bodies in oversized anoraks, some with plaid patterned shirts wrapped around their waists and boots tied together with string lay motionless, still clutching their AKs, the last painridden seconds of their lives captured in their staring bloodshot eyes.

The RSM had led his party to within 300 metres of the command building in good time. As the battlefield area became more constricted, Jason and Jock looked to their right and got their first glimpse of the RSM. Their reaction was similar to Gordon's. 'Where the fuck did he come from?' said Jock in amazement, knowing the RSM was supposed to be at the FUP. While taken aback by his arrival,

Jock also realized more manpower on target might come in handy when the SAS reached the HQ.

'He couldnae resist it,' Jock chuckled to himself, knowing how the RSM must have felt stuck at the back and that he would have got equally frustrated in his position.

A Squadron's approach towards the HQ had to be discussed, and as quickly as possible. 'What's happening?' said Jock.

He was told by another soldier: 'You and the rest of your troop head towards the two mud huts on the flank. ****'s [the RSM's] party will take the command centre. Understood?'

'Yeah, whatever.'

Through the dirt and clouds of smoke the SAS assault parties could see Al Qaeda retreating behind the huts and headquarters. The huts would be taken one by one, each needing to become a mini-FSB covering those advancing ahead. The attack was going to become more of a CQB (Close-Quarter Battle).

The men did another weapons check, detaching and shaking magazines and where necessary carefully snapping a new one into the main body or replenishing the magazine with bullets from half charged ones. Others tightened their helmets and allowed themselves just a few minutes to take in the enormity of the battle.

The RSM advanced, out of Jason and Jock's sight. They had veered left towards the huts. The next human voice they heard screamed, 'Man down, man down.'

Instinctively Jason glanced right. 'Fuck, it's **** [the RSM]. He's hit.'

Jock looked briefly in his direction as well before shouting furiously, 'Fuckin' get on with it, Jase, ye twat, or you'll get a fuckin' bullet as well.'

There was no time for a speech. Jock knew taking casualties was inevitable. It was with no disrespect that the

Scot did not care who was down. There was nothing he could do to help. Some 'localized' A Squadron guys did not even bother looking across; they were spread out too far and wide to see who had been hit on the opposite flank.

Everyone's primary concern had to be winning the battle. Jock had to make sure that Jason, who as a young trooper looked up to the RSM, kept his mind on the job and not the casualty.

The RSM was in agony, having been shot in the calf. It was what troops call a flesh wound, meaning the round nicked him rather than going all the way through his leg. He hobbled in excruciating pain on his other leg, his courageous attempt to push on and increase the attack's momentum having backfired.

As the RSM was the leader of the troops, the CO's right-hand man on the battlefield, his death would have meant restructuring the CO's command structure. That is why he was supposed to stay at the back. He was much more than just another senior NCO, he was the soldiers' father figure, the head of the clan who held a unique position in the Regiment. Now he was trapped in open ground, in such pain he was incapable of moving on his own. It was a race between the SAS soldiers in the RSM's vicinity and the Al Qaeda snipers as to who could get him first.

'Fucking pull him out of there,' screamed one SAS man, struggling to be heard over the sound of the active support weapons on the FSB and the personal weapons of both the SAS and Al Qaeda.

A Kiwi from G Squadron, picked by the RSM to leave the FSB, sprinted from dead ground to his side. Amid shouts of 'Get him into fucking cover', the New Zealander wrapped his arms around his senior colleague as enemy bullets fizzed past them. Taking a second casualty merely indicated the lack of cover and served as a reminder of the danger of advancing across such open ground. While it was not as flat as Iraq, described as 'like a snooker table', there was precious little natural cover around the opium plant. More artificial cover, in the form of smoke grenades, was required.

It was peculiar that the RSM was shot in the calf, raising questions as to which direction he was travelling in when hit, and who shot him. If it was forward, towards Al Qaeda, then it is likely the RSM was shot by one of his own men. For the enemy to have hit him in the calf he would have had to have been running away, and that was definitely not the case.

'Fuck me,' thought Jock, 'two guys down and a shite load of heavy fighting to come around the HQ.'

This was rapidly becoming a serious fire fight, the test of SAS soldiers, young and old, that everyone in the Regiment wanted.

This generation of SAS men had to prove they were as good as their CO believed, as fit, determined and skilled in battle as those who had worn the sandy beret before them. Jock had little sympathy for the RSM, not that the Regimental Sergeant Major would be looking for any, for he knew the chance he was taking as he left the FUP for the front line, via the CO's position and the FSB.

H+2.00 hrs

The SAS was gaining the advantage in this private contest between approximately 200 men who all got one hell of a kick out of fighting. To win its biggest scrap since the Second World War – biggest in terms of men and weaponry on target – would take a lot more warrior spirit and good fortune, especially if they wanted to emerge victorious without suffering heavy losses.

It was the contest Jason and Jock feared they would be

denied. The younger man was growing in stature through the ordeal, his senses on fire, he felt so alive. The pre-operation tension had been so high that now, more than two hours into the battle, its decisive phase provided a dramatic adrenalin rush and came as a huge relief.

They continued to pour forward. To a man, their 'offensive spirit' was coming to the fore; the ultra-confidence brought about by the Regiment's training regime and their abilities as individual soldiers. As the military theorist Clausewitz said of the best soldiers, 'the whole object of his sleeping, eating, drinking and marching is simply that he should fight at the right place and at the right time'.

This was the only place and time in Afghanistan they were going to get a battle. They had to make the most of it. They would have been devastated to miss out on the opportunity to put hundreds of hours of training into practice, even though it meant putting their lives at risk, Al Qaeda having shot at least one of the two wounded SAS men and demonstrating their prowess at hitting moving targets. They were advancing into what is known in military terms as the 'area of breakthrough', running over lifeless bodies, detached limbs, discarded weapons and thousands of bullet cases lying in clusters like rabbit droppings.

The precision of the fire and manoeuvre drills was critical; to move fast enough to stabilize the new line or object of defence, in this case the mud huts. The SAS would then fan out as an expanding torrent of soldiers, exploiting new territory and going in for the kill.

13. DEATH RATTLE

H+2.15 hrs

There were hidden pockets of Al Qaeda resistance dotted around the headquarters, those who abandoned the trenches having taken up new firing positions. The plant finally within reach, Jock and Jason's troop riddled the mud huts with small-arms fire. Prominent among the pillaging horde enclosing the enemy fortress were members of the RSM's party, shorn of their leader. Twenty-five minutes after his fall they remained in the thick of the fighting, advancing deep into Al Qaeda territory under heavy fire.

As the guerrillas' bullets tore up the ground, one man was shot twice through the left knee as he charged forward. The rounds ripped through the muscle and bone and exploded out of the back of his leg. Dropping to the ground, he screamed as blood gushed from the huge wound. 'Man down, man down,' shouted a colleague nearby. The trooper, one of the RSM's party, lay prone to enemy fire, clutching his crippled limb and in excruciating pain. How long before more Al Qaeda rounds found their target? His nearest comrades were pinned down as well. Any rescue attempt would render those running to the G Squadron man just as vulnerable.

Two more of the RSM's soldiers, also G Squadron guys, carried out Operation TRENT's bravest act. They sprinted across the barren ground as Al Qaeda attempted to pick them off with AK47 fire. They grabbed the ex-Para, hauling his arms around their shoulders, and pulled him towards the nearest point of cover. His leg was an appalling sight, blood soaking through his combat trousers and pouring on to the dirty ground. He screamed in agony at the top of his voice.

One man applied direct pressure forcefully to the wound, to restrict further blood loss, as another pulled out his shell dressings, the large square-shaped bandages made of lint and cotton wool. They are so named as they are designed to treat large wounds caused by shell fragmentation.* This moment demonstrated why all SAS men become expert medics.

'Come on, get it in,' said one, seeing the shell dressing being unwrapped and stuffed into the gaping, bloody hole, the bandage immediately swamped with blood. 'Tape him up and get that leg raised,' added another as he ripped through the victim's combat smock. He needed clear access to one of his arms to get a drip into a vein.

With every casualty came the realization that this was a proper fire fight against a more than capable enemy. Back in Hereford, whenever that would be, they could justifiably claim to have had a decent contact; the biggest in 22 SAS's history. But without the Regiment taking casualties, the B and D Squadron guys would dismiss the battle.

H+2.30 hrs

In stark contrast to A Squadron's predicament, life was a breeze at the FSB. As their colleagues fought for their lives a few hundred yards away, some of the troops sat idly

---

* When a man is wounded, soldiers tending to him use his medical kit, not their own.

having a brew – their first since Bagram. Blasé perhaps, but unprofessional it was not. Those brewing up were unable to fire as A Squadron troops and the RSM's party had encroached into their arcs. They were neither under fire nor able to assist those ahead of them. It was one of those lulls when the only weapons fired on the FSB were the Barretts.

A parched Gordon spotted guys on the adjacent Pinkie getting their brew kits out. Excitedly he jumped off the wagon, beckoning Phil to follow. 'Good fuckin effort,' Gordon shouted, adding: 'Mine's NATO standard.'*

He ran to the back of the Pinkie to find his mess tin and burner. As a smile spread across his face at the thought of a mug of sweet tea, he tried again to get Phil involved: 'Come on, mate, we can't do fuck all and I'm bloody thirsty.'

'Nah, you go on. I'm staying put,' was the reply.

Disillusioned, Phil was in no mood for laughing with the rest of the guys. He slumped over his GPMG, staring ahead at the mayhem he so badly wanted to be part of. He had half a mind to grab his personal weapon and join Jason and Jock – that was what the RSM had done after all. The FSB was remarkably quiet; no more US jets screeching through the skies or chorus of pounding .50s. Phil felt restless and alone; a spectator. What did this battle amount to? Firing a GPMG into an empty space as his colleagues went eyeball to eyeball with the enemy. That was it. Not enough to satisfy. 'I might as well be on the range,' Phil thought.

The third casualty had been dragged to a position of relative safety. Eventually he would be carried back to the FSB. He was given an opium-based drug as a pain reliever. To the wounded man in his nauseous state, it felt as though it merely skimmed the surface of his pain. The irony of the situation struck home. 'There's us blowing up an opium

---

* NATO standard tea: white, with one sugar.

plant and what are we giving him? An opiate!' one soldier remarked. An outburst typical of SAS humour in battle.

The injection is believed to have been Omnopon, a drug containing opium alkaloids, morphine and codeine. As the victim had lost so much blood, it was injected intravenously. The drug was diluted and fed into his system gradually.

Fifteen minutes after the third casualty's fall came the fourth. Closing in on the headquarters, another ex-Para who advanced with the RSM was shot twice, in the chest and left wrist. Like Jock, he had opted to wear a ceramic plate as part of his body armour – a life-saving decision. An Al Qaeda 7.62-mm bullet pinged off his chest leaving a strike mark. He was knocked off his feet, but still alive. Jason and Jock were too busy keeping the attack going to think about the four casualties. Neither knew much other than that the third man, ex-Para like them, seemed to be in the worst state.

Although both mud huts had been bludgeoned by SAS fire they could still be occupied. Jason and Jock's task was to work in twos and close in on the nearest one. Whichever pair from their troop got there first would 'go firm,' allowing rear A Squadron elements to advance towards the second hut under covering fire.

H+2.45 hrs

There was one heroic Al Qaeda guerrilla who stuck out at this point. Taller than most of his comrades, lean and bearded as they all were, he was, much to the SAS' amusement, the most animated of the enemy in battle. Jason and Jock watched him darting from trench to trench, retreating as A Squadron took more ground, but seemingly losing none of his appetite for the contest as he did so. Firing his RPG even with the SAS at close range, he typified Al Qaeda in battle, more threatening in spirit than as conventional soldiers. Jock shook his head and could not help but smile.

'The guy is fuckin' crazy, possessed, man; do you know what I mean?'

'He's a twat,' said Jason bluntly, adding, 'He'd be better off grabbing an AK than firing that stupid thing.'

Jason watched him scampering around behind the buildings, motivating his remaining comrades. He seemed to be the enemy's inspiration.

'Look at the rag-head now, Jock.' Al Qaeda's 'cheerleader', as the SAS soldiers referred to him, fired a rocket up in the air and screamed 'Allah Akhbar' at the top of his voice. 'He's a fuckin' nut case.'

'The cocky bastard,' said Jock in a tone conveying that amusement had given way to annoyance. 'He's fuckin' saying we should take him on!'

Amazingly, the Al Qaeda leader was beckoning the SAS to run towards him. 'I've had enough, that fuckin' loony is gonnae get it,' the Scot added angrily.

The cheer-leader was better at ducking shots than firing his RPG and he kept up his routine of calling the SAS forward and screaming praise to Allah for at least half an hour. That he kept missing or that his comrades were being slotted left and right of him never dented his enthusiasm.

'I keep fuckin' missing 'im,' Jock.'

By now Jock was laughing again. 'You know, Jase ... he's so brave they should give him the Al Qaeda MC [Military Cross] when this is all over.' With that they both laughed out loud.

It would have to be a posthumous award as even he was slotted eventually as A Squadron closed in and the pepperpotting continued. Jason screamed, 'Moving,' and jumped to his feet from behind a rock, sprinted forward and dived to the ground. Now static, he shouted, 'Move!' to Jock who replied, 'Moving,' as he got to his feet, with Jason now laying down covering fire. They had got lucky, catching Al Qaeda unawares and gaining 25 metres in a matter of seconds. The enemy must have been changing magazines, or running out of them; barely a shot was fired.

The next pair to advance were not so lucky, rounds whistling past their ankles and ricocheting off rocks behind them as they charged on. They adopted the smallest body positions possible, running forward and keeping their heads down. Those wearing helmets – and by no means all the SAS men were – felt more protected.

H+3.00 hrs

'Right, Jase, that other pair are gonnae go for the first mud hut, we'll cover 'em and try and take the second. OK?'

'Sure, Jock.'

With the sound of Jason and Jock lying down supporting fire behind them, the two leading men ran forward, hunched over their rifles and peppering the hut which already had hundreds of holes in its clay-coloured walls. Could any enemy have survived inside? Highly unlikely; but a wrong assumption might be fatal. They would clear the target then hold it, making the first mud hut a staging post for the HQ assault.

A high-explosive grenade lobbed inside exploded with a huge 'Boom'. One man ran up to the wall and fired through the window. After an internal search for live enemy and booby traps the shout went up, 'Building clear.' Job done; the makeshift SAS FSB was up and running. The first of the opium plant's buildings was SAS territory, reward for over three hours of fighting and heaven knows how many hours in transit before that: 'an empty shithole' as the men recalled. They would 'go firm' there for the remainder of the assault.

'Go, go, go, Jase,' said Jock as the men ahead signalled for them to advance. Their routine would be: bludgeon the position, advance under cover, search and clear. The Regiment would then have two mini-FSBs from which to back up to the RSM's party as it took on the final objective.

Jason ran ahead and threw a grenade through the mud hut entrance, the explosion rocking the building to its foundations. He followed it up with bursts of small-arms fire through the dust clouds, keeping his shots as low to the ground as possible, thinking any surviving Al Qaeda would be lying on the floor.

'On me!' he shouted, beckoning Jock forward; now they both riddled the position with bullets. Jock looked inside, the sight of his rifle tracing across the bloodstained hovel: empty, no need to double-tap anyone. 'Room clear!' shouted Jock. The stench inside was incredible and overpowering, the aroma of human excrement mingling with cordite, horrid to inhale. He wished momentarily he did not have a sense of smell.

There were still Al Qaeda in and around the plant, fighting, while one or two opted to run for it, in doing so providing sport for the FSB snipers. The matchstick men scurrying frantically were opportune targets for the deadeyes, not to be missed. They were slotted and died where they fell, huge Barrett rounds shattering their skulls like water melons.

The Colt M203s were particularly useful in this final stage. The single-shot 40-mm grenades, fired from a barrel beneath the main body of the automatic rifle, exploded on impact around the HQ. They were accurate and easy to use from as far out as 800 metres. The SAS had customized the M203s, fitting reinforced barrels for longer lifespan and high-spec optical sights.

*

H+3.15 hrs

The HQ was a single-storey walled building, similar in size and shape to the warehouses dissected so clinically by the US rocket attack three and a quarter hours earlier. The search had to be conducted with the professionalism that had kept the soldiers alive thus far. Once sealed off, a party of at least four men would pull it apart for any sign of enemy intelligence. This was the only phase of Operation TRENT CENTCOM was interested in. An intelligence cache might justify the operation's huge risk and expense. Easily forgotten, but intelligence-gathering was Operation TRENT's 'official' aim.

Although the sheer force of the SAS's onslaught made it unlikely, it was impossible to ensure that all enemy inside the HQ were dead. The search had to proceed while this remained a risk factor. The immediate area was cordoned off and protected from every angle of possible Al Qaeda retaliation. Points east, west and south of the target were by now cul-de-sacs of SAS firepower, but the slopes of Spot Height 2213 to the north still offered cover for the enemy. A Squadron's troops were alive to the threat of perhaps just one hidden Al Qaeda guerrilla who had kept his head down until now, seeking the satisfaction of killing an infidel at this late stage.

Poised to return any enemy fire, Jason and Jock protected one arc from the second mud hut. As the sun beat down, sweat dripped from Jason's forehead on to his eyelids. He wiped it away with his forearm, taking off the last layer of cam cream with it. He scanned the rear of the HQ for any movement amid the sharp outcrops of rock.

The search team did not have time on their side, a maximum of fifteen minutes, as the CO was wary of the potential risk of Al Qaeda reinforcements arriving on target. Booby traps inside the HQ were a major concern; fleeing enemy might have laid charges linked to trip wires or

strapped explosives to dead comrades which would deto-
nate when the corpse was moved. The search had to be
conducted with speed, but not at the expense of security.

Soldiers from the RSM's party took the lead, all of them
familiar with the drills; the Method of Entry SOPs for room
clearance and the 'Actions On' encountering 'unfriendlies'.
If there was any suspicion a corpse had been rigged, the
SAS soldier would lie on the body then roll over, pulling it
with him, ensuring the enemy acted as a human buffer.

The men rifled through the flat-roofed building and
located the CP (Command Post), the room from which Al
Qaeda operations and the opium plant were run. The admin
centre had windows but no glass in the frames. Like the
mud huts, it stank of body waste and explosives. It had
been trashed, and was now a mess of paperwork.

H+3.30 hrs

Time stood still for Jason and Jock, the latter particularly
uncomfortable while waiting for the search to be completed.
After the slog of the advance to contact, being static and not
shot under fire seemed strange. Jock felt more vulnerable
with apparently no enemy in sight. He did not want to
be caught out. 'Where are the little fuckers hiding?' he
wondered.

'What the fuck are they doin' in there?' said Jason
minutes later, eager like his older 'oppo' to get the job
finished.

'Come on, guys, it's time to get the fuck out of here,'
replied Jock, looking at his watch, his mind racing through
all the worst-case scenarios.

Finally the bounty was uncovered: two lap-tops and a
mass of documents, all of which would have been destroyed
instantly by US air strikes. It would be for the Int Cell back

at HQ Bagram – known by the SAS as 'spooks' – and the CIA to decipher them. The troops put the computers into 'grab sacks' and headed out of the building, as methodically as they had entered it, scanning every room, corridor and corner for enemy.

While the search party went about its business, the CO was thinking two and three steps ahead. As commander he had to manage the next phase of Operation TRENT and this point in the battle was a critical test of his generalship. There was no instruction to hold the target, or any point in doing so; as it was 250 kilometres south-west of Kandahar, where the Taliban were holding out, and of no strategic or tactical importance. With Camp Rhino set up at the same time as Operation TRENT, CENTCOM had its forward-operating base in this corner of Afghanistan. It was of far greater importance that the third casualty was airlifted to a field hospital.

The CO got on the radio and set up an RV with a US CH-47 Chinook helicopter. It would meet an SAS party, including all four casualties, in a position designated safe and sufficiently removed from the Operation TRENT target – another hairy moment as Al Qaeda were perfectly capable of taking out a helicopter with a Stinger or an RPG.

H+3.45 hrs

The CO gave OC A and OC G 'prepare to move' orders which filtered down the chain of command, followed by an immediate order to withdraw. The FUP packed up and it was time for A Squadron and the RSM's party to make the first, exhaustive phase of the exfil on foot, back to the Pinkies, covered all the time by the FSB.

'Right, Jase, let's get the fuck out of here!' shouted Jock, urgency abounding.

'Right, Jock,' replied Jason, adding, 'Where the fuck's our wagon?'

'Fuckin' miles away by the look of it, laddie.'

This was a tactical withdrawal; the soldiers did not just turn around and take a leisurely jog back to their Pinkies. That meant members of A Squadron covering each other and not taking any chances that the Al Qaeda who lay 'dead' on the ground were not clinging to life and still capable of firing a weapon.

Jason and Jock were exhausted, running on adrenalin alone. Jock's legs were stiff, 'maybe this soldiering *is* a young man's game,' he thought as he legged it over the rocky, sandy battleground. The 50 pounds of kit and weapons he carried felt like twice that weight but Jason did not look much sprightlier. There was no let-up in the QBOs (Quick Battle Orders), the NCOs determined to keep the pace of the withdrawal up: 'Fuckin' move it, come on! What are you waiting for?'

Some of the troops got lucky, finding their wagon drivers had pushed up during the assault to put down suppressive fire and hit the particularly troublesome Al Qaeda bunker which had Jason, among others, trapped.

Jason did not want to be beaten back to the wagon by Jock. He drove on, still fired up from the battle and summoning reserves of energy. He saw some troopers getting on any wagon they could find, some ended up with four on board.

Jock issued a warning: 'Think about it, Jase,' he said as he puffed along, weapon in hand, 'We've gottae have at least three guys on each Pinkie to fire the twin Gimpys. Find our wagon if ye can.'

'Sure thing, Jock.' Jason nodded.

'Where is the bastard?' said Jock, who was dying for a smoke and a brew.

'Got 'im,' replied Jason.

'Thank Christ for that,' said Jock, lumbering forward.

H+4.00 hrs

Jock hauled himself into the front seat and said to the driver, who had by now spent four hours stuck on the Pinkie awaiting their return, 'Get us the fuck out of here, will ye?'

Ideally the CO would have wanted to stick to the ground he and his men knew on the exfil. After considering local issues he overruled it. He knew the eastern flank but he did not want the convoy getting stuck in the sand again. The forty-vehicle file would head further west, through the area known as Garmsel, which means 'warm wind'. A Squadron would lead the order of withdrawal, with the Colonel in the centre of the file. The nearest permanently housed local population were situated at Malah Do Kand, a desert outpost 25 kilometres north-east of the target. To the northwest was the Margo Desert and the Nimruz Province, which bordered Helmand. Another reason for heading west was to take the SAS as far away from Malah do Kand as possible, the town being a likely source of Al Qaeda reinforcements.

'Keep fuckin' switched on, Jase,' Jock reminded Jason at least half a dozen times as the wagons bounced over the rocky ground during the 15-kilometre journey to the LZ (Landing Zone). Like the drive from TLZ to target, this was a mobile defensive operation; in other words, the convoy was entirely responsible for its own protection. Again, the outriders on their Honda XR400R and CR250R trail bikes provided a protective or reconnaissance screen around the flanks, front and rear of the column.

The riders, the most vulnerable members of the giant

SAS party, would provide the CO with an indication of enemy strength and intentions if Al Qaeda approached. In terms of mobility the Regiment might have found itself at a disadvantage; Al Qaeda's pick-up trucks were faster and lighter than the Pinkies and Acmacs over the desert terrain. With that in mind, the 'mother ships' were set in the middle of the file and either end of the column was protected by wagons armed with twin GPMGs for rapid and heavy return of fire.

As they left the opium plant behind, Jason and Jock spared a thought for the wounded. When A Squadron had reached their wagons Jock grabbed a word with a guy who had treated one of the casualties during the fire fight. He passed on the news to Jason: 'He says there's not much to worry about with three of 'em, but it's a wee bit worse for ****** [the third casualty], who got hit twice in the knee. Touch and go apparently . . .'

Jason frowned, and could not think what to say. Casualties and fatalities were part and parcel of operations but, that said, the guy was someone he knew from the Parachute Regiment. He realized for the first time how lucky he had been not to get hit.

H+4.30 hrs

Both parties, the SAS and the US Chinook, arrived on time at the LZ from where the four wounded were taken to a US base in northern Pakistan. A 150-kilometre journey lay ahead over the mountains on the border between Afghanistan and Pakistan and the Chagai Hills. The base was also part of the disputed Baluchistan territory and its airstrip, built in the 1930s, was used for both civilian and military air traffic. The area was just as sandy as Garmsel and Registan and, worrying from the casualties' point of view, particularly susceptible to dust storms, which would make landing hazardous.

Although every man remained 'tactical', i.e. in a permanent state of readiness to respond to any Al Qaeda counter-attack, after having successfully completed the RV with the US CH-47 the troops instinctively felt that the battle was finally over and they had won. A sense of relief and euphoria swept through them. The LUP was a further 50 kilometres away from the LZ site. The closer they got to it and the further they were from the target, the better they felt.

Gordon was chuffed with his day's work. There was no doubt the FSB had performed well and personally he felt a huge wave of satisfaction that finally, after eighteen years in the Army, ten of them in the SAS, he had been in a contact and put all that training and preparation to the test. A tremendous weight had been lifted from his shoulders.

'I've done a Dead Reckoning fix,' he shouted, map in hand and turning his head towards Phil, who as usual was doing the driving.

'Yeah? What?'

'Should be at the LUP some time after 17.00 hrs, I reckon. It's pretty flat around here; we're going faster than we were this morning.'

'OK, Gordon. It's all the middle of nowhere, isn't it?'

'Suppose so. The CO's chuffed with us, mate, and the OC. We did a good job there, all of us, did what we had to do . . . and how many fuckin' times have we trained for it? At last! No thanks to the Yanks, eh, Phil, fuckin' hell! What are they like?

Phil agreed. 'Can't fuckin' believe it. Fuckin' amazing that it didn't take out a Pinkie; ours wasn't far away. There would have been hell to pay if they'd have taken some of us out. The boss would have gone spastic for a start; and me.'

The drive continued over similarly sandy and grey terrain towards the LUP. The men were keen to get there as soon as they could. It had been a long day and night before. They were hungry, thirsty and tired. There was only so long they could continue running on adrenalin.

'What does the boss man [OC G] think?' Phil asked, as he continued his fight with the ground to steer the Pinkie in the right direction.

'He's impressed, apparently. Pleased about how we did the job – everyone worked well together, he says. The contact was worth all the hassle getting here. It was a massive operation, mate; we'd have been in the shite if it had gone tits up. Thank fuck it didn't. And no one else has had a fuckin' contact like that out 'ere, 'ave they?'

'True, I suppose,' said Phil, preoccupied.

Gordon just carried on talking. 'What about those twats on the broken-down Pinkie? Ha, ha, how fuckin' pissed off must they be. They'll have to send a heli out for 'em.'

'Yeah, mate,' said Phil, adding, 'They were going mental. Don't blame them. All that fuckin' way, only eight clicks [kms] from the target!'

Thinking about their predicament made Phil realize that perhaps he had not been that unlucky after all. 'Thank fuck we had that contact, Geordie,' he said.

'Too true, mate. That was down to Downing Street, y'know, that fire fight was thanks to them, Phil.'

'The hierarchy have to get something right now and again. Group [UKSF] were still grumpy about the risk factor though.'

'Twats,' said Gordon, adding, 'It was fuckin' worth it. We got a lot of kills too, the sniper team especially. They're claiming twelve apparently.'

'Lucky fuckers,' said Phil. 'What's the point of having us here if we don't get used? That's what it's all about, hitting the baddies.'

Gordon said, 'Yup. Pity A took so fuckin' long gettin' across that flank. Made a meal of it, didn't they?'

H+6.30 hrs

On arrival at the LUP the vehicles would be parked up in a similar defensive formation as they had been in the night before, which after the events of the day, seemed one hell of a long time ago. Gordon was not far off with his map-predicted ETA at the LUP as the convoy arrived at around 17.30 hrs. They were exhausted – not that any of the men was going to show it or admit to it.

Jason and Jock's Pinkie arced around from the LUP's vehicle entry point. Jock had been playing down the contact with Jason, who was buzzing. He wanted him to stay focused on the all-around defensive SOPs that now came into practice. It would have been easy for Jason to switch off, having been in a contact for the first time.

If either of them could have heard Gordon groaning, even jokingly, about A Squadron's performance, they would have punched the Corporal's lights out. Spirits on their Pinkie were running high, back-slapping and bravado abounded, the pair of them having closed with the enemy and emerged victorious.

The wagon pulled up as part of the formation at the LUP, and Jock jumped off to offload some of the kit. They would need camouflage nets to cover the Pinkie that coming night and he was dying for a brew.

'For fuck's sake, let's get this shite sorted and we can have a cuppa tea,' he said, adding, 'Get on with it, Jase.' He need not have worried about Jason switching off though; he was too professional for that to happen.

'No problem, Jock.'

'It was about doin' our job today, Jase, nothing more. We're here to hit people. Simple as that. Don't get too cocky.'

'Me? Cocky?' said Jason, smiling.

'Yeah, you. I'm not saying you didnae do well, ye did; but just think about what might be around the corner. Gottae be ready if we get another one.'

'For sure, Jock.'

'What about **** [the RSM], though, eh, he's gottae be feelin' a wee bit stupid. Should have stayed where he was, at the FUP. He wanted a bit of the action, didn't he?'

'Don't blame 'im, Jock. Wouldn't you if you were stuck where he was?'

'Maybe! Those rag-heads were like a bunch of headless chickens, covered in shite, no problem for us. We didnae need him in there as well.'

H+9.00 hrs

It was important the de-brief took place as soon as possible. The soldiers' accounts would be pulled together to create an official account of Operation TRENT, to be filed at Stirling Lines. The troops were asked to recall the enemy's dress and equipment, calculate the numbers killed, enemy weapons captured and who fired first. Those who had entered the HQ described the documents and intelligence sources found. The CO would later write an in-depth report detailing precisely the target, the enemy's movements, the whereabouts of his forces in relation to Al Qaeda, the progression of the battle and the time it had taken to capture the opium plant.

*

H+22.00 hrs

Most of the guys got a well-earned kip that night, stag-watch commitments aside, and after leaving the LUP the following morning both squadrons received a much needed resupply by RAF Hercules.

Jason and Phil bumped into each other awaiting the resupply of water, ammunition, food and fuel: this was their first meeting since the altercation in the hangar at Bagram.

'I 'eard about the blue on blue,' said Jason, who had been far enough away at the time to find it amusing.

Phil hesitated before answering. Jason was behind him when he started talking and it took him a split second to turn around and realize who it was. 'Jason,' he thought, 'not my favourite person in the world.' But he was a little more philosophical about the fire fight and his role in it having had a night's kip.

'Yeah, bit of a fuck-up,' he responded, smiling as he lifted a metal box full of 7.62-mm for his Pinkie's twin GPMGs. 'Slot anyone, then, Jase?' he added.

'I reckon so. You?'

'Couldn't tell. I was keeping heads down. Making sure they didn't fire many rounds at you.'

'They never fuckin' stopped firin' rounds at me, Phil! All I can remember is gettin' shot at constantly for four fuckin' hours!'

'That's why it took A so long to take that flank, then. You always were a bit slow.'

'Fuck off, Phil,' Jason said half-jokingly. 'I'll tell you what it's like to be in a proper fire fight, over a beer in "H". Feels good, mate.'

'Whenever that is, Jase. Who knows? Couple of weeks' time, maybe?'

'Something like that. Hope we get another scrap before then. At least you weren't on that fuckin' Pinkie that broke down.'

'For sure, Jase.'

'They were fuckin' pissed off, especially when I laughed at 'em when we drove past!'

'That's typical you, typical you. That gob of yours is going to get you chinned.'

As he began to walk away Jason added, 'You know what the only shame is, Phil?'

'No, what?'

'That they weren't bigger fish in the overall battle picture.'

'Oh right, yeah, I suppose. It was still a high-threat enemy target, though, Jase, and the only decent contact anyone's had out here.'

H+24.00 hrs

News was passed down the chain of command from the Colonel that following Operation TRENT's success, CENT-COM wanted the Regiment to carry out further anti-opium operations in the days to come. The bad news for the guys was that these were expected to be unopposed. The troopers in A and G were also told they would be back in Hereford before Christmas.

14. NEWS BREAKS

From dusty Dalbandin, where the third of the four casualties received emergency treatment and his condition was stabilized, the quartet was airlifted to a US base in Germany and finally back to the United Kingdom. Their next port of call was the Centre for Defence Medicine at the Queen Elizabeth Hospital, Selly Oak, Birmingham, a £30 million thirty-six-bed facility which had been opened by the Princess Royal seven months earlier. Surgeons with specialist training in operating on gunshot wounds amputated the third casualty's left leg, below the knee.

The scene of the drama switched from southern Helmand to the House of Commons. Hereford MP Paul Keetch, who as well as being the Regiment's local Member of Parliament was the Liberal Democrat Defence spokesman, was as eager as anyone to hear of his constituents' activities. Being well connected in the Regiment, he did not just have to rely on Geoff Hoon, who gave nothing away under questioning. As always, he stuck rigidly to the Government's stance of non-disclosure of information pertaining to Special Forces operations.

Before a busy Chamber on the afternoon on Monday, 26 November, Keetch asked: 'Given the reports over the weekend about some British casualties in Afghanistan – the Secretary of State will know I spoke to his office about that this morning – is he able to tell the house any more about that?'

Hoon replied: 'As far as casualties are concerned, I will deal with that matter in due course. I can confirm that British forces are on the ground in Afghanistan working alongside United States forces and I will explain a little more about that in due course.'

Yeovil MP David Laws tried again, asking the Secretary of State: 'Will he tell us whether any of the British casualties have been evacuated back to the United Kingdom?' Hoon said they had.

It was quite uncanny, and entirely coincidental, that in the same session the respected Labour backbencher Tam Dalyell asked: 'What guidelines have been given to our forces to try and find the hoards of opium that are said to be in the possession of both the Taliban and the Northern Alliance? Is due account taken of the fact that the farmers will be deciding whether to sow crops of poppy, because it would be highly desirable to give them an incentive to sow something else?' The SAS had certainly done that.

Dalyell's pertinent question put Hoon in a tight spot. What could he possibly say? 'British forces are not there to track down hoards of opium, but they are there to destroy support for terrorism and the Al Qaeda organization, which has extensive involvement in drug smuggling. There is little doubt that in tracking down Al Qaeda and destroying its facilities we will in the process also destroy its ability to supply drugs into this country and elsewhere.'

Within a couple of days of Operation TRENT a fifth SAS soldier was wounded. He was one of the few who had remained in north-west Afghanistan, where the main body of A and G Squadrons were on Operation DETERMINE. The casualty, in his thirties, severely injured his shoulder when his Pinkie skidded off a dirt track. There was nothing unusual about that, but the driver had to take evasive action to avoid being crushed by a US CH-47 Chinook helicopter, thought to have been part of the US Marine Corps, which otherwise would have landed on the Pinkie, killing him and the other SAS men on board. The Chinook was supposed to airlift the victim and his colleagues to assist in a CIA operation. It was similar to the blue on blue on Operation TRENT in that the accident resulted from a communication error between UK and US forces.

The injured SAS man was casevaced back to the United Kingdom. He was too badly hurt to resume regimental duties and months later began legal action seeking damages from the US Defense Department, without his Regiment's support. Predictably, this caused uproar with the MOD and UKSF, which, it seemed, did not want to embarrass or upset the US military by revisiting the incident. The victim sat at home in Hereford planning life in civvy street while his lawyers did battle in Whitehall to get MOD backing.

Paul Keetch MP took up the fight, saying at the time, 'One of my constituents was injured as a result of an accident involving US forces. While it is understandable the MOD do not want to discuss the accident, it cannot deny it took place. It is better to be open and straight-forward in these situations. It would only seem right that if one of our troops was injured, albeit by accident by coalition forces, he should be compensated. The MOD should be supporting his right to adequate compensation, not trying to block it.' A financial settlement was eventually reached late in 2002.

Back in southern Afghanistan, A and G Squadrons patrolled the desolate moonscape of the Margo Desert, the *Dasht-i-Margo*, or 'Desert of Death', hoping against hope for another fire fight. As anticipated the assaults on the smaller opium dens were uneventful. They were 'walk-throughs' – unopposed assaults on what had been until recently Al Qaeda positions.

However, there was to be one further SAS engagement, albeit an entirely unexpected and accidental one.

Three days after Operation TRENT, two fully armed troopers riding motorcycles ahead of an SAS convoy approached a small fort. Intelligence indicated that the Afghans occupying the position in the dusty desert basin were 'friendlies', non-Al Qaeda.

Perhaps nobody had told them that the SAS was paying a visit as the Regiment's outriders came under attack, from small-arms fire from AK47s.

The riders were just a couple of hundred yards from the building. Immediately they swerved into cover and dismounted. In the ensuing fire fight two of the 'friendlies' were killed and the remainder at the fort surrendered to the SAS.

The eyes of the world were upon the United Nations-sponsored peace conference from 27 November in Bonn, Germany, hosted by the UN's Special Representative for Afghanistan, Lakhdar Brahimi. The crucial meeting was attended by twenty-five tribal leaders, and British, French, German, Russian and US diplomats. With Northern Alliance leader Burhanuddin Rabbani refusing to attend, the chances of peace seemed slim. However, Northern Alliance negotiator Younis Qanuni surprised international diplomats, backing the United Nation's draft for a new government without the approval of Rabbani. The elder statesman of Afghan politics, who had self-importantly remained in his Presidential Palace in Kabul, had been sidelined.

The upshot of five days of negotiations was the creation of a six-month interim Government, Hamid Karzai's appointment as Prime Minister, the selection of ministers for the twenty-nine-member Cabinet and arrangements for the international peace-keeping force. The interim Govern-

ment would be replaced by a 'transitional authority' sitting
for two years. Democratic elections are anticipated in 2004.

With the SAS out of action again following Operation
TRENT, next into battle was the MOD which on Wednes-
day, 28 November was granted a High Court injunction
banning the *Sun* from identifying the four wounded SAS
men. As a responsible newspaper, which in the past has
reported the Regiment's actions accurately, the *Sun* would
never have named the four, as its executives insisted, and it
had never done so before. A spokesman for the *Sun* called
the MOD's action 'macabre' and 'appalling'.

The ban applied to the entire media, although legislation
was and remains in place banning the publication of the
identities of serving UKSF personnel. The MOD was taking
the fight to the press, as if to warn off the *Sun* and other
publications from reporting the Regiment's activities. It did
not succeed.

Defending the legal action, a MOD spokesman said: 'We
take the security of our personnel extremely seriously. We
want to be sure security on operations such as this one is
not compromised. There was a worry that the *Sun* and other
newspapers might put the identity of some of them at risk.
This is serious stuff – people have been targeted before
because others have pieced together information about their
identity.'

Denied accurate information by the MOD about the
operation, newspapers were left to make informed guesses
about its nature. Operation TRENT was attracting more
column inches than any SAS operation since the shooting of
the IRA terrorists in Gibraltar – yet virtually all that was
published was wide of the mark.

The assumption was made, understandably, that the
Regiment would be at the cutting edge of Allied ground

operations, not fighting an isolated battle on the other side of the country. That the SAS was in action in Tora Bora, eastern Afghanistan, seemed the best bet as it was also reported that CIA-backed Afghan warlords there were closing in suspected sightings and intelligence reports on bin Laden. The consensus of Fleet Street opinion was that the four SAS men were wounded while 'knife-fighting' in a 'cave battle'.

Tora Bora is approximately 800 kilometres from the Operation TRENT target and the SAS was never anywhere near catching Osama bin Laden. It was as simple as that. The Regiment would, of course, have jumped at the chance of hunting for bin Laden but neither it nor the Americans had the intelligence to get close to him.

There was no mention of an attack on an opium plant near the Pakistan border as, for example, the *Sunday Times* reported on 2 December: 'Two SAS men were wounded before the cave entrance had been reached. Moving in teams of three along the walls, the SAS troopers inched their way through the cave mouth as fire was poured down ahead of them. Four hours later, eighteen Afghans lay dead and four SAS soldiers were wounded. Dozens of terrorists were wounded and captured. The defeated men emerged outside at gunpoint, their hands cuffed behind the back with plastic strips.'

The British public scarcely learnt any more from Hoon's response to written questions submitted by Llew Smith, MP, who, as *Hansard* records, asked:

To the Secretary of State for Defence pursuant to his answers of 26 November 2001, Official Report, column 668 on Afghanistan, if he will provide details of (a) the number of British armed forces casualties suffered to date (b) where, and under what circumstances, the casualties were caused, (c) when the injured personnel were evacu-

ated back to the United Kingdom and (d) what injuries
were suffered; and how many (i) injuries and (ii) deaths
have been caused to allied forces operating in
Afghanistan.

On 5 December Hoon replied:

I can confirm that four British military personnel were
wounded on operations in Afghanistan, one seriously.
They are all now back in UK receiving treatment. An
additional member of the armed forces has also had to
return to UK for medical assessment. I am withholding
further details of the circumstances and the injuries in
accordance with Exemptions 1 and 12 of the Code of
Practice on Access to Government Information. It would
not be appropriate for me to provide information about
the casualties sustained by other coalition members.

The Taliban's five-year rule officially ended on 6 December,
with the fall of Kandahar, its spiritual home and birthplace.
The surrender was signed at interim Government leader
Hamid Karzai's base, north of the city. He pronounced: 'The
Taliban leadership has decided to surrender Kandahar to
me and in return we have offered them amnesty so that
they can go to their homes safe without any trouble. We
only arranged to discuss the transfer of power. In order to
prevent chaos, in order to prevent unnecessary confusion,
the transfer of power will be done in a slow and orderly
manner.'

Taliban spokesman Abdul Salam Zaeff said: 'Mullah
Omar has taken this decision for the welfare of the people,
to avoid casualties and to save the life and dignity of the
Afghans.'

Karzai offered Omar protection in return for him den-
unciating terrorism: 'If he does not, then he will not be safe.

He must make it explicitly clear that terrorism has brutalized Afghan society and destroyed our country. That is our demand. If he does not meet the demand, that means he is party to terrorism, then he must face justice.'

His gambit infuriated President Bush who wanted him brought to justice regardless. As neither Karzai nor Zaeff could find him, the difference of opinion barely mattered. Omar fled, and at the time of writing, remains on the run. An embarrassed Karzai responded: 'Last night was his last chance before the transfer of power. He remains to be committed to his association with terrorism. They [the Taliban] have committed crimes against the Afghan people and against the international community. They must leave my country, and they must face justice, international justice.'

Under General Franks's instructions US forces remained outside Kandahar, waiting for the situation inside the city to, in his words, 'stabilize'. It was the sensibly cautious option – but one which put paid to hopes of catching Omar. Speaking at CENTCOM on 7 December, the sixtieth anniversary of Pearl Harbor, Franks said: 'The situation in Kandahar reminds me of the situation in Mazar-i-Sharif some weeks back. We have seen the surrender of a great many Taliban forces inside Kandahar. We are not yet sure, we do not yet have a sense of comfort that there is stability in the city and I don't expect that we will have a sense of comfort for perhaps two or three days, until we get a valid assessment of exactly what is going on in Kandahar. I will not say that we anticipate the US Marines going in Kandahar.'

Franks was also typically vague about Omar's whereabouts, adding, 'I don't think I would say that Mullah Omar has vanished. I think we've said all along, I think the President said that we'll either bring him to justice or bring justice to him. So that is what I believe about Mullah Omar right now.'

Where was bin Laden? Franks admitted: 'I will tell you honestly, no, I'm not sure where bin Laden is right now.'

Kandahar's fall coincided with the flood of Al Qaeda fighters through Tora Bora into western Pakistan, perhaps with bin Laden among them. With only 1,300 troops in the country, the United States was ill-equipped to cope. It had been shelling Tora Bora since 1 December. By the 5th it had recruited 3,000 locals belonging to warlords Haji Abdul Qadir, Haji Zaman and Hazrat Ali. Stories emerged of some fighters running off with their wad of dollars. It was a farce.

On 9 December, US intelligence detected radio transmissions from Tora Bora caves of a voice believed to be bin Laden's. Did he disappear in the ceasefire which followed in the area? Possibly; but we will never know.

Other intelligence, obtained from Al Qaeda prisoners, pointed to him leaving Afghanistan on 27 November, the eleventh day of Ramadan, when he apparently drank tea with his supporters and told them before fleeing, 'Paradise is on the way. Fight until death.'

By 18 December members of A and G Squadrons were back in 'H'. Many saw the Channel 4 pictures of the Qala-i-Jangi fort uprising which resulted in the deaths of around 400 Taliban. It was the war's most controversial episode and the SAS troops were furious to be accused of shooting at prisoners. The British forces shown on the film, made by an Afghan cameraman, were not, according to my sources, SAS men, as Channel 4 and many newspapers assumed. Typically, the MOD did nothing to refute the reports. The British voices clearly audible on the film must have been either SBS or British Secret Service personnel.

As Amnesty International and left-wing MPs called for an inquiry into the deaths of the Taliban at Qala-i-Jangi, the military operation there was not one the Regiment wanted to be associated with. It was, in the words of one SAS man, 'a one-sided bloodbath, and nothing to do with us'. As the uprising coincided time-wise with Operation TRENT, the Regiment could not have been 'in strength' at two places at once.

Hoon declined to name the British unit involved, preferring to give an overview of events: 'After Taliban fighters held at Qala-i-Jangi fort overpowered their captors and seized armoury, British troops went to the aid of their US colleagues and attempted to recover, under heavy fire, two US personnel apparently captured by Taliban fighters.'

The incident left America mourning its first victim of enemy fire in Afghanistan, CIA agent Johnny 'Mike' Spann. The thirty-two-year-old ex-US Marine was killed attempting to separate local Taliban from foreign fighters, linked to Al Qaeda. The Afghan Talibs had been promised freedom by the Northern Alliance, while the mainly Arab outsiders were heading for the US prison camp, Guantanamo Bay, Cuba.

After killing Spann the prisoners grabbed arms and a battle ensued. The US response was swift. Air strikes over three days reduced the fortress to rubble, in the process injuring five American soldiers who had to be airlifted to US bases in Germany via Uzbekistan. Waves of strafing fire from AC-130 Spectre gun-ships finally ended Taliban resistance while Northern Alliance forces fired mortars. Among the survivors was Californian Talib John Walker Lindh.

Amnesty's request for an inquiry under UN auspices was rejected in London and Washington. Leader of the House of Commons Robin Cook, MP defended Allied actions: 'International law is clear: prisoners' human interests and needs should be respected. However, it is also robust in providing that those who are combatants need not expect to be treated as prisoners of war. The matter for debate is whether the response was appropriate for prisoners who had armed themselves with Kalashnikovs, mortar guns and a tank, in those circumstances, whether it is right to regard them solely as prisoners.'

Amnesty responded: 'The rejection of an inquiry by the United Kingdom into what is apparently the single bloodiest incident of the war, during which serious abuses of international human rights and humanitarian law may have been committed, raises questions about their commitment to the rule of law. By blocking an inquiry the UK Government and others are adding to a suspicion that something seriously untoward took place. A proper investigation could clear the air and potentially offer useful lessons on the question of how best to hold and transport prisoners and also how best to safeguard the lives of both prisoners and prison guards. What can there be to fear from the inquiry except the truth and a clear message that impunity will not be tolerated.'

On 3 January, it was announced that former SAS CO Lieutenant General Cedric Delves would replace RAF Air Marshal Jock Stirrup as the senior British officer at CENTCOM. With his impeccable SF pedigree – he won a DSO in the Falklands War as OC D Squadron before becoming CO 22 SAS in 1986 – Lieutenant General Delves' appointment was seen as symbolic of the war's changing nature; an indication that finally, after the hullabaloo, Allied troops were going to close with Al Qaeda. Of course this was not the case as the SAS had exfiled back to UK, having fought one battle and struggled to get clearance to fight it.

Delves became the highest-ranking non-American at Central Command. Unfortunately the enemy had by then all but disappeared from Afghanistan. Having Delves at CENCTOM three or four months earlier might have helped the two SAS squadrons play a more significant role in Afghanistan.

The Regiment did go on to hunt for Al Qaeda in Yemen

in 2002 and Delves played a part in directing those operations. A US Defense official said: 'I think the fact that you have a three-star Spec-Ops general at the table means the SAS and your other guys are not about to pack up and go home when other countries come into our sights.'

On 13 January 2002, the *News of the World* published the author's first account of the opium plant mission.

15. BACK IN 'H'

Talk of the Regiment's first Victoria Cross (VC) since the Second World War, coming in 22 SAS's Golden Jubilee year,* was in full swing by February 2002; and by the tone of some newspaper articles the award of Her Majesty the Queen's highest gallantry medal was a mere formality. Such expectations were based on ridiculous, fantastical accounts of actions which never took place, dreamt up either in newspaper offices or deep within the MOD. Had members of the Regiment been involved in knife fights against Al Qaeda deep inside Tora Bora's pitch-black caves tracking the world's most wanted man, the award of the VC might have been a certainty.

In such an historic year there was enormous pressure to use the award of VCs not just to recognize actions in Afghanistan but in previous conflicts as well when SAS men with more valid claims for a VC missed out. To some, such a decoration was suitable compensation; others in Hereford

---

* The 22nd Special Air Service Regiment, as it exists today, was formed from the Malay Scouts in 1952. The first 'SAS' unit, known as L Detachment, SAS Brigade, was founded in July 1941 by Lieutenant A. D. Stirling of the Scots Guards in North Africa. Upon founding the unit, the former Ampleforth and Trinity College, Cambridge student became a Captain and eventually a Colonel. He was knighted in 1990. He never married. The Regiment celebrated its fiftieth birthday twice; most recently in 2002.

argued it would cheapen the VC. The Regiment's serving members, back from the world's most inhospitable country and with their Afghan desert tans even more conspicuous than usual in Hereford, knew the truth behind the secrecy, false accounts and propaganda. From senior soldiers, the RSM and the likes of Jock, to fresher-faced young troopers such as Jason and Phil, they knew that tales of hand-to-hand fighting and clashes with knives were figments of the imagination of civil servants and journalists and they did not want a single VC awarded for Operation TRENT.

Since the VC's institution in 1856, 1,354 have been awarded to British and Commonwealth soldiers all by royal assent and presented by the monarch. The 1.375-inch Maltese Cross, sometimes referred to as a 'cross patte', is crafted by the royal jewellers Hancocks and Co., Burlington Gardens, London, from the remains of the bronze cascabels* from two Russian cannons captured at Sebastopol during the Crimean War.

The stipulation for the award of the Victoria Cross is as follows: *'The Cross shall only be awarded for most conspicuous bravery or some daring or pre-eminent act of valour or self-sacrifice or extreme devotion to duty in the presence of the enemy.'* At least three witnesses must provide sworn written statements acknowledging the act, and this should, where possible, include a senior officer.

The first recipients were decorated by Queen Victoria in Hyde Park on 26 June 1857. 'For Valour' is engraved by hand on the front of the medal, which is attached by a suspension bar to the crimson ribbon, while the recipient's name, rank, number, unit and date of the action are etched into the reverse. In July 1877 a VC was awarded for gal-

---

* The cascabel is the knob at the rear of the cannon to which a rope is attached.

lantry in Baluchistan, where the SAS had fought, to Captain
Scott of the Bengal Staff Corps

As media pressure intensified to award the VC for
these 'daring exploits in the caves', the author wrote a
piece for the *News of the World* on 3 February 2002, head-
lined: 'SAS: Keep your VCs'. The report quoted an SAS
source who explained how the soldiers on Operation
TRENT were stunned by the furore, the false accounts and
all the hype about medals. He noted: 'Our four-hour fire
fight couldn't have gone much better' and 'we didn't lose
a man'. These are two important points since VCs tend to
be awarded posthumously – as an act, or series of acts,
genuinely worthy of a VC are likely to be a soldier's last –
or when such a staggering act has dramatically swung a
battle in favour of the recipient's unit, allowing it to pluck
victory from the 'jaws of defeat', as it were. He added: 'We
all think it is very important that the Victoria Cross is not
devalued in any way and we believe it would be if one
was awarded in this case. The VC should not become a
political award.'

As if being wounded, and some colleagues questioning
his actions at the opium plant, was not a sufficient burden
for the RSM to carry, the *Mail on Sunday* published over the
course of 2002 a number of inaccurate articles about him.
On 24 March its front page headline screamed: 'Secret VC
for Hero of SAS Cave Battle' and its opening paragraph
read: 'An SAS hero is to be secretly awarded the Victoria
Cross for amazing bravery in Afghanistan. He is the first
living recipient of the VC for thirty-three years. The soldier,
a Regimental Sergeant Major whose name will never be
made public, continued fighting Al Qaeda terrorists despite
being shot.

'He was part of a ninety-strong SAS force which, outnumbered two-to-one, won what became known as the
Battle of the Caves in an Al Qaeda hideout in the White

Mountains. The vicious fighting involved hand-to-hand combat and the entire enemy were either killed or captured.'

If, as the *Mail on Sunday* suggested, the RSM was to be awarded, or had even been nominated for a VC, he would have been hugely embarrassed and unable to live it down. Back in the real world, it had been the RSM's decision to leave the FUP and head for the front line; his actions were not to remedy a dire situation, it was a personal choice made when the Regiment was winning the battle. As Jock suggested at the time, 'He couldnae resist it.'

In the Regiment a soldier may get a slap on the back and a beer, if he is extremely fortunate, for displaying notable valour, whether wounded or not. Gong hunting is a major *faux pas* in Hereford, and seldom done. Clichéd as it no doubt sounds, SAS soldiers do not look to Whitehall for praise or reward. Earning and maintaining their fellow soldiers' respect is what they aspire to. Any lack of humility is frowned upon. It came as no surprise to the SAS community that the media got it so wrong. The vast majority of soldiers past and present share a pretty low opinion of the press. The Vice-President of the SAS Regimental Association, and former member of 16 Troop (D Squadron's Air Troop) told the author in no uncertain terms: 'Journalists are an anathema to soldiers.' His attitude is the norm and the 2002 UKSF Unauthorized Disclosure Policy Review (covered in detail in the following chapter), described media speculation about the regiment as 'increasingly pernicious'.

The RSM was particularly angry that newspapers printed exact details about his family status and 'door-stepped' him, to use the Fleet Street vernacular, seeking an interview with him at his home. As far as the SAS was concerned, the media had overstepped the mark, jeopardizing the security of one of its soldiers. This incident was also condemned by the DA-Notice Committee, the joint media and MOD body which oversees reporting on the military and security services. As a result of media reports surrounding the issue of SF gallantry awards, 'serious measures had to be taken to enhance the security of them and their families. There had also been an emotional impact, on the families in particular,' the Committee reported. The minutes of the DA-Notice Committee's November meeting added: 'The Ministry of Defence representative returned to the problems caused after the announcement of SF gallantry awards, by the publication of sufficient details of two of those decorated for them to be easily identified by hostile intelligence.'

In October 2002, almost a year after Operation TRENT, it finally became clear that no VCs would be awarded. Having told tales of derring-do, so great that only VCs would be sufficient reward for the participants, the press had little choice but to suggest that members of the SAS had been cruelly denied their merited decorations.

On 29 October the *Daily Telegraph* suggested: 'The lack of a VC will be seen by members of the SAS and SBS as evidence that whatever they do they are unlikely to receive the highest award for gallantry.' The newspaper added: 'The servicemen involved were warned earlier this year that they would not be receiving the VC despite the fact that their deeds clearly qualified under any sensible interpretation of the criteria.'

There was no fanfare for the awards the SAS did receive for Operation TRENT and other operations elsewhere. The decorations were squeezed in at the bottom of a list of awards for members of the Armed Forces from the period 1 October 2001 to 21 March 2002, for 'services in Northern Ireland, the former Yugoslavia, Sierra Leone, the Gulf, the Congo, Georgia, at Sea and Afghanistan'. All recipients from non-UKSF units were named and ranked. The last paragraph of the MOD's announcement read: 'In addition the following awards are announced for gallantry and distinguished service between 1 October and 31 March 2002: 1×DSO, 1×CBE, 2×MBE, 4×CGC, 2×GM, 5×MC, 3×DFC, 8×MID and 8 QCVS.' There were no names of service personnel. The units covered in this anonymous section were the SAS, SBS and the RAF's 7 and 47 Squadrons based at RAF Lyneham who work with UKSF. These awards were not just for Operation TRENT but were won by all those units over that six-month period and may not all have been for actions in Afghanistan.

The absence of a VC was welcomed. Paul Keetch, MP said: 'A sigh of relief was certainly blown in Hereford. Such an award would have devalued the VC and caused uproar in the Regiment. Some members of Government would have enjoyed the prestige of such a medal; the action did not merit it. We must be thankful the SAS, UKSF and the Ministry of Defence stood firm.'

The main awards for the SAS on Operation TRENT were two CGCs, a DSO, two MCs and a number of MIDs. The CGC is second only to the VC in the order of medals for courage. Instituted in October 1993, it was first awarded in 1995 to Corporal Wayne Mills of the Duke of Wellington's Regiment for his actions in Bosnia as part of the United Nations' Peacekeeping Force. It consists of a silver cross, with the royal crown in the middle, imposed on a circular laurel wreath.

The DSO medal, a white and gold cross with the royal crown set against a red background and surrounded by a laurel wreath, is given to officers in recognition of outstanding command in battle and under enemy fire. The MC, awarded for exemplary gallantry and command on the operation, is an ornamental cross with broad finials, hanging from a white ribbon with a vertical purple strip.

Just a few days short of Operation TRENT's first anniversary, 21 November 2002, Her Majesty The Queen and Prince Philip visited Stirling Lines, meeting soldiers who fought at the opium plant and their families. SAS children attending local schools were given the day off to attend. The Queen's visit marked her Golden Jubilee and the 22 SAS's fiftieth birthday. On what was her first visit to the new barracks she unveiled a plaque marking the SAS's new aquatic centre's official opening. Her Majesty was one of many royals, most memorably the Prince and Princess of Wales, who enjoyed trips to the old Stirling Lines, just off the A49 Ross road on the other side of Hereford. Soon after the Iranian Embassy siege in 1980, Princess Diana's blonde hair was singed by live rounds in a shooting demonstration at the 'Killing House'.

Another article by the *Mail on Sunday* on 15 December 2002 caused dismay, as it claimed: 'An SAS hero is quitting the crack Regiment because his commanding officer accepted a military honour for bravery after he modestly turned one down.'

The newspaper got the CO's decoration wrong, suggesting he was to receive a CGC, not a DSO. The DSO is a command, rather than a bravery award. Though the RSM and CO had fallen out, the RSM was due to leave the Regiment anyway, at the end of his two-year stint in that role and having been commissioned. His decision to leave had nothing to do with the CO's award. The *Mail on Sunday* clung to its 'account' of the SAS's battle in Afghanistan, saying: 'The Sergeant Major was hurled to the ground after being shot but, wedging his back against a cave wall, he rose to his feet and continued firing at the enemy with blood pouring from his wounds. The SAS man then hobbled into the thick of battle, drawing his 9-inch knife and, as his men ran out of ammunition, he led them into hand-to-hand combat with the enemy.'

As serving soldiers, neither the CO nor the RSM was in a position to right the wrongs and though the CO had his critics he was, overall, a respected commander of the SAS.

Glory-hunting is simply not in his nature. The MOD's single contribution was its frequently trotted-out line: 'We never comment about our Special Forces.' If only it did. Paul Keetch, MP, who knew both men, said: 'The point about the *Mail on Sunday* is it has been creating stories about the Regiment which have little factual back-up in order to sell newspapers. Also, from talking to people involved in the fighting, which undoubtedly was fearsome, I heard nothing to suggest the VC would have been the right medal to award.

'The action of certain newspapers in sanctioning the door-stepping of members of the Regiment was deplorable. While newspapers and journalists may claim to have the welfare of the British Armed Forces at heart, this was a disgraceful breach of the SAS's entitlement to security.'

Major Anders Lassen is the only SAS man to have won the VC. A Danish officer who joined the British Army at the outbreak of the Second World War, he served in 1 SAS, which became part of the Special Boat Squadron – the forerunner of today's Special Boat Service (SBS). Lassen was killed at Lake Commachio, northern Italy on 9 April 1945, by which time he had been awarded an MC and two bars, signifying a staggering three acts worthy of the medal.

A brief assessment of Lassen's VC winning endeavours, those of the few SAS to have subsequently missed out, and accounts of the last two recipients of the VC indicate why the medal was not awarded after Operation TRENT. Although the distribution of gallantry medals is never entirely meritocratic, there was a huge gulf between Lassen's quite staggering actions and those of anyone in Afghanistan. Lassen was an eccentric, innovative and heroic soldier who surprised those who fought alongside him with his skills and ideas. On Commando training in Scotland he caught a stag single-handed before killing it with a knife.

Lassen even wrote a paper for the War Office advocating the use of a seemingly outdated weapon in guerrilla warfare, which he used expertly – the bow and arrow. Lassen fought with the SAS and SBS in the Adriatic, mainland Greece and Italy in 1943–4. He met his end shortly before the conclusion of the Second World War. The mission at Lake Commachio was to destroy a number of German pillboxes.

His citation read:

Major Lassen himself then attacked with grenades, and annihilated the first position containing four Germans and two machine-guns. Ignoring the hail of bullets sweeping the road from three enemy positions, an additional one having come into action from 300 yards down the road, he raced forward to engage the second position under covering fire from the remainder of the force.

Throwing in more grenades, he silenced this position, which was then overrun by his patrol. Two enemies were killed, two captured, and two more machine-guns silenced. By this time the force had suffered casualties and its fire power was very considerably reduced. Still under a very heavy cone of fire Major Lassen rallied and reorganized his force and brought his fire to bear on the third position. Moving forward himself, he flung in more grenades which produced a cry of 'Kamerad' – surrender. He then went forward to within three or four yards of the position to order the enemy outside to take their surrender. Whilst shouting to them to come out he was hit by a burst of spandau fire from the left of the position and he fell mortally wounded, but even whilst falling he flung a grenade, wounding some of the occupants, and enabling his patrol to dash in and capture this final position.

Major Lassen refused to be evacuated as he said it would impede the withdrawal and endanger further lives, and as ammunition was nearly exhausted the force had to withdraw. By his magnificent leadership and complete disregard for his personal safety Major Lassen had, in the face of overwhelming superiority, achieved his objectives. Three positions were wiped out, accounting for six machine-guns, killing eight and wounding others of the enemy and two prisoners were taken. The high sense of devotion to duty, and the esteem in which he was held by the men he led, enabled Major Lassen to carry out all the tasks he had been given with complete success.

Since World War Two, a handful of SAS soldiers have missed a VC by a whisker. Perhaps the men most unfortunate in this regard were Captain Mike Kealy (see p. 70), who led the Regiment's force, known as the BATT team (British Army Training Team), at the Battle of Mirbat on 19 July 1972, and one of his men, the Herculean soldier from the Southern Seas and SAS legend, Labalaba. If the war in Oman had not been so secret, the pair might both have received VCs. In his autobiography, *Looking for Trouble*, General Sir Peter de la Billière – Kealy's CO at the time – pointed out why he was so unlucky:

> When I myself went out to Mirbat soon after the battle and spent a night in the BATT house, I realized all the more clearly that Kealy's own conduct had been beyond praise. I should have liked to recommend him for the Victoria Cross, but this was politically impossible, for a VC would have attracted far too much attention and publicized our presence in Oman to an unacceptable degree.

At the time of the Battle at Mirbat, B Squadron had been in Oman for three months and G Squadron was to replace them on the day the eight soldiers, led by Kealy, were attacked. A force of around 300 *Adoo* approached the BATT house position near Mirbat. Ridiculously outnumbered, their chances of survival hinged on the fort's 25-pounder gun which, incredibly, the huge Fijian Labalaba kept firing and loading alone despite having his jaw shot off. Such was the nature of the man, that Laba made light of his injury, telling Kealy over the radio in his matter-of-fact way: 'Enemy now very close, I've been chinned but I'm all right.'

Kealy, Trooper Tobin, 'T', another Fijian trooper (his identity is known to the author but I have chosen not to name him), and Omani soldier Walid Khalfan ran to support Laba from their positions, running hundreds of yards across open ground in range of *Adoo* fire. 'T' was shot in the back but survived, Laba was shot again, this time in the neck, and died of his injuries. Tobin, who ran forward to give medical assistance to 'T', also died. Kealy had radioed for support before running from the fort to the gun, and finally 22 G Squadron troops arrived by helicopter from Salalah and the rebels retreated.

The SAS killed thirty-eight *Adoo*. Kealy was awarded the DSO, Trooper Tobin a posthumous Military Medal, Trooper 'T' a Military Medal, and Labalaba a mere posthumous MID. With a handful of local fighters they had held out against an attacking force almost ten times their size. Until 1977, only the VC and the MID could be awarded posthumously; that stopped Laba being given a higher award. He missed a VC for the same reason as Kealy and no announcement was made about the Mirbat medals until 1976. In the view of many of today's SAS men, if there was to have been an award of a VC to mark the Regiment's fiftieth anniversary, Laba would have been the most worthy candidate, not the RSM or anyone else on Operation TRENT.

Three of the four wounded soldiers on Operation TRENT were former members of the Parachute Regiment. This comes as no surprise as the two most recent recipients of the VC, awarded posthumously after the Falklands War, were also paratroopers. Lieutenant Colonel Herbert 'H' Jones, CO 2 PARA, was killed during the monumental battle at Goose Green on 28 May 1982. Sergeant Ian John McKay, of 3 PARA, died on Mount Longdon on the night of 11/12 of June.

Once again, the bravery of these men surpassed any act in Afghanistan. Lieutenant Colonel Jones's citation, which appeared, in accordance with tradition, in the *London Gazette*, on 11 October 1982, read:

> During the attack against an enemy who was well dug in with mutually supporting positions sited in depth, the Battalion was held up just south of Darwin by a particularly well-prepared and resilient enemy position of at least eleven trenches on an important ridge. A number of casualties were received.
>
> Colonel Jones encouraged the direction of his Battalion mortar fire, in an effort to neutralise the enemy positions. However, these had been well prepared and continued to pour effective fire onto the Battalion advance, which by now held up for over an hour and under increasing heavy artillery fire, was in danger of faltering. Colonel Jones immediately seized a sub-machine-gun, and, calling on those around him and with total disregard for his own safety, charged the nearest enemy position.
>
> This action exposed him to fire from a number of trenches. As he charged up a short slope at the enemy position he was seen to fall and roll backward downhill. He immediately picked himself up and again charged the enemy trench, firing his sub-machine-gun and seemingly oblivious to the intense fire directed at him. He was hit by fire from another trench which he outflanked, and fell dying only a few feet from the enemy he had assaulted. The devastating display of courage by Colonel Jones had completely undermined their will to fight further.

Sergeant McKay's actions were equally heroic. He sacrificed his life for others and ensured the success of the battle.
From his citation:

> Sergeant McKay was platoon sergeant of 4 Platoon, B
> Company, which after initial objectives had been secured,
> was ordered to clear the Northern side of the long East/
> West ridge feature, held by the enemy in depth, with
> strong, mutually-supporting positions.
>
> The enemy fire was still both heavy and accurate, and
> the position of the platoons was becoming increasingly
> hazardous. Taking Sergeant McKay, a Corporal and a few
> others, and covered by supporting machine-gun fire, the
> Platoon Commander moved forward to reconnoitre the
> enemy positions but was hit by a bullet in the leg, and
> command devolved upon Sergeant McKay.
>
> It was clear that instant action was needed if the
> advance was not to falter and increasing casualties to
> ensue. Sergeant McKay decided to convert his reconnais-
> sance into an attack in order to eliminate the enemy
> positions. He was in no doubt of the strength and deploy-
> ment of the enemy as he undertook this attack. He issued
> orders, and taking three men with him, broke cover and
> charged the enemy position. The assault was met with a
> hail of fire. The Corporal was seriously wounded, a
> Private killed and another wounded.
>
> Despite these losses Sergeant McKay, with complete
> disregard for his own safety, continued to charge the
> enemy position alone. On reaching it he despatched the
> enemy with grenades, thereby relieving the position of
> beleaguered 4 and 5 Platoons who were now able to
> redeploy with relative safety. Sergeant McKay however
> was killed at the moment of victory, his body falling on
> the bunker. Without doubt Sergeant McKay's action
> retrieved a most dangerous situation and was instrumen-
> tal in ensuring the success of the attack. His was a coolly
> calculated act, the dangers of which must have been too

apparent to him beforehand. Undeterred he performed
with outstanding selflessness, perseverance and courage.'

At no point during Operation TRENT was the degree of
sacrifice displayed by Lieutenant Colonel Jones or Sergeant
McKay required for the battle to be won. Lieutenant Colonel
Jones's battalion were outnumbered by Argentine forces at
Goose Green, whereas the SAS had at least a 2:1 advantage
against Al Qaeda. The SAS also had a fearsome array of hi-
spec weaponry whereas the rag-heads were merely armed
with AK47s and RPG7s. While the bravery of the RSM and
others at the opium plant was commendable, their actions
were seen in Hereford in the context of the battle and the
odds, which were strongly in its favour.

The media also suggested in October 2002 that SAS men
had been denied VCs in Afghanistan because there was no
'conclusive proof' of their actions as the warrant for the
medal stipulates. As the two squadrons were together on
Operation TRENT this was simply not the case. All the
men's actions were judged on their own merits.

16. POST-OPERATION ANALYSIS

Operation TRENT's aims had been fourfold: destroy the enemy and its opium, establish a presence in its territory, and recover intelligence from its headquarters. Although denied 'optimum military effectiveness' by strategic disadvantages such as the setting of 'H-hour' at 11.00 hrs and the immediacy of the operation ruling out CTRs and OPs, the SAS still achieved these objectives.

The enemy on target was destroyed, as many as forty Al Qaeda killed in the fire fight and more by the Regiment's mortar teams and the US air strikes. An unknown number of 'runners' escaped the carnage. The SAS did not hang around the target counting the dead bodies, so this estimate is based on accounts of those on the FSB and advancing on foot. A huge quantity of opium was destroyed, denying Al Qaeda, the Taliban and drug dealers a share of tens of millions of pounds.

Such a brutal and clinically executed attack did indeed establish a presence in Al Qaeda territory; a short-lived one but sufficient to ensure the smaller-scale assaults on other opium dens that followed were unopposed. Intelligence was also recovered in the form of lap-tops, maps and documents, though the value of these materials in the war against terror remains unclear. Does that make Operation TRENT a success? Does it justify the huge logistical operation, four wounded SAS and all the risks involved? Not necessarily.

One must judge the mission against Operation ENDURING FREEDOM and Operation VERITAS* criteria.

President Bush had made his primary war aim crystal clear: bin Laden, 'dead or alive'. As a non-military man he failed to appreciate the importance of setting operational objectives appropriate to the means available to ensure their attainment – i.e. the required manpower, weaponry, time and logistical support. One should credit CENTCOM chief Franks who, under huge political and public pressure to find bin Laden, opposed his President's position. He was criticized for saying, 'We have not said Osama bin Laden is a target of this effort'. Franks knew bin Laden was the ultimate prize but also what was and what was not possible militarily. Bush, it seemed, did not. As far as Franks was concerned, Operation ENDURING FREEDOM was about: 'the destruction of the Al Qaeda network, as well as the Taliban that provide harbour to bin Laden and Al Qaeda' which was far more realistic.

When Franks said 'we' he was speaking for the US military community, the men on the ground, not the politicians in Washington. With the White House dead set against a large-scale US military presence in Afghanistan, Franks was never given the tools for the job, the 'boots on the ground' to cut off the Al Qaeda leader's escape routes.

Like Bush, the MOD put bin Laden's capture top of the list of Operation VERITAS's 'campaign objectives':

(a) to bring OBL and other Al Qaeda leaders to justice; (b) to prevent OBL and the Al Qaeda network from posing a continuing terrorist threat; (c) to this end to ensure that Afghanistan ceases to harbour and sustain international terrorism and enables us to verify that terrorist training has ceased and that the camps where

* Operation VERITAS was the name given by the MOD for British operations in Afghanistan.

terrorists train have been destroyed; (d) assuming that Mullah Omar will not comply with the US ultimatum we require sufficient change in the leadership to ensure that Afghanistan's links to international terrorism are broken.

As Operation VERITAS set out to bring bin Laden to 'justice' and, at the time of writing he is still at large, the Operation was therefore a failure. Apart from killing around forty hardcore Al Qaeda, which air strikes alone could have accomplished, it is difficult to see what Operation TRENT contributed towards Operation ENDURING FREEDOM. CENTCOM was aware that the SAS's sole mission would not further its main cause – as the Regiment knew as well – hence A and G Squadrons were only given an hour's top cover and at such a peculiar hour. Operation TRENT appears almost objective-less from CENTCOM's perspective and does not fit in with Operation VERITAS's agenda either.

At least by destroying the opium – estimated street value £50 million – the SAS made a valuable contribution to the war against drugs. Opium production was one of Afghanistan's few industries to prosper during the Soviet occupation and in the civil war that followed. The country became the world's leading producer, overtaking Burma, Laos and Thailand. By the year 2000, Afghanistan accounted for 72 per cent of the world's illicit opium crop, producing 3,656 metric tonnes for exportation. The following year opium production fell to just 185 tonnes – UNODCCP (United Nations Office for Drug Control and Crime Prevention) figures – as it appeared the Taliban was finally enforcing its own ban on opium cultivation, bowing to huge international pressure.

Or was it? The Taliban switched from producing opium to hoarding it, in enormous quantities at plants such as the SAS's target, which was one of Afghanistan's largest drug-storage facilities. Al Qaeda's best troops were stationed there to protect the harvest. As 'hardcore' Al Qaeda were used, one can make the direct link between the terrorist organization and global narcotic trafficking.

Although only 10 per cent of its land was open to cultivation, Helmand, named after the 1,130-kilometre river flowing south-west through the province, was still Afghanistan's largest opium producer. Since 1993, opium production in Helmand had risen by 800 per cent.

Weeks before CENTCOM approved Operation TRENT, US Drug Enforcement Agency chief Asa Hutchinson told Congress: 'Due to warfare-induced decimation of the country's economic infrastructure, narcotics are the primary source of income in Afghanistan, a country dependent on agricultural production where opium is the most popular cash crop.

'The relationship between the Taliban and bin Laden is believed to have flourished in large part due to the Taliban's substantial reliance on the opium trade as a source of organizational revenue. While the activities of the entities do not always follow the same trajectory, we know that drugs and terror frequently share the common ground of geography, money and violence. The sanctuary enjoyed by bin Laden was based on the Taliban's support for the drug trade, which is the primary source of income in Afghanistan.'

Eighty per cent of heroin in Britain in 2001 originated from Afghanistan and it paid for tens of thousands of weapons. There seemed to be some political will to do something about it, as Tony Blair told the House of Commons in September 2001: 'The arms the Taliban are buying today are paid for with the lives of young British people buying their drugs on British streets. That is another part of the regime we should seek to destroy.'

This was more of a gesture than a commitment to stamp out opium production, however; not enough has been done to this end following the fall of the Taliban to suggest that stopping heroin exportation was a primary concern. Tackling drugs was buried in the small print of the MOD's campaign objectives document released at the beginning of hostilities. The priorities have already been quoted, its wider objectives were:

(a) to do everything possible to eliminate the threat posed by international terrorism; (b) to deter states from supporting, harbouring or acting complicitly with international terrorist groups; (c) reintegration of Afghanistan as a responsible member of the international community and an end to its self-imposed isolation.

Only later does it mention: 'Reconstruction of Afghanistan could take 5–10 years to complete. Only sustained international development effort has any chance of ridding Afghanistan of heroin and the domination of warlords.'

Opium production rose eighteen-fold following Mohammed Karzai's inauguration, rising from 185 tonnes in 2001 to 3,400 tonnes in 2002. This was despite tens of millions of pounds being donated to Afghan farmers to compensate them for the supposed lack of their opium crop – a move defeated by fraud as farmers exaggerated the size of their land holdings. Helmand was once more among the most productive provinces.

There was more of a point to the Regiment's hearts-and-minds programme, post-Operation TRENT, when rice and flour were distributed to needy 'friendlies'. There remains dreadful poverty in Helmand and hundreds of thousands of people still owe their existence to UN food and water distribution programmes. Operation TRENT coincided with a drought, which brought the Helmand River down to a sixth of its normal level, explaining the dried-out stream beds which the SAS troops dived into for cover from enemy

fire and view. The Mercy Corps, an NGO, went into the
province just weeks after the SAS attack and its spokesman,
Scott Heider, reported: 'People in Kandahar are trying to
get on with life, but in Helmand the situation is much
worse. People there need pretty much everything, and we
are currently assessing the situation to prioritize those
needs. Our people were shocked at the conditions these
people were forced to live in.'

So who or what benefited most from Operation TRENT?
The SAS, quite simply, which got the fire fight its troops
and the CO wanted so desperately. That the White House
and CENTCOM were persuaded to facilitate it can be
interpreted in one of two ways: either as testament to
London and Washington's 'special relationship', and an
indication of the Regiment's remarkable political clout on
both sides of the Atlantic, or that British units, Special Forces
even, are so peripheral to 'US military think' that its commanders do not mind if they set their own agenda.

Either way, two full squadrons engaged the enemy, fired
their weapons in anger and were shot at; experiences to
serve all those present well on future operations. The longer
the fight lasted, the less sophisticated it became and the
more the danger of the Regiment losing soldiers increased.
With A Squadron and the RSM's party directly on target,
this phase of Operation TRENT was an old-fashioned infantry battle, soldiers firing in close proximity, primarily with
small arms.

The US air strikes and the awesome array of firepower
on the FSB were no longer factors. Those guns were silent.
It was as even a contest as the war could have thrown up –
precisely the scenario the SAS was after and what the
United States was avoiding: putting troops in situations
where no technological advantages came into play. In vir-

tual isolation, the SAS and its enemy fought an extremely aggressive private contest for survival and the glory of victory; the same offensive spirit driving the SAS forward and encouraging Al Qaeda to hold ground. Stripped to the core, Operation TRENT was a scrap between approximately 200 men who all got a huge kick out of fighting.

The experiences of Jason and Jock were in stark contrast to those of Gordon and Phil. Studies of infantry battles have concluded that only 10–15 per cent of soldiers actually close with the enemy and fight. Jason and Jock both did so, although neither really came face to face with Al Qaeda, and there was no hand-to-hand fighting on Operation TRENT. Jason and Jock got their kills at a range of approximately 50–200 metres. In any given combat situation the majority of soldiers merely put down harassing fire and do not see the enemy. Gordon fired his GPMG in the direction of Al Qaeda trenches, which gave him great satisfaction, but Phil had the worst of it, firing into an empty arc to keep it clear. Jock returned to 'H' quietly satisfied, but Operation TRENT was for him a 'passing satisfaction'. Jason felt 10 feet tall, as he had experienced combat, performed well under fire and felt his senior colleagues respected him for it. Gordon was relieved, and Phil disillusioned that the contact had not provided the thrills he anticipated.

The post-op de-briefs assessed the battle plan's merits, and what went wrong and right, with a view towards eradicating mistakes. There were both formal and informal de-briefs at squadron and troop level, and A and G Squadrons also received an overview of Operation TRENT by the CO. It had been a four-phase mission (Phase Five, the withdrawal, is not considered technically as one of the battle-plan phases), lasting some forty-five hours, from when the HALO team left Bagram to the CO giving the immediate order to withdraw from the target. The basic plan – to establish static FSB in support of infantry advancing from the flank – worked well. Considering the geography, lack of cover, and the Al Qaeda bunkers, A Squadron's advance to contact was skilfully and bravely executed.

The plan to dovetail A and G Squadrons' attack with the US air strikes, requiring precise timing and co-ordination, was, in the absence of a CTR, extremely difficult. Due to the soft sand, the SAS had very little time to spare.

The proximity of the US fire to the FSB was RHQ's biggest issue to chew over. Why were the US pilots not made aware of G Squadron's advance? Why were the US Navy F/A-18s not using LTM (Laser Target Marking), which would have provided more accurate fire? These were grave errors. The Regiment and the US Navy got away with it, but they may not be as fortunate next time. SAS troopers claimed later that such was the low priority the United States gave Operation TRENT, the Hornets with activated LTM were prioritized on other bombing missions.

Sufficient time had been 'factored in' to the length of journey predictions to cope with an incident such as the broken-down Pinkie. Good planning also ensured the squadrons took all their firepower with them in case a wagon or two dropped out. One vehicle out of forty breaking down was not considered too bad a record. Those armed with twin GPMGs, being the most effective weapons on target, were at a premium. Back in Hereford, the squadrons were given new Pinkies.

That four casualties were taken on the advance to contact was non-contentious for the CO and his men, their uncompromising attitude towards combat being what it is. They expect casualties, as if a fire fight without casualties or fatalities is not really a fire fight at all. When the Colonel pulled the Regiment together back in the United Kingdom, he made his position clear. Casualties and the risk of death

were, he told them, 'the price the SAS has to pay for being
at the forefront of operations worldwide'.

Bravado aside, the SAS being so small it cannot afford
to lose too many men, something the UKSF top brass gave
more thought to. SAS personnel are trained at huge public
expense primarily for anti-terrorist, reconnaissance, small-
scale search and destroy missions – not full-frontal offensives carrying a greater risk of casualties. UKSF's view is
that there are too few SAS soldiers for the Regiment to
engage in conflicts or contacts of attrition, which is fair
enough and explains why the CO was, I understand, 'ticked
off' by those above him for spending 'too long' on the
target.

That the RSM was wounded was a point of contention.
Many of the men, like Jock, suggested he should not have
been at the front, RHQ personnel being supposed to remain
out of the way when the bullets are flying. This point was
alluded to by Gulf War RSM Peter Ratcliffe in his memoir,
Eye of the Storm. He recalled the DSF's reaction to finding
out he had been ordered behind Iraqi lines in 1991:

> RHQ passed on to me the response in London to my
> having been sent into action. The Director of Special
> Forces, a very jovial brigadier, had refused to believe the
> report given to him by the ops room in London. The
> Director was a real character, a genuinely funny man
> who was both very gregarious and extremely good com-
> pany. 'You must be fucking joking,' was his first com-
> ment to the ops officer. 'The RSM's role in war is ammo
> and POWs. What the hell are you talking about?' So far
> as I could gather, when his ops officer insisted that I had
> indeed been sent into Iraq to take over a patrol, the
> Director told him, 'Don't be so damned stupid. RSMs
> don't fight in wartime. It's an outrageous suggestion.
> Either that, or they've all gone stark raving mad out
> there.'

Others backed the RSM, insisting that SOPs 'are there to be broken' and that soldiers at all levels in the chain of command should seize the initiative. 'You can't have everyone standing around, staring at their bergens,' one man said. There was consensus on the 'no CTR or OPs' issue. These procedures are cornerstones of successful SAS operations, whether the Regiment is acting as a reconnaissance unit for a larger military force or, as on Operation TRENT, tasked to attack a position itself. Plans for the crucial Phase Four, the assault on the opium plant, had to be turned around at the last minute because the squadrons were unaware of the nature of the terrain in the target's immediate vicinity. The lesson was learnt the hard way: 'Sat Int' and aerial photography are not adequate substitutes for 'Hum Int' when it comes to planning an assault.

That A Squadron had to leave the TLZ first, not G Squadron as the battle plan dictated, was a minor matter, caused by the state of the ground where each squadron's vehicles were situated. The order of march was switched *en route* and did not cause difficulties.

There were a huge number of pluses to be taken from Operation TRENT, greatly outweighing the negatives. The squadrons and the RHQ had seized an opportunity to show the Americans what was possible, to plan and execute a giant logistical operation, including a long infil and battle, and with a fair amount of panache, as the HALO jump showed. There was a great deal of satisfaction for everyone involved – from the QM who received an MBE for his organizational skills, the freefallers and the soldiers decorated with CGCs for pulling the third casualty to safety.

The fire fight itself was proof of success; in the CO's words, the Regiment's 'warrior spirit' was still there as nobody had 'flinched or faltered'. How the likes of Jason reacted under fire showed that the right soldiers still passed SAS Selection and the Regiment's exhausting and brutal training regime remained effective. The Colonel also acknowledged the challenge of operating in Afghanistan, a military environment in which the 'definitions of success and failure are finely balanced' – a comment aligned to Operation TRENT's relative success against Operation ENDURING FREEDOM and Operation VERITAS's disappointments. Aside from an obvious scalp such as bin Laden's capture it was also difficult to gauge what represented success and failure. Al Qaeda, the CO told his men, were a 'chameleon-like' enemy and, in a comment which touched on some of Donald Rumsfeld's views on 'old think versus new think' military strategy, he described the war against terrorism as one in which 'the battle lines are not clearly drawn'.

There was a huge sense of relief in Hereford that after such a barren period the Regiment had been tested operationally on a large scale. The casualty count – three wounded Paras and one wounded ex 'Amphibious' forces (the RSM) was the cause of much of what passes for SAS humour: 'The three Paras received wounds to the front as they were going forward, towards the enemy. The other soldier was shot from behind. He must have been running away!'

The CO had done extremely well, thoroughly deserving his DSO. His 'generalship' or 'operational art', to use two terms favoured by war's armchair analysts had been tested throughout. This young Lieutenant Colonel organized in double-quick time a complex, large-scale manoeuvre under great pressure from above and below in the chain of command. At stake on Operation TRENT were his men's lives, the Regiment's reputation, Operation ENDURING FREEDOM's momentum and, to a significant extent at this delicate time, relations between Blair's Government and the Bush Administration, London having put such pressure on Washington to secure the SAS a contact. The request having been granted, albeit somewhat reluctantly, there would have been fury in the US Government and military if any incident or accident on Operation TRENT had impacted adversely upon the overall mission.

SAS deaths, high numbers of casualties or, heaven forbid, defeat, would have sent shockwaves around the world, severely affecting the Allies' limited capability on the ground and boosting Al Qaeda and the Taliban's morale. Such a politically and militarily risky mission was only made possible by the CO's absolute confidence in his men's fighting abilities. In the aftermath of the Operation, his tenure as CO over, he left the Regiment as one of the most popular, successful and respected commanders in its recent history. Time will tell whether he emulates former SAS COs, de la Billiere, Rose and Delves – in going on to bigger though not necessarily better things, after Hereford.

Having given in, CENTCOM did not let the SAS have everything its own way. The plant was to be hit immediately with no time for the SAS to assess the target itself, the intelligence to plan the mission would be second-hand, from Predator drones and satellite cameras. Over the course of the Operation, the CO proved his leadership qualities and judgement. Three examples:

At **H − 0.45 hrs**: The CO stopped the convoy and took the most sensible course of action, bearing in mind the time and his troops' vulnerable position. He was reluctant to radio for support, knowing that the F/A-18 Hornet thundering over the SAS column would alert Al Qaeda. The SAS simply could not afford to be late for the battle. This decision went a long way to ensuring it was not.

At **H − 0.30 hrs** it fell upon him to carry out his own instant CTR, assess terrain, thickness of cover and hidden ambush positions. Without a second to lose, he made the right decision, to switch flanks.

At **H+3.00 hrs** his men were winning and the headquarters about to be searched. But he also had four wounded, one of whom required immediate casevac. The Colonel had to weigh up the value of staying on target for a longer fire fight against the risk of holding a position the US Generals would have been happy just to bomb.

The CO was right to withdraw when he did – and should have left sooner according to his bosses. The battle had been won against a courageous enemy, dug in, well armed – albeit with less sophisticated weaponry but with no shortage of ammunition – and perhaps most importantly of all, enjoying extremely high morale, as Napoleon quantified it: 'Morale is to the material [physical] as three is to one.'

Was Operation TRENT a wise deployment of UKSF troops? Not entirely, but the Regiment believed it had no choice but to lobby hard when nothing else was on offer. Prior to the Regiment's first deployment, such a two-squadron attack would have seemed an unlikely tasking. Most of the troops expected smaller, lightning-strike raids to be the order of the day. These simply did not materialize.

Operation TRENT could and nearly did lose a lot more than there was to gain, as only good fortune prevented a devastating 'blue on blue' on the FSB at just before **H+1.00 hr.**

Putting 120 guys into the line of fire was a gamble. Would the United States have done likewise? That is very unlikely, certainly not unless it greatly furthered the overall operation. The plant was manned by 'hardcore Al Qaeda', while the troops referred to them as 'a bunch of druggies', typical soldiers' bravado which says more about them than the troops they faced. The enemy were Al Qaeda elite but, crucially from the US point of view, not 'Tier One Personalities', members of its war council, such as bin Laden, Al-Zawahiri, or Khalid Sheikh Mohammed. There would have been top cover throughout the mission if the likes of that trio had been present and in all likelihood the United States

would have insisted on having a presence on the ground as
well.

The diplomatic fallout of US planes killing any number
of SAS – by common consent the world's best soldiers – on
a mission to capture bin Laden would have been great, let
alone a mission which had nothing to do with Operation
ENDURING FREEDOM or Operation VERITAS's core aims.
Such an incident would have been incredibly embarrassing,
would have caused the military campaign in Afghanistan to
stutter and impacted upon the planning and execution of
future US/UK operations such as Gulf War II.

Fratricide – the killing or injuring by friendly forces of
service personnel on the same side – is a key issue in
modern warfare. During the 1990–91 Gulf War nine British
soldiers were killed and twelve injured when a US A-10
Tankbuster mistook APCs (Armoured Personnel Carriers)
belonging to the 3Bn RRF (Royal Regiment of Fusiliers) for
Iraqi troops. A verdict of 'unlawful killing' was returned at
an inquest into the deaths in 1992. The soldiers' CO, Lieutenant Colonel Andrew Larpent (Rtd), has campaigned on
the 'friendly fire' issue ever since.

Such is the Regiment's international renown, its position
in the military hierarchy and the British public's obsession
with it that the impact would have been greater had as
many G Squadron soldiers been killed or injured. The MOD
had also had a decade since the Gulf War to equip British
Army frontline vehicles, tanks, APCs or the SAS's Pinkies
with an effective IFF (Identification Friend from Foe) system, which it has always insisted it is 'working on'.

That the US Navy was less to blame than the SAS may
have been overlooked, especially as American pilots had
already struck non-enemy targets by late November, inadvertently bombing civilian areas in Kabul and a Red Cross
warehouse. On 5 December, less than a fortnight after
Operation TRENT, three US Green Berets were killed and

the future Afghan President Hamid Karzai injured when B-52 bombs struck a coalition position near Kandahar. Rear Admiral Stufflebeem said: 'This is one of the potentially most hazardous type of missions that we use as a military tactic. Calling in air strikes nearly simultaneously on your own position, on enemy forces that you're engaged in close proximity to, is a hazardous business and takes very fine control and coordination and precision.'

On 20 December US jets fired rockets at elders heading to Karzai's inauguration ceremony in Kabul (the Pentagon insisted they were Al Qaeda members). The worst case was on 17 April 2002, when four Canadian soldiers were killed when a USAF F-16 accidentally dropped a 227-kilogram laser-guided bomb on them. They were taking part in live-firing exercises in a recognized training area near Kandahar airport. These accidents occurred despite the Pentagon spending $200 million on investigating how to eradicate 'friendly fire' incidents. Fifty US and British troops were killed in 'blue on blue' attacks in the first Gulf War – 20 per cent of all US casualties. Lawyers for the US National Guard pilots court-martialled over the Canadian incident blamed the accident on the amphetamine pills given to the airmen, which were intended to help them concentrate on longer flying missions. Realistic estimates of the civilian casualty count in Afghanistan between October and December 2001 vary between 3,000 and 5,000.

As there were so few combat operations during Operation ENDURING FREEDOM in which Allied troops actually closed with Al Qaeda, the SAS was grateful for the opportunity and recognized its good fortune. No other unit would have been allowed to veer off at a tangent to fight a private battle. Whatever Jason, Jock, Gordon and Phil's frustrations on Operation DETERMINE may have been, there was no policy to keep the SAS out of action. What the SAS wanted did not fit into how CENTCOM wished to run the war. Understandably, as the war was a direct consequence of 9/11, US troops would be prioritized to carry out ground attacks, such as the botched assault on Mullah Omar's compound on 19/20 October. Why was Operation TRENT's success not a springboard for other SAS combat missions inside Afghanistan? Because there were no more opportunities to use the Regiment in search-and-destroy operations in December than there were in October or November.

General Franks and Defense Secretary Rumsfeld came under sustained criticism for not stopping more Al Qaeda – and perhaps bin Laden – fleeing Tora Bora in early December. In their defence, intelligence reports suggested that bin Laden was in locations throughout southern Afghanistan and Pakistan, just as they do today. It was impossible for the United States to know which were correct.

Both men were given a rough ride by the US Senate Armed Services Committee on 31 July 2002. Franks stressed he did not have enough troops to follow every lead – that was the White House's fault, not his, though he did not say so. The SAS remained in south-west Afghanistan, much closer to Kandahar than to Tora Bora. As Kandahar was the Taliban's spiritual home and its leader Mullah Omar had been protecting bin Laden it made sense to keep the squadrons where they were.

Franks explained: 'On Tora Bora, early December 2001, United States of America at that time had about 1,300 Americans in country in seventeen different locations. Kandahar was, as of that time, still not fully under control. We had our Marine forces acting out of Camp Rhino, which was our initial point of entry into Afghanistan. We were very mindful – and I guess I'll take credit or blame for this

– I was very mindful of the Soviet experience of more than ten years, having introduced 620,000 troops into Afghanistan, more than 15,000 of them being killed, more than 55,000 of them being wounded.

'It was the Afghans who wanted to attack in the Tora Bora area. We had Special Forces troopers with those Afghans, to be sure. We had linkage with the Pakistanis, who some would say, although not much reported at the time, had in the vicinity of 100,000 troops on the western Pakistani border along a great many of the points of exfiltration. Did the enemy get out of Tora Bora? Senator, yes, to be sure. I am satisfied with the way this operation was conducted. No, I won't say that. I am satisfied with the decision process that permitted the Afghans to go to work in the Tora Bora area.'

The excuse of the Red Army's 'defeat' in Afghanistan is a poor one. Nobody expected 620,000 Allied troops to be deployed, not even 62,000, but 6,200 US and British infantry soldiers with the requisite support arms focusing on a specific area and acting upon good intelligence could have made a significant difference. The Red Army's losses over that period are most respectable. Between December 1979 and 1989 they lost one soldier for every 45,000 deployed. The Red Army was predominantly a conscript force and the occupation coincided with the Soviet Union's gradual collapse. Neither the soldiers nor most of the politicians in Moscow during the Gorbachev era wanted them to be there. At any one time the Soviet Union had between 94,000 and 104,000 troops in Afghanistan – half the US strength in Vietnam in a land five times as big.

Franks's 'co-accused', Rumsfeld, took a pasting from Democrat Max Cleland, a crippled Vietnam veteran, who said: 'Mr Secretary, for me, Operation ENDURING FREEDOM has become Operation ENDURING FRUSTRATION.

I think it is fine to nation-build or liberate Afghanistan. For me, the frustration continues because we still have not killed or captured Osama bin Laden and his terrorist cadre.

'One of the things I learned in Vietnam is that if a terrorist doesn't lose, he wins; which is why I'm so committed, personally, to making sure his end is in sight. And it troubles me, I'm frustrated that his end is not in sight, nor is the end of his terrorist cadre in sight. That, for me, is mission number one for our government, and mission number one for our military.'

Rumsfeld replied angrily: 'Mission number one you say ought to be Al Qaeda and the Taliban. That is exactly what we are doing and we are doing it across the globe. People are getting arrested every day, arms caches are being discovered every day, people are being interrogated, people are being detained. It seems to me that the United States armed forces were designed to deal with armies, navies and air forces. Doing a single manhunt is a different type of thing. The intelligence community is working hard on it, General Franks is working hard on it, people across the globe are working hard on it. You can be frustrated if you want but I'm not. I think that we've got a serious effort going on and serious work is being done.'

Preparations for March 2003's invasion of Iraq distracted attention from the failure to find Osama bin Laden. At least until November 2002, when the Democrat–Republican consensus over Al Qaeda was shattered by a scratchy, three-minute audio-tape from *Al-Jazeera*, the Arab TV station, which signalled bin Laden's return. According to the NSA (National Security Agency) experts, the voice which said, 'As you kill, you will be killed, as you bomb you will be bombed,' was almost certainly Bin Laden's. He mentioned the Bali terrorist attack and the Chechen takeover of a Moscow theatre, saying, 'These actions were carried out by the zealous sons of Islam in defence of their religion and in response to the order of their God and prophet, may God's peace and blessings be upon him.'

Future Democrat Presidential candidate and former Majority Leader in the Senate Tom Daschle responded: 'We haven't found bin Laden, we have not made any real progress in many of the other areas involving the key elements of Al Qaeda – they continue to be as great a threat today as they were a year and a half ago. So by what measure can we say this has been successful so far? It is bin Laden's messages that we are listening to and it is bin Laden who is still the spokesperson. It was the President himself who said that we will not be successful until he is found dead or alive. Those were his words. Well, I guess I would say the time has come to ensure that happens.'

If only it were that simple. The crime is not the failure to capture bin Laden, because a global manhunt is extremely difficult and the Al Qaeda leader has effectively been on the run, evading justice, for a decade, but the failure to capitalize on the best opportunity to do so – which occurred in Afghanistan in 2001. The SAS could also have played a much greater part than it was allowed to. In no way did Operation DETERMINE or Operation TRENT enhance the chances of catching bin Laden or any other Al Qaeda leaders. Both missions were a sideshow in that regard, and that is why the latter is only remembered with passing satisfaction, even though viewed in isolation, it was a great success from start to finish.

What has changed in Afghanistan since Operation TRENT and Operation ENDURING FREEDOM, and what has remained the same? Al Qaeda's camps have returned to the south-east of the country, as a terrorist organization it remains a global threat, and the majority of its leaders are still at large. Beyond Kabul's city limits, Afghanistan is a lawless, impoverished state, a despot's paradise with enough arms and ammunition to sustain any number of terrorists and porous borders with its neighbours. There is little its President Hamid Karzai can do about this, for simply staying alive is his everyday concern. Not only are old Al Qaeda training camps being used again but new ones are being built in the east of the state to train a new intake of volunteers.

According to the United Nations there is considerable room for improvement in the extent of international co-operation to prevent Al Qaeda from recruiting, rearming and financing terrorist atrocities across the world. Its coffers remain flush and hidden while it has also 'localized' its methods of money-making to avoid detection. The United Nations is also getting wise to the link between Al Qaeda and the opium industry. It has calculated that 68 per cent of Afghanistan's potential opium harvest will come from areas where the Taliban is supported. There is enormous potential for Al Qaeda to make money in this area. This may lead to the SAS returning to the Helmand province for a repeat performance.

Malah Do Kand is 250 kilometres from the Iranian border where guards have been involved with 'drug smugglers' armed not just with AK47s but 14.5-mm heavy machine-guns, US-made night vision equipment and anti-tank and anti-aircraft missiles (probably RPGs). As the UN monitoring group concluded in December 2002,

Bearing in mind the areas inside of Afghanistan from which the majority of the traffickers are emanating, the likelihood of elements of the Taliban and Al Qaeda once again having easy access to weapons and drug proceeds cannot be ignored. Recent reports from intelligence services indicate that Al Qaeda is regrouping and setting up training facilities inside Afghanistan, close to the Pakistan border. This would suggest that Al Qaeda will probably require additional arms and ammunition.

Although Cofer Black, the US State Department's counter-terrorism co-ordinator, admitted, 'Al Qaeda is still planning attacks, despite the solid progress the danger persists,' there are many positives to consider as well. Terrorist attacks worldwide declined significantly in 2002, from 355 reported incidents to 199, and the number of strikes on US interests overseas fell from 219 to 77 (although the main reason for this was fewer attacks on US oil pipelines in Colombia). Over 300 arrests of Al Qaeda suspects were made after 9/11, the most significant being Khalid Sheikh Mohammed's capture in Pakistan on 1 March 2003. Mohammed is thought to have been the mastermind behind the hijackings. There will be new recruits to fill his shoes and neither the United States' phased withdrawal from Saudi Arabia, nor the publication of the 'road map' for peace between Israel and the Palestinians, will appease Islamic fundamentalists. It remains to be seen whether the US plan to introduce democracy to Iraq will precipitate a rise of the rule of law and religious freedoms in other Islamic states and whether these changes will be a force for stability or instability.

17. REGIMENTAL FUTURE

It is the perfect moment to disband the SAS. The Gulf
War will almost certainly prove to have been its last
hurrah. I know what the SAS can and cannot do, and I
honestly can't see a useful future for it in its present form.
The SAS finds itself increasingly marginalised. Quite
apart from other problems, the Regiment is also grossly
overstaffed.

This was written in 1998 by the SAS's longest-serving
soldier, Ken Connor, and is taken from his book *Ghost Force,
The Secret History of the SAS*. Connor was no mug, nor was
he the only member of the 'old and bold' to argue along
these lines. I am not mocking Connor for thinking the
Regiment was finished, rather I quote him to emphasize
how less certain the SAS's future appeared prior to 9/11,
which inspired a dramatic change in the United States'
foreign policy. America, and to a lesser extent Great Britain,
thought it was secure, confident that its advances in technology and information extended its peace. It paid a heavy
price for this complacency, which, as its invasion of Iraq in
March 2003 demonstrated, it is determined not to pay twice.
There is nothing America will not do to ensure its security
regardless of the United Nations' Charter and the opinion
of the international community. In the hawkish Bush administration, the 'U' in United Nations stands for Useless.

Before 9/11, the SAS wondered where its next battle was coming from. Today the challenges are stacking up, be it assisting the United States in seeking to overwhelm rogue states possessing WMDs (Weapons of Mass Destruction) or tackling international terrorist organizations such as Al Qaeda. In Gulf War II, B and D Squadrons, 22 SAS, along with the SBS's Maritime Squadron, were deployed throughout Iraq in a reconnaissance role, searching in vain for WMDs which failed to materialize. The troops became frustrated as while they were marooned in the Western Desert looking for non-existent Scuds, Delta Force linked up with Israeli military intelligence agents in Baghdad to orchestrate the assassination attempts on Saddam Hussein and the arrests of the senior members of his regime. It was the SBS that hit the headlines, and for the wrong reasons. While members of the Maritime Squadron were resting up at an LUP 50kms from the Syrian border 100 Iraqi Republican Guards overran its position. In the scramble to safety a Pinkie, a Quad bike and multi-million-dollar high-tech communication equipment were left behind. Two men failed to make it to the ERV, having escaped the LUP and made their own way to Syria. Foreign Office Minister Mike O'Brien was dispatched from Whitehall to secure their release.

The campaign against Osama bin Laden's forces will, as the CO said in the MBR, last for 'generations'. It may also be fought not only in the Middle East and Central Asia but closer to home. By the Government's admission, Al Qaeda cells are active in the United Kingdom, men schooled at bin Laden's camps before the World Trade Center attack and those who may have travelled to Afghanistan since, after these training centres resumed. Mainland Britain could become the new Northern Ireland for the SAS. For Belfast in the 1970s and 1980s, perhaps read Birmingham, Manchester and London in future.

The preparation for, execution and aftermath of Operation TRENT highlighted areas of concern for the Regiment; when under US command it must be able to plan and execute its operations 'the SAS way', and the secrecy for secrecy's sake attitude should be relaxed. The former will save lives and prevent a fatal 'blue on blue'; the latter may prevent millions of people whose taxes sustain the Regiment from being misled.

The Regiment must also maintain its current manpower level and, its autonomy, and whatever the pressure to do otherwise, or how many good soldiers still fail, never lower the standard required to pass SAS Selection. It should also, along with the rest of the armed forces, greatly improve the level of care provided to victims of battlefield accidents and those wounded by friendly or unfriendly fire. One former 264 (SAS) Signal Squadron member, who survived the Sea King helicopter crash in the Falklands War, has suffered terrible Post-Traumatic Stress Disorder for twenty years yet has been unable to obtain sufficient funds for the specialist treatment his condition requires.

The rather romantic view of the Regimental head shed is that despite huge cultural and behavioural changes in Britain, post-Second World War, the SAS has stayed pretty much the same. Perhaps it is blinkered by sentiment. While as an institution the SAS is as cut off from everyday life as the Benedictine monastic community at Belmont Abbey, just a few miles from Stirling Lines, no body, whether it consists of highly trained killers or contemplative monks, is entirely impermeable to such shifts. The SAS recruits from an entirely different British society today than it did in its infancy and inevitably this is reflected in the actions and attitudes of its soldiers during and after service.

Recent years have seen the passing of the Regiment's 'unofficial' fines system, the creeping of the compensation culture – reference the post-Afghanistan dispute between the fifth SAS casualty with the MOD and US Marine Corps – and petty squabbles between the official SAS Regimental Association and the more recently established Special Forces Association. Hereford, it seems, is not big enough for the both of them as the two bodies use the letters pages of local newspapers to throw mud over who is entitled to erect official monuments to fallen comrades. The drinking culture more prevalent in past decades has subsided, Selection candidates do use waterproofs, the course itself has never been harder, and consequently today's SAS men are considered fitter than those of yesteryear. Physically, they have gone from resembling long-distance runners to more heavily muscled decathletes.

The SAS's soldiering skills remain of the highest standard and yes, the ethos of the Regiment, as defined by Stirling, is intact. The troops' desire to experience combat and test themselves to the very limit of their capabilities is just as strong. It was what the SAS's founder referred to as the 'unrelenting pursuit of excellence'. His ideals have long been inbred in Hereford. The soldiers may not all get on, but they respect one another's abilities to the point that some are in quiet awe of their peers. Though many SAS missions have had mixed results, few have failed outright, and when things have gone wrong the soldiers' comradeship, courage and initiative have limited casualty numbers and degree of failure.

The SAS has always had the advantage over its international equivalents, Delta Force included, of recruiting from a superior regular force. The British Army is the world's most highly skilled and professional, bar none. Its ability is proven, most recently in two Gulf Wars. It deploys rapidly into any climate, often with substandard kit compared to US issue; yet it achieves excellent results.

One unhealthy development for the SAS and the British Army as a whole is that ex-Paras today account for over 50 per cent of the Regiment's 'badged' strength, a matter which should be addressed for operational and political reasons; if only there were a simple solution. As its soldiers' specialist skills require their deployment in a different capacity, the SAS is seldom tasked in a full-frontal infantry assault role – Operation TRENT being the proverbial exception to prove the rule. This is what the Parachute Regiment does best – striking rapidly and deeply into enemy territory and killing enemy. The SAS's operational priorities, the anti-terrorist defence of Britain, reconnaissance gathering and 'S & D' require its troops to be not just as fit, indeed fitter than Paras, but also more adept at planning and lateral thinking, and considerably more patient.

It is important to remember that Stirling was not a Para, nor were General Sir Peter de la Billière, or General Sir Michael Rose, Lieutenant General Delves or the CO who orchestrated Operation TRENT; all are men who have to varying degrees shaped the Regiment. Though all but a few will fail SAS Selection, the door to Britain's most elite unit must be as wide to applicants from all units, and long may the British Army uphold its record of service and serve the Regiment so well.

One of many benefits of Gulf War II will be that thousands of British servicemen and women will be better soldiers for having experienced combat, whether from a tank, an artillery position or on the frontline. However, the fact will remain that a soldier from a tank or artillery regiment will still be less likely to be suitably prepared to tackle SAS Selection than a Para.

The Parachute Regiment is the best combat unit outside Hereford and, with the Royal Marines, gets the toughest assignments. Bearing in mind P Company (the exhausting finale of Parachute Regiment basic training) and greater likelihood of having experienced close-quarter combat, a Para's advantages over the non-Airborne soldier are obvious. Efforts to tackle the Para dominance could also be detrimental. It is a terribly vague concept to select recruits on the basis of potential; such a policy risks accepting soldiers into the Regiment who are too far below the requisite standard.

With that in mind, should Training Wing, which runs the bi-annual courses, be criticized for passing those who are closer to the 'finished product' over those who, as a result of inferior service history if not soldiering ability, may require more continuation training? With so much invested in the Regiment's ability to perform anywhere, at any time on the most high-risk missions, there can only be one standard to join the SAS, and that is the highest possible.

A Para-centric SAS lends itself towards being dissolved into the 10,000-strong 16 Air Assault Brigade, of which the Parachute Regiment is part. If this happened, the Regiment would lose some of its distinctive character and identity, and the link with the Stirling era. With SF units expensive to run, few in the MOD would bemoan such a move, while the SBS could easily slip back into 3 Commando Brigade's organizational hierarchy. 16 Air Assault Brigade is Britain's rapid reaction force, invading enemy territory by parachute or Apache attack helicopter. It includes, at any one time, two of the three battalions of the Parachute Regiment, 7 RHA (Royal Horse Artillery) and the 23rd Engineer Regiment (RE). There would be no need for UKSF.

The future size of the SAS is as contentious an argument. There is increasing pressure upon the Regiment to expand, as its resources are stretched beyond capacity. Inevitably, media reports have suggested it will do so – by as much as 400 per cent. Talk of a 'manpower crisis' in Hereford is, however, as old as the Regiment itself. There will never be 'enough' SAS men as they are the best. Any report that the SAS can go from a strength of 350 (500 if one includes two Territorial Army squadrons, the London-based 21 SAS and

Birmingham-based 23 SAS), to 2,000 to cover future operations against Iraq or as part of the global war on terror, is
far-fetched. There is no question of the SAS relaxing its
entry requirements in order to ensure its number can
increase.

As a proposal this is an absolute non-starter, not just
because an insufficient number of troops would pass Selection, even if the bar was lowered slightly, but for logistical
reasons as well. For every SAS man on the ground, two or
three are required generally in support roles. If a fifth sabre
squadron was introduced, providing sixty troops for frontline operations, 264 Signal Squadron, the RAF squadrons
attached to the SAS and all the RE, RAMC personnel
strengths would need to be expanded as well.

In the opening chapter of *The Special Air Service*, published in 1971, the author Philip Warner wrote:

> Although the Special Air Service regiment has been in
> existence for nearly thirty years, and has fought with
> distinction in Africa, Europe, the Middle East and the
> Far East, very few members of the general public have
> heard of it, and fewer still understand how and why it
> functions.

Today, by stark contrast, the SAS is the world's most famous
yet misunderstood unit – its hard-won recognition and
reputation have come at a cost. Every detail of its activities
that escape from beneath the cloak of secrecy in Hereford is
lapped up by the British public which seems to have an
insatiable appetite for tales of the SAS in action. To feed this
hunger, as was the case after Operation TRENT, reports of
its actions which are based on few if any facts appear in
many British newspapers, across the divide of tabloids and
broadsheets.

In some respects the first three decades of the SAS's

history must today seem like halcyon days; the Regiment could get on with its business in private. This will never again be the case. The turning point was, of course, the storming of the Iranian Embassy in 1980, pictures of which, like the atrocities of 9/11, were flashed around the world. Before 9/11 Operation NIMROD was probably the most dramatic political or military event ever shown live on British television. In 2003, as the public's demand to be informed about the Regiment increases, it becomes more concerned about secrecy, seemingly beyond the level required for reasons of operational security and the future safety of SAS soldiers.

While the Regiment has proved itself to be innovative with regard to planning and executing operations, the use of equipment and command structures, it has failed to address the media obsession it generates. Some inside the SAS fear that the media pose a threat to its unaccountability, or unruly autonomy, that newspapers would audit its actions given the chance: too true. Understandably the Regiment wants to remain a self-policing band of brothers and only with great reluctance is the SAS community bracing itself for some degree of change. Yet why should the two squadrons on Operation TRENT not receive the public congratulation they deserve, as this was not a covert mission? They are entitled to it and they took no satisfaction from reading the fictitious accounts of cave battles. Opinions in Hereford are divided over whether increased openness is a wise course of action.

It is a question of when, not if, the SAS modernizes its media and public relations, as the minutes from the DA-Notice* Committee meeting, November 2002, reveal:

* The DA (Defence Advisory) Committee is the joint Official/Media committee overseeing the reporting of military matters. The Committee Secretary may advise any broadcast organization or newspaper that publication or screening of material could endanger

The MOD representative explained why the policy on reporting matters which could genuinely endanger the security of SF personnel and operations could not be changed in the heat of the moment, and that MOD had a responsibility to its people and their families to ensure their security. The Chairman acknowledged that the current policy was sometimes less than helpful to both MOD and the media, and that a change might reduce the kind of damaging reporting seen recently.

Such sentiments are the first steps on a long journey, but one that is worth making. A more open policy has its pros and cons. Behind the scenes, options for change are afoot and the SAS had paid close attention to the gradual modernization at MI5. The 2002 UKSF Unauthorized Disclosure Policy Review presented a number of models of media interaction, or distance, and options for greater control of 'the Circuit'.

One idea is for non-operationally sensitive material to be disclosed to a selected cadre of 'trusted' journalists, the radical alternative is for the Regiment to encourage the Government to introduce legislation making it a criminal offence for publications to discuss or report UKSF matters. The report suggests that media interaction via an official channel would allow UKSF to 'effect some influence over it [the media]'. It would also reduce the ability of 'third parties' to 'write what they wish without fear of contradiction'. It would put UKSF in a better position to 'discredit rogue reporting (in whatever form)' – of which there was a great deal in Afghanistan.

Media reporting in Gulf War II was less of a concern for

---

national security if he considers it would breach guidelines protecting service personnel and ensuring requisite operational secrecy.

UKSF. With newspaper and broadcast organizations*
embedded with non-SF units, the media got its fill of heavy
fighting. There was not such a need to glorify any British
units with hypothetical tales of derring-do.

UKSF is also pursuing damage limitation and media
manipulation techniques, as the report adds: 'Operational
success probably generates an audience more sympathetic
to the arguments of tight restraint. This may be eroded in
instances of failure, particularly if there are perceptions of
ineptitude or illegality.' A better relationship with the media
may be most advantageous at the time of: 'the bad news
tale'. Applying the UKSF 'media interaction' model to
Afghanistan, a detailed report of Operation TRENT could
have been given, as it was not a covert mission, though
such a brief would probably not have included any mention
of the close shave on the FSB from the F/A-18 strafing fire.
All the nonsense about cave fights and VCs might never
have appeared.

The head sheds are also weighing up options to scrutin-
ize the activities of ex-SAS personnel, appointing a 'watch-
dog' to investigate possible cases of disclosure and to
observe 'The Circuit' – the clique of ex-Airborne and Special
Forces soldiers who monopolize top-bracket security jobs in
London and the Middle East. UKSF has expressed the view
that there is a genuine risk of SAS tactics being taught to
discredited regimes and foreign nationals. While the SAS is
rightly concerned that there is no legislation to control UK
private security or military companies active overseas, the
best solution is not to make it more difficult for serving
members of the Regiment to find employment post-service,

---

* Around 2,000 journalists covered Gulf War II – 700 more than the
number of US troops deployed in Afghanistan in 2001 to find Osama
bin Laden.

and the knowledge and techniques born out of combat experience are their intellectual copyright. Former members also have the moral standards to pick and choose their clients.

The introduction of confidentiality contracts for current and ex-SAS personnel was entirely at odds with the concept of soldiers 'serving' the Regiment. In October 1996, after the success of Andy McNab's *Bravo Two Zero* and Chris Ryan's *The One That Got Away*, the following DCI (Defence Council Instruction) was issued by the MOD:

> From the date of this DCI all Armed Forces personnel serving currently or in future on the establishment of units under the operational or administrative command of Director Special Forces will be required to sign a contract binding the signatory to a lifelong commitment not to disclose, without prior permission of the MOD, any information gained during Service with Special Forces.
>
> All personnel required to sign will be issued with written guidance explaining the nature of the require-ment. Failure to sign will result in the individual con-cerned being reported through the chain of command to the Director Special Forces. If after a fixed period of review any objections to signature cannot be resolved, the individual concerned will be deemed unsuitable for duties with UK Special Forces and will be 'returned to unit'.

SAS soldiers were not given copies of the contracts, or allowed to seek legal advice before signature, and signing the contracts remains part of 'Regimental Part One Orders' in the SAS's rulebook. The SAS Regimental Association polled its membership about the contracts, and 96.8 per cent of respondents (who were 73 per cent of the membership) voted in favour. The contracts were standardized, as follows:

> Between MOD and (*Insert soldier's name*)
>
> In consideration of my being given a (*insert agreed length of service*) posting in the United Kingdom Special Forces from (*date*) by MOD, I hereby give the following solemn undertaking binding me for the rest of my life: -
>
> (1) I will not disclose without express prior authority in writing from MOD any information, document or other article relating to the work of, or in support of, the United Kingdom Special Forces which is or has been in my possession by virtue of my position as a member of any of those Forces.
>
> (2) I will not make any statement without express prior authority in writing from MOD which purports to be a disclosure of such information as is referred to in paragraph (1) above or is intended to be taken, or might reasonably be taken, by those it is addressed as being such a disclosure.
>
> (3) I will assign to MOD all rights accruing to me and arising out of, or in connection with, any disclosure or statement in breach of paragraph (1) or (2) above.
>
> (4) I will bring immediately to the notice of MOD any occasion on which a person invited me to breach this contract.

There was every reason to increase security in the 1970s and 1980s to meet the threat posed by the IRA, less as a knee-jerk reaction to McNab and Ryan's bestsellers. For despite many bitter disputes between soldiers and the Regimental hierarchy, few genuinely damaging nuggets of information have been released into the public domain, prior to, or regardless of, the contracts.

In March 2003 another B20 (Bravo Two Zero) survivor known as 'R', a New Zealander, appealed to the Privy

Council to overturn a decision by Court of Appeal judges in his home country that while he could publish his account, he could not claim any profit from its sales as he had signed a confidentiality contract. The ex-A Squadron trooper argued the contract was invalid as he had not been allowed to seek legal advice prior to signing it and it had been made clear he would be RTU'd if he did not. 'R' said this amounted to 'duress' and 'undue influence'. The head shed in Hereford, who had expected to lose the case, received a pleasant surprise.

Five law lords making up the Privy Council upheld the decision by a majority of four to one. 'R', who has adopted the pen name Mike Coburn, may still choose to publish *Soldier Five* abroad to avoid the MOD claiming its bounty. To publish in the United Kingdom he will need clever accountants. 'R' said: 'Their Lords' decision that legal advice is not required when an employee is forced to sign a contract that limits his freedoms for the rest of his life defies description.' This messy dispute over a mission which was a succession of cock-ups looks set to rumble on and on, twelve years after the disputed actions took place.

Considering the high esteem in which the Regiment is held today in political and military circles on both sides of the Atlantic, it seems remarkable just how many times during its history the SAS's future has been in doubt. Even after its breathtaking achievements in the Second World War, during which Hitler remarked: 'These men [the SAS] are very dangerous. They will be hunted down and destroyed at all costs,' it was disbanded in October 1945. After fighting heroically and with great success in the Malayan Campaign during the 1950s it looked as though time was up for the 'jungle bunnies' as they were known in the newly formed 22nd Special Air Service Regiment as the Army Council questioned whether there was any need for it. Luckily the SAS, under the command of Lieutenant

Colonel A. J. Deane-Drummond, was dispatched to Oman in 1958 and given a new lease of life.

Each time its future has been in doubt, the Regiment has adapted to serve in a new theatre of war. In the decades ahead its soldiers must not only be as courageous, selfless and professional as those who have served in the SAS before them, but also as innovative. Of course, if it had not been for Stirling's breathtaking vision there obviously would not be an SAS at all, but since his era, the foresight of the likes of the late Andy Massey and of General Sir Peter de la Billière kept the Regiment one step ahead of politicians who questioned the need for such a peculiar little unit.

Early in 1972 Massey, then a Captain, was tasked by DLB to undertake a feasibility study on the Regiment setting up a specialist anti-terrorist team capable of responding to any hostage or siege. His document, codenamed Operation PAGODA, was passed by DLB to the Director, Special Forces Group – a forerunner of UKSF – but shelved by MOD. After the Israeli hostage crisis at the Munich Olympics the report was dusted off for Prime Minister Ted Heath who was desperate to know how Britain could respond to a similar event here. The answer came eight years later in fifteen minutes of breathtaking action at Princes Gate, Knightsbridge.

The world's future security has seldom seemed as uncertain as it does in 2003, while the art of war has never been as complicated. Perception is all in the media-dominated battlefield. It is not sufficient just to win or inflict a few civilian casualties. The entirely healthy distaste for conflict in the West requires our forces to emerge victorious having killed as few enemy as possible as well. Hence the United States, with Great Britain in tow, seeks to scare them into submission by using 'shock and awe' tactics. The present generation of SAS soldiers must meet this and many other challenges, but none will be harder than those they set for themselves. Their commitment to the unit is total. They are only satisfied when they outperform every other military unit in the world having fought the 'SAS way', with guile, cunning and bravery, outthinking as well as outfighting the enemy and living up to the Regiment's traditions.

The view from the blue mountain is never enjoyed for long; there is always another summit to scale. Such a passion for fighting battles is easy to admire but difficult truly to understand. Whatever the old and bold think, the SAS will have a glorious future based on the unrivalled quality of its officers and men. There will be many more battles, though when and where they take place and against whom nobody can say. The true stories of them will be a long time in the telling.

Glossary of Terms

Adoo	Arabic for 'Enemy'
AOD	Automatic Opening Device
AOR	Area of Responsibility
APC	Armoured Personnel Carrier
AQT	Al Qaeda/Taliban
BATT	British Army Training Team
CAS	Close Air Support
Casevac	Casualty Evacuation
CBE	Companion of the Order of the British Empire
CDS	Chief of Defence Staff
CENTCOM	United States Central Command
CGC	Conspicuous Gallantry Cross
CIA	Central Intelligence Agency
CINC	Commander-in-Chief
CINCCENT	Commander-in-Chief, Central Command
CO	Commanding Officer
CP	Command Post
CPO	Command Post Operator
CQB	Close-Quarter Battle
CTR	Close Target Reconnaissance
DFC	Distinguished Flying Cross
DPM	Disruptive Pattern Material
DSF	Director, Special Forces
DSO	Distinguished Service Order
DTG	Date, Time, Group; used in radio communications
'Duff Gen'	Poor or inaccurate intelligence
DZ	Drop Zone
ERV	Emergency Rendezvous

ETA	Expected Time of Arrival
Exfil	Exfiltration/Exit
FAC	Forward Air Controller
FBI	Federal Bureau of Investigation
FOB	Forward Operating Base
FSB	Fire Support Base
FUP	Forming Up Point
GM	George Medal
GPMG	General Purpose Machine-Gun
GPS	Global Positioning System
'H'	Hereford
HALO	High Altitude Low Opening
'Hat'	Para term for non-Parachute Regiment troops
HE	High Explosive
Head shed(s)	Slang term for those in charge, the 'bosses'
HMG	Her Majesty's Government
HUMINT	Human intelligence, as opposed to intelligence gathered by 'artificial means', satellite or Predator drone
IC	In Command
IFF	Identification Friend from Foe
Infil	Infiltration/Entry
ISAF	International Security Assistance Force
INTBRIEF	Intelligence Briefing
INTREP	Intelligence Report
ISI	Inter Services Intelligence
JDAM	Joint Direct Attack Munitions
Jihad	A holy war for Muslims against non-believers, or infidels, and the absolute test of a Muslim's faith and religious observance
LO	Liaison Officer
LTM	Laser Target Marking
LUP	Lying Up or Laying Up Point/Position
LZ	Landing Zone
MBE	Member of the Order of the British Empire
MBR	Main Briefing Room
MC	Military Cross
Medevac	Medical Evacuation
MFC	Mortar Fire Controller

MID	Mention in Dispatches
MOD	Ministry of Defence
MRE	Meal(s) Ready to Eat
Mujahideen	'Army of God'
NATO	North Atlantic Treaty Organisation
NCO	Non-Commissioned Officer
NGO	Non-Governmental Organization
NSA	National Security Agency/Advisor
NVGs	Night Vision Goggles
OAS	Organization of American States
OBL	Osama bin Laden
OC	Officer Commanding
OP	Observation Post
Op	Operation
Op ABLATE	The mission to rescue British hostages in Sierra Leone
Op BLOOD	The SAS' return to Afghanistan, November 2001
Op CORPORATE	The Falklands campaign, April and May 1982
Op DESERT STORM	US operation to liberate Kuwait in 1991
Op DETERMINE	The SAS' infil into Afghanistan, October 2001
Op EAGLE CLAW	Delta Force mission to rescue US hostages in Tehran, April 1980
Op ENDURING FREEDOM	US operations in Afghanistan 2001
Op FAVIUS	Shooting of IRA terrorists in Gibraltar, 1988
Op GRANBY	UK operations to liberate Kuwait in 1991
Op NIMROD	SAS hostage rescue mission at the Iranian Embassy in 1980
Op PAGODA	The setting up of the Regiment's anti-terrorist unit in the 1970s
Op TRENT	SAS assault on the opium plant, November 2001
Op VERITAS	UK operations in Afghanistan 2001
OSA	Official Secrets Act
PAF	Pakistani Air Force
PE	Plastic Explosive
PJHQ	Permanent Joint Headquarters
PJI	Parachute Jump Instructor
QAC	Quick Action Commands

QBOs	Quick Battle Orders
QCVS	Queen's Commendation for Valuable Service
QM	Quartermaster
RAF	Royal Air Force
RAFO	Royal Air Force of Oman
RAMC	Royal Army Medical Corps
RE	Royal Engineers
REMF	Rear Echelon Mother Fucker
RHQ	Regimental Headquarters
RIC	Royal Intelligence Corps
RM	Royal Marines
RPG	Rocket Propelled Grenade
RSM	Regimental Sergeant Major
RTU	Returned to Unit
RV	Rendezvous
SAM	Surface to Air Missile
S & D	Search and Destroy
S & R	Surveillance and Reconnaissance
SAS	Special Air Service, or Speed, Aggression and Surprise, Supply and Stores, Sports and Social, or Self Appreciation Society
SASRA	Special Air Service Regimental Association
SATCOMMS	Satellite Communications
SB, SBS, 'Shaky Boots'	Special Boat Service
SF	Special Forces
SITREP	Situation Report
SOCOM	US Special Operations Command
SOPs	Standard Operating Procedures
SP	Special Projects
SQMS	Squadron Quartermaster Stores
Sqn	Squadron
SSM	Squadron Sergeant Major
TA	Territorial Army
TAB	Tactical Advance to Battle
TACBE	Tactical Beacon, used for surface to air transmissions, also SARBE
TACSAT	Tactical Satellite Communications
TAP	Tactical Assault Parachute
TAR	Tactical Air Reconnaissance
TAT	Tactical Air Transport
2IC	Second In Command

TLZ	Tactical Landing Zone
'Tom'	Airborne term for the most junior soldiers
UAV	Unmanned Aerial Vehicle
UKLF	United Kingdom Land Forces
UKSF	United Kingdom Special Forces
UN	United Nations
USLO	United States Liaison Officer
VC	Victoria Cross
WMD	Weapon(s) of Mass Destruction
WP	White Phosphorous, or 'Warm Persons'
WSBA	Western Sovereign Base Area (Cyprus)

Notes

2. DEAD OR ALIVE

p. 19: Diane Feinstein, *CNN*.

p. 20: Richard Durbin, *Time*, 27 May 2002.

p. 21: Condoleeza Rice, *Dubya's Posse*, Channel 4, September 2002.

p. 23: Hanan Ashrawi, *Daily Telegraph*, 18 September 2001.

pp. 23–4: Roger Heacock, ibid.

p. 24: Dick Cheney, *Meet the Press*, NBC, 16 September 2001.

p. 26: Colin Powell, *Dubya's Posse*, Channel 4, September 2002.

p. 26: Dick Cheney, *Meet the Press*, NBC, 16 September 2001.

p. 27: Donald Rumsfeld, US Defense Department Briefing, 8 October 2001.

p. 27: General Wesley Clark, *Time*, 24 September 2001.

p. 27: Condoleeza Rice, *Dubya's Posse*, Channel 4, September 2002.

p. 28: Major General Alexander Lyakhovski, *Time*, 1 October 2001.

p. 29: Frank Donatelli, *Daily Telegraph*, 22 September 2001.

pp. 31–2: Major General Leo Baxter, *Associated Press*, 8 October 2001.

p. 32: General Tommy Franks, *Daily Telegraph*, 10 October 2001.

p. 32: General Sir Peter de la Billière, *Storm Command*, Collins, 1992.

p. 34: General Ralston's 'affair' allegation, *Daily Telegraph*, 19 September 2001.

3. THE ELVIS OF THE EAST

p. 35: Issam Abdullah, *Sunday Times*, 8 September 2002.

p. 44: Mohammed Atta's 'letter', *The Washington Post*, 28 September 2001.

4. 'ON MY ORDERS'

p. 46: Edmund McWilliams, *Newsweek*, 5 November 2001.
p. 46: Hamid Gul, ibid.
p. 47: Robert McFarlane, ibid.
p. 47: Defense Department spokeswoman, *San Francisco Chronicle*, 10 October 2001.
p. 50: Merrill McPeak, *Online News Hour*, 8 October 2001.

5. OPERATION DETERMINE

pp. 68–9: Use of the SAS, *Sunday Telegraph*, 16 September 2001.
p. 72: National Audit Office report Exercise *Saif Sareea* II HC1097, Session 2001–2002: first quotation from para 4 of the Executive Summary, the second from Section 4: Joint Task Force Command Structure, subsection 'other elements', para 1.22.
p. 72: Lieutenant Colonel Angus Taverner, *Daily Telegraph*, 27 September 2001.

6. BLAIR GOES TO WASHINGTON

pp. 86–7: Rear Admiral John Stufflebeem, Defense Department briefing, 24 October 2001.
p. 87: Senator John McCain, *Wall Street Journal*, 26 October 2001.
p. 88: General Tommy Franks, Pentagon briefing, 8 November 2001.
pp. 88–9: Ronald Reagan on Abdul Haq, *Newsweek*, 5 November 2001.
p. 89: Richard Holbrooke on Haq, ibid.
p. 89: Donald Rumsfeld on Haq, ibid.
p. 93: Kofi Annan, *UN Information Centre*, 13 November 2001.
p. 95: Tony Blair, Downing Street news conference, 13 November 2001.
p. 95: Donald Rumsfeld, US interview, 13 November 2001.

7. OPERATION BLOOD

p. 97: Geoff Hoon, *Today*, BBC Radio 4, 16 November 2001.

14. NEWS BREAKS

pp. 219–20: Paul Keetch, Geoff Hoon, David Laws and Tam Dalyell, *Hansard*, 26 November 2001.

p. 221: Paul Keetch, interview with the author.

p. 223: Spokesman for the *Sun* and MOD spokesman, from the *Daily Telegraph*, 1 December 2001.

p. 225: Geoff Hoon, *Hansard*, Defence Questions, 13 December 2001.

pp. 225–6: Hamid Karzai and Abdul Salam Zaeff, international press reports.

pp. 228–9: Robin Cook, Statement in the House of Commons reproduced by the *Worldwide Socialist Web Site*: 'Why Britain should be indicted for war crimes: The SAS' role in the Qala-i-Jangi massacre'.

p. 229: Amnesty International statement, released 30 November 2001.

p. 230: US Defense official, *Daily Telegraph*, 4 January 2002.

15. BACK IN 'H'

pp. 239–40: Lassen citation, *The Special Air Service*, by Philip Warner.

16. POST-OPERATION ANALYSIS

p. 246: General Franks, Pentagon briefing, 8 November 2001.

pp. 246–7: Operation VERITAS objectives, from MOD press release, 16 October 2001.

p. 259: Rear Admiral John Stufflebeem, Pentagon briefing, 5 December 2001.

p. 265: Cofer Black, introducing the US State Department's 'Patterns of Global Terrorism' report, May 2003.

17. REGIMENTAL FUTURE

pp. 277–8: Soldier 'R' aka 'Mike Coburn', *The New Zealand Herald*, 20 March 2003.

Bibliography

Asher, Michael, *The Real Bravo Two Zero*, Cassell, 2002.

Bergen, Peter, *Holy War, Inc: Inside the Secret World of Osama bin Laden*, Weidenfeld and Nicolson, 2001.

Billière, General Sir Peter de la, *Storm Command*, Collins, 1992.

—— *Looking For Trouble*, Collins, 1994.

Bowyer, Richard, *Dictionary of Military Terms*, Peter Collin Publishing, 2002.

Connor, Ken, *Ghost Force: The Secret History of the SAS*, Cassell, 1998.

Corbin, Jane, *The Base*, Simon & Schuster, 2002.

Cowles, Virginia, *The Phantom Major: The Story of David Stirling and the SAS Regiment*, Collins, 1958.

Curtis, Mike, *Close Quarter Battle*, Bantam, 1997.

Davies, Barry, *The Complete Encyclopedia of the SAS*, Virgin Publishing, 1998.

—— *Heroes of the SAS*, Virgin Publishing, 2000.

Geraghty, Tony, *Who Dares Wins, The Special Air Service, 1950 to the Gulf War*, Warner Books, 1993.

Griffiths, John. C., *Afghanistan, A History of Conflict*, Andre Deutsch, 2001.

Heyman, Charles, *The British Army, a Pocket Guide*, Pen and Sword, 2002.

Horsfall, Robin, *Fighting Scared: Para, Mercenary, SAS, Sniper, Bodyguard*, Cassell, 2002.

Howard, Michael, *Clausewitz: A Very Short Introduction*, Oxford University Press, 2002.

Huntington, Samuel, P., *The Clash of Civilisations and the Remaking of the World Order*, Simon & Schuster, 1997.

Kemp, Anthony, *The SAS: Savage Wars of Peace 1947 to the Present*, Penguin, 2001.

Kitson, Frank, *Low Intensity Operations*, Faber & Faber, 1971.

McNab, Andy, *Bravo Two Zero*, BCA, 1993.

Rashid, Ahmed, *Taliban*, Pan Macmillan, 2001.

—— *Jihad, the Rise of Militant Islam in Central Asia*, Yale University Press, 2002.

Read, Tom, *Freefall*, Little, Brown, 1998.

Rose, General Sir Michael, *Fighting For Peace*, Harvill, 1998.

Ryan, Chris, *The One That Got Away*, Century, 1995.

Virilo, Paul, *Desert Screen: War at the Speed of Light*, The Athlone Press, 2002.

Warner, Philip, *The Special Air Service*, William Kimber, 1971.

Woodward, Bob, *Bush at War*, Simon & Schuster, 2002.

www.dnotice.org.uk

Index